ASK ME IF I'M HAPPY

AN ACTOR'S LIFE
PETER BOWLES

**SIMON &
SCHUSTER**

London · New York · Sydney · Toronto

A CBS COMPANY

First published in Great Britain by Simon & Schuster UK Ltd, 2010
A CBS COMPANY

1 3 5 7 9 10 8 6 4 2

Simon & Schuster UK Ltd
1st Floor
222 Gray's Inn Road
London WC1X 8HB

www.simonandschuster.co.uk

Simon & Schuster Australia
Sydney

A CIP catalogue record for this book is available
from the British Library.

Hardback ISBN: 978-1-84737-767-8
Trade Paperback ISBN: 978-84737-880-4

Typeset in Bembo by M Rules
Printed in the UK by CPI Mackays, Chatham ME5 8TD

For
Guy, Adam and Sasha;
and their children
Jasmine, Michael, Emily, Arden, Ben and Teddy;
and Sue.

CONTENTS

INTRODUCTION

M y life is divided into two parts and in some ways divided into four. The first two are before and after recognition and great popular success. That is interesting in my case because my first life didn't end until I was forty-three and had a teenage family. The second part of my life has been vastly different, as though I had drawn Excalibur from the stone. Not within my family, but in the outside world, both in what I found myself capable of and in other people's attitude towards me, both good and bad.

Two other dividing parts of my life, which I wish to show, and that inevitably had a strong effect on my character and development, was that through my parents I experienced both extremes of the British class system. My parents both came from very ordinary working-class backgrounds, but at an early age they were quite intimate servants of the most powerful people in Britain. They were still in this position until the war broke out and I was three years old.

Then a strange split in my development occurred. When I was about six, I moved from a small country cottage to Nottingham, first to a two-roomed digs and then to a terraced house – no bath, outside lavatory – in one of the poorest working-class districts of the city. Inside the house my parents, in contrast to everyone around them in both factory and street, despite having very little money, had seen and experienced 'the other side of the moon'. I was pitched into the wonderful hurly-burly of a society who knew their place, knew no envy but certainly had in comparison, quite severe poverty. This has produced a dichotomy in my character that is in my personal and professional life to this day.

Memories are as real as any good film you have seen. While you are watching this good film you are drawn into its reality. A reality which will last two or three hours. My own film – that is, my life – that my memories have drawn me into, has lasted seventy-three years so far. Although I have diaries, letters, papers and so on, I have not referred to them because the only truth I live with and want to share with you are my impressions and memories of events. Just as you wouldn't want to see behind the camera of any film whilst you watched it, because it would spoil the reality, so checking my old diaries would be sure to spoil my memories, my only reality, my only truth. If someone reading this book remembers some of these things differently, then that's their film. That's their life.

What I am about to tell you is mine.

CHAPTER 1

THE BEGINNING

My father was the youngest of six children born and brought up in Huntingdon. I believe Cromwell's old school, which is now a museum, was still being used as a primary school, and was where my father started his education. The then county town of Huntingdon was (and still is) overshadowed by the huge and imposing Hinchingbrooke Castle, country seat of the Earl of Sandwich, which was to have such an influence on my father's life, as it did for Samuel Pepys, who came from the nearby village of Brampton. Both my father and Pepys began their working life in the employ of an heir to the Earldom and were taken with them to London.

My Grandfather Bowles was born in 1864 and died in 1948 so I got to know him well on the holidays we had in my grandparents' little terraced cottage. Among many things, which included going to America at seventeen to fight the Red Indians, and seeing the first train arrive in Huntingdon as a little boy, was the fact that he was a coach driver as a young man. The large hotel he worked for, which is still there, was filled with ladies of pleasure from London at the weekends. That is, all the weekends when the students were up at Cambridge University. My grandfather ferried the better off and randy students in his coach and four from Cambridge to Huntingdon for the weekend and then back again on Sunday evening, or maybe Monday morning! It must have been a very jolly coach drive going out and a hungover one coming back.

My grandfather, who was well retired when I knew him, had a special daily habit when his family were there. After coming back from his allotment at the end of the day, usually with me, he would go into the tiny scullery, put on a kettle, strop his cut-throat razor and then shave. He would then go upstairs and put on his Sunday best, his only suit I suppose, attach a stiff collar and put on a tie. All I've described would have taken place before six o'clock. My grandparents had no radio, or wireless as it was then called, and no electricity, only gas mantles downstairs (two rooms) and candles upstairs (two rooms). On coming downstairs all spruce and smelling of shaving soap, he would pick up a glass tumbler from the sideboard, and go on his own into the front room, the best room, which was only used on special occasions. After half an hour, the family were asked to come into the room and sit as we could. My grandfather would stand with his back to the empty fireplace and tell us the six o'clock news.

It was wartime; the six o'clock news was of tremendous importance. My grandfather told it beautifully in his strong Huntingdon accent, every detail, we were rapt. I am certain I inherited whatever talent I have from my grandfather and then from my father, who was a tremendous raconteur, both men having a flashing sense of humour.

But how did he know the six o'clock news? I found out, as I grew older, that the people next door had a radio and that it was placed near the party wall. My grandfather used the glass, placing the flat end to his ear and the open end to the wall, to hear the BBC newsreader. Then in his suit, collar and tie, boots shining, he would deliver this oh-so-important world war news to his little family of listeners. I did love him so.

My mother was the eldest of four daughters, all of whom were strikingly beautiful. I can tell you, the Mitford Girls would have found them very stiff competition.

Mum was brought up in a tiny Scottish hamlet of seven houses in Dumfries and Galloway, and just as my father's town was dominated by Hinchingbrooke Castle, so my mother's hamlet was by the country seat of the Earl of Galloway, Cumloden House.

My mother walked four miles to school and back in all weathers. No school run in those days. It is extraordinary to think that I now have had several neighbours who drove their boys aged thirteen or fourteen to St Paul's School, only one or two bus stops down the road.

As it had with my father, the Big House beckoned, and Mum at sixteen took employment at Cumloden. At first an under-nanny, she then moved on to become full nanny to the Lady Jeanne Campbell, the baby daughter of Lord Ian Campbell, heir to the Duke of Argyll, and his wife Janet Aitken, daughter of Lord Beaverbrook. Lord Beaverbrook, apart from owning Express Newspapers, was a very powerful figure in British politics. Janet Aitken Campbell was to become, two marriages later, Janet Kidd, grandmother to today's famous ex-model Jodie Kidd.

My grandparents in Scotland I got to know well, because grandad worked on the huge estate and I spent many happy summer holidays there climbing trees or just wandering around on my own, wary of the bellowing rutting stags and basking adders. I also formed a close relationship with my mother's youngest sister, who in fact was only five years older than me, and still a schoolgirl. This aunt, like her sisters, grew into an exceptionally beautiful young woman, and was runner-up for the Miss Scotland title in the early 1950s.

My mother came to London with her employers to look after baby Jeanne and often spent time at Cherkley, the home of

Lord Beaverbrook. I think quite a lot of time was spent there because Ian Campbell left his wife soon after the child was born. Lord Beaverbrook made it quite plain that he found Nanny very attractive and would often sit on Mum's bed at night for a chat before he retired to bed himself. What more can I say?

Meanwhile destiny moved on, and my father too came to London with his employer, but not before working as a butcher's delivery boy and teaching the young future Aga Khan (the one who married Rita Hayworth) to ride a butcher's bicycle. The teenager lived near Huntingdon, and had been forbidden a bicycle in case he hurt himself. My father taught him how not to hurt himself for 2s. 6d. an hour.

My father was now the valet/companion/chauffeur to the young Drogo Montague, the handsome, hell-raising second son of the Earl of Sandwich. I say hell-raising only in that Drogo, who was of a similar age to my father at this time, adored women and the nightlife of the twenties and thirties London. I know that my father thought him a terrific chap and often went out dancing with him. Sometimes they raced each other in Drogo Montague's two cars, a Rolls and a Rolls Bentley, around the darkened streets of London. Then, after a short marriage to Tanis Guinness, Drogo began to court Janet Aitken Campbell, and this is how two servants, my parents, met. My father told me that one day he had delivered a message from Drogo to Janet Campbell's house. She was then living in Carlton House Terrace. (Mum pointed out the house when she came to watch filming of *The Charge of the Light Brigade* in a nearby house.) Somehow my mother took the message and my father, after walking away from the house, went back and asked my future mum to the Servants' Ball. Although I have never read about this anywhere it seems there was at this time an Annual Servants' Ball at the Albert Hall, and the legend is that their masters served the drinks.

It must have been an absolutely marvellous topsy-turvy Lords of Misrule occasion. There were tens of thousands of servants in London at this time and a ball at the Albert Hall gave them a chance to dress up and be grand themselves.

Drogo and Janet Campbell became Drogo and Janet Montague and went to live in a house built for them in what is now Chelsea Square but was then called Trafalgar Square. Strangely enough, when my mother showed me the house a few years before she died, I realized I had often parked my car right outside it on my way to the Queen's Elm pub. Of course the young child Lady Jeanne Campbell was with them and later a son, William Montague, was born, and my mother joined all the other nannies in Hyde Park only a shortish walk away. Janet Aitken Montague was quite a woman all her life, and I know that she liked to give my father (who had kept his employment with Drogo) his daily duties whilst lying in the bath. My father was very tall and very handsome and two years younger than his 'Mistress' so she must have enjoyed it, and I don't think my father minded.

My parents married and had to leave their employment as my father was sleeping above the garage and my mother of course lived inside, by the nursery.

Many, many years later, Janet Kidd, as she now was (having divorced Drogo Montague and married Johnny Kidd), gave a large exhibition of her paintings at Harrods. For some reason I was invited and because I knew Mum had enjoyed many happy years working for her I asked Mum, who like Janet Kidd was well into her eighties, if she would like to come with me. She would, and did, but I had a tremendous stomach-churning shock when, on introducing my mother to Janet Kidd, my mother, as she took her outstretched hand, went into a deep curtsey and called her 'My Lady'. Oh dear, that was a bad moment.

I also met Lady Jeanne Campbell, Mummy's 'first baby', in New York, not long before she died. We had tea together and she was happy to chat of those days before I was born. She had become quite a girl herself and, as well as marrying Norman Mailer, was reported to have slept with Nikita Khrushchev, John F. Kennedy and Fidel Castro. Not, as far as I know, at the same time. Mum was so pleased to know that I had met and talked to her.

My father's next employment was with the Margesson family, who had a large manor house called Boddington Manor in Warwickshire and of course a London house. Captain Margesson was at this time Chief Whip and Leader of the House, and a close friend of Neville Chamberlain.

Although I was born in London the Margessons gave Mum and Dad a little thatched cottage in the grounds of Boddington Manor and my father worked there as butler/chauffeur.

I remember my father, after serving at one dinner, telling us how surprised he'd been to find among the evening suits and dresses a man wearing 'a sheet', as Dad described it. It was, of course, Ghandi.

Many years later, on a publicity shoot for *To The Manor Born*, I visited the cottage. It was much smaller than I remembered it. The people now living there gave me a leather-bound Day Book which they had found in a chest of drawers bought at the Boddington Manor auction. There, written in October 1936, supposedly by Captain Margesson, was 'Bowles to London to attend the birth of his child'. Then, some days later, 'Bowles back with his wife and newborn son' (me). It's nice to have.

When war came my father, who was a fully trained Rolls-Royce chauffeur and able to strip a Rolls engine and rebuild it, was sent to the Rolls-Royce Aero-engine factory in Hucknall, Nottingham, and Mum and I were allowed to stay on in Boddington for another two years. The Margessons quickly had very young Austrian Jewish refugees under their roof – away from the Jew-hating Nazis. They were my playfellows. One was Fritz Spiegel, who became a celebrated musician and broadcaster. I know this because, shortly before he died, he approached me in the Garrick Club in London with a photograph of us playing together in 1940.

Sometime during the spring of 1939 my father drove Lady Margesson to Berchtesgaden, and apart from complaining about his brown-shirted, gun-toting drinking companions, he brought me back a little pair of lederhosen. It was a very warm summer in 1939, and when I got molten tarmacadam on them from the road it's the only time I remember my father being really cross with me. I've still got the lederhosen. They've still got tar on them.

I learnt to read at a very early age. There was a little village school with one classroom and from the age of three I sat on the teacher's lap (I can still feel the warmth of her thighs) as she taught the five to ten year olds the three R's. I mention this early reading because by the time I went to regular primary school in Nottingham at six or so I could read fluently and was always being asked to 'get up' and read something. I think this may have influenced my desire to be an actor.

Not long ago I was recognized and approached by two elderly ladies outside the National Theatre who said they had both been to the Boddington School with me, and told me that my teacher with the warm thighs had only recently died, in her nineties.

Mum and I must have moved up to Nottingham in 1943 and we lived for a couple of years in Dad's digs – just two rooms, I remember.

Then life changed for me in a most marvellous way. Whilst in digs on the outskirts of Nottingham, at least two miles from the primary school (yes, I walked there), I had no playmates nearby, but now my father had saved and bought a lease on a classic terraced back-to-back house. Small yard, outside lavatory, no bath, two-up two-down house in a long cul-de-sac of similar houses in Hyson Green, Nottingham. Although once again the school, Berridge Road Juniors, was some way away, the street was packed with children. No one had a car, of course, so we could all play in the street, hopscotch, whip and top, football, cricket. The girls, tucking their skirts in their knickers, and playing and singing wonderful rhyming songs whilst skipping and doing amazing tricks with tennis balls against the walls. There was also a large air raid shelter in the middle of the road, and it became our clubhouse, which we lit with candles and 'defended' when we were storing our Guy Fawkes bonfire wood inside. I remember the wonderful VE Day celebrations with many tables and masses of food in the street.

The street was heaven, lots of friends, tremendous warmth and a feeling of community. And although I and certainly my parents knew there was another world in Britain, no one in Hyson Green did. There was poverty, of course – a clog shop at the top of the street, a 'Government kitchen' in the church nearby where you could have a three-course meal for 3d. – but everyone in that working-class *Saturday Night and Sunday Morning* Alan Sillitoe community felt reasonably content. There was no feeling of envy, or feeling deprived, none of the 'why haven't I got one, I deserve it' sort of attitude that exists today. All brought on, I suppose, through the invention of television and in particular commercial television.

Naturally we went to the pictures, Saturday morning pictures, but the characters in those films were seemingly from a different planet; and as for violence, if there was a photo of Roy Rogers holding a gun in a film 'still' outside the cinema, they stuck a piece of sticking plaster over it!

It was at Saturday morning pictures that I first felt the full power of art. In this case music. An orchestra played Tchaikovsky's Piano Concerto in B flat minor (I learnt its name years later) and it reduced this nine-year-old to tears. I wanted desperately to learn how to play the piano, begged and begged my poor parents to buy me a piano, but that was impossible. Then I won a scholarship to the city grammar school, the only boy in my street to do so. That required a uniform. That made me different, and I started to learn how to defend myself.

Nottingham High Pavement was an old grammar school established in the eighteenth century and it was very disciplined. I didn't like it scholastically but it had the most marvellous drama and sports side, and at least one wonderful teacher who came onto my *This is Your Life*. He was the late Stanley Middleton who was for many years a prize-winning novelist of Nottingham life.

This school unfortunately does not exist any more and even more unfortunately was in the news a few years ago when I was very shocked to see the photograph of a teenage schoolboy wearing 'my' school uniform. A boy who grew up to be the most prolific mass murderer this country has ever known. His name was Dr Harold Shipman.

My mum stayed home as she had always done, at first to look after me and then my sister, Patricia, who had been born just before we moved to Hyson Green. We are proud of Patricia because she went on to be awarded an MBE for her work in the NHS. Dad had been taking engineering exams and was beginning to move up from the factory floor and work on metal fatigue and something called 'the Flying Bedstead', which later became the Harrier Jump Jet with vertical take-off. He became a quality engineer and whenever I took a plane and saw RR on the engine I knew I'd be safe as far as the engines were concerned. My dad was very proud to have worked for Rolls-Royce.

When I was around the age of thirteen my father saw a card in a shop window advertising that someone wished to swap their council house in a place called Highbury Vale, again on the outskirts of Nottingham, for a house in Hyson Green. There was no comparison – was the advertiser mad? The house was on one of the more beautiful 'ideal' council estates built between the wars. Front and back gardens, inside lavatory and bathroom. Many of the houses were built around large planted

squares, although our house looked straight onto the vast playing fields of the county grammar school, Henry Mellish. My
parents were so thrilled by the swap that, after taking the coal
out of the bath, we moved in at a rent of 10s. 6d. a week (50p
a week). I don't know what that would be with inflation, but I
think my dad was earning around £8.50 a week at this time.

I loved it there too, and became best friends with a local boy
who was also making the long trip to my school. His name was
Terry Brooks and he was the loveliest of young men. He introduced me to Charles Atlas and the concept of fitness and
bodybuilding, something that has remained with me all my life
and has been a tremendous help in my career both for confidence and deportment. Incidentally, another young boy lived
just down the road from us. He had won a scholarship to the
Nottingham High School – a private school. He was Kenneth
Clarke, now the famous politician, but he didn't, I think, want
to reminice about this aspect of his life when I tried to engage
him in 'memory lane' chat at the Garrick Club recently.

At the age of fifteen I began to have severe pains in my
abdomen. Our local doctor wouldn't come and see me so I had
to take a bus, and remember only too well having to crawl on
all fours along the pavement from the bus stop to his surgery.
He diagnosed constipation and prescribed a strong laxative. In
the middle of the night my parents rang for an ambulance. My
appendix had probably burst. I can remember the ambulance
bells ringing as we drove to Nottingham General Hospital. I
can also remember reciting some Shakespeare as I was wheeled
into the operating theatre. Everything seemed quite normal to
the nurses and doctor after the operation, and quite soon I was
being encouraged to walk to the bathroom. I began to be in
extreme pain as days went by. The pretty nurses called me a cry-
baby as they helped guide my stooped body to the lavatory. I
became so unwell that I began crying out with pain in my bed.
A doctor was finally called. He took one look at my blackened,

distended belly and called for a scalpel. He immediately cut me open, then and there. I can still remember the spurt of evil-smelling fluid that shot into the air covering him and his two nurses. I had severe, well-established peritonitis.

Well, I've described that a bit too vividly, I suspect, so suffice it now to say I had further complications. My parents were told I would probably die, and I was in hospital for many weeks. I didn't die, but I was left with a lasting suspicion of doctors and a touch of hypochondria. Then back to school and the school plays; my future was beginning to germinate.

I'd just like to finish this chapter by saying that I had a very happy childhood with extremely loving parents. The only unhelpful thing that they taught me (because they had come from ordinary country stock, and had worked for years as servants) was that I should always show great respect for my betters. The 'betters' were naturally schoolteachers, policemen, vicars, doctors or any university-educated figures of authority. When I came into the acting profession every director I worked for was a university-educated figure of authority. It held me back terribly. I always naturally thought they were right when they directed me because they were 'educated'. I was about forty before I realized that I had at least equal intelligence and something more important, something called talent and instinct and my own style. They can't teach you that at university, or drama school for that matter.

CHAPTER 2

RADA

Digs and holiday jobs

Although appearing in school plays and amateur plays at the wonderful Nottingham Co-op Arts Centre, at the age of sixteen I still had no idea that I could, or might, make acting my career or profession. In fact, not thinking I was clever enough to be a doctor, I was planning to be a dentist. But only because they earned the magical £1,000 a year.

Although I had been many times to the pictures, the actors appearing in them seemed to be from another world. America was another world. London was another world. I didn't go as a schoolboy to the 'old' Nottingham Playhouse, although I had seen Laurel and Hardy at the Nottingham Empire, and I certainly had no idea there was such a place as a drama school. This was to change when an announcement was made by the headmaster at morning assembly that an old pupil, John Turner, had won the coveted 'Kendall Prize', awarded to the most promising actor of the year at the Royal Academy of Dramatic Art. I had seen John Turner in a school play not long after arriving at High Pavement. He played Shylock and he had been wonderful; then presumably he had left school as he was several years older than me. (John Turner, now retired, had a distinguished career in Shakespeare and is married to the great actress Barbara Jefford.)

I made enquiries of my drama teacher at the Co-op Arts Centre and, with the kind but bewildered encouragement of my parents, wrote off to RADA for a prospectus. I learnt you had to audition and pay to go there unless you won a scholarship. My parents had no money so I would have to get a scholarship.

In order to improve my accent and verse speaking I attended evening elocution classes at the Mechanics Institute. I was joined by another aspiring actor from school, Philip Voss, with whom I'd been in several school plays, and a boy from the Co-op Arts Centre called Bill Monk. I discovered that another pupil in that small class was someone who had already spent one year at RADA and was now finishing off his national service in the RAF. His name was Alan Bates. I was immediately and consciously struck by Alan's physical beauty and his exceptional talent for verse speaking. Alan's best friend met him after class every week and we all went to the Kardomah for coffee. His friend was called John Dexter. Philip Voss went to RADA and became a successful actor. Bill Monk changed his name to Conrad Monk, went to RADA and, after a brief spell acting, was rumoured to have founded the Knobs and Knockers chain of shops. Alan Bates became an international star and Knight of the Theatre, and John Dexter, apart from running the New York Metropolitan Opera, became one of Britain's most celebrated and respected theatre directors. He famously said to Arnold Wesker at one rehearsal, 'If you don't shut up, Arnold, I'll direct this play the way you wrote it.' Another boy who was also in the school plays with me was John Bird, but he didn't go to RADA. He won a scholarship to Cambridge. It didn't divert him from becoming a successful actor/performer and a very successful writer, in addition to founding the famous Establishment Club with Peter Cook.

Although accepted, I didn't win a scholarship to RADA so I applied for help from Nottingham Council, but they decided they couldn't help me as I hadn't taken my A levels. This meant my parents could only afford to send me to RADA for one term, 23 guineas was the fee. The only desperate hope for me was to win the one scholarship that was to be awarded to the student who showed most 'promise' at the end of that first term. We accepted the place not realizing there would be at least a hundred students in that intake. RADA made its money that way then, slowly dropping students until only twenty-five were left at the final term two years later. It's very different now. Far, far fewer students, much, much higher fees, even allowing for inflation, and the course is three years.

At around this time I had appeared as Mark Antony in the school play, *Julius Caesar*, with John Bird playing Brutus. I remember the enormous suffusion of happiness, sitting on top of a trolley bus, knowing that I was, that night, to be playing Mark Antony in the city of Rome. That happiness has never been surpassed by anything I have done in my whole career. I received very good notices in the local papers, and as a result, although still a schoolboy, was asked to appear in the Nottingham Playhouse's production of *Julius Caesar*, playing Young Cato and Trebonius. So my first unpaid 'professional' debut was really in 1953 when I was sixteen, and I made my first professional mistake in this production. I made it because I was a sixteen-year-old amateur who prompted a seasoned leading professional. Derek Godfrey, who later became a leading actor at the RSC, was playing Antony and on the first night he dried in the 'Friends, Romans, countrymen' speech. I was one of many Roman citizens crowding round him, and as I had just played Antony, I gave him the line. He gave me a withering look and called 'Prompt' to the stage manager in the wings. This was not forthcoming so I again gave him the line. He ignored me, cut a few lines and continued. In the interval I was called to his dressing room and given the worst dressing-down of my life! Schoolboys do not prompt leading professional actors. The sooner I went to RADA the better! It was shortly after this production I saw Robert Eddison in a new verse play at the Playhouse. The impact of his mellifluent dark-treacle and honey voice made a deep impression on me and spurred my ambition on.

The first thing I discovered at RADA, apart from the heaven of being with other young people who felt exactly like I did, was young women, beautiful young women, young women who looked just like the young women I had seen in my mother's magazines. Young women who looked like models, and who for the most part spoke with very posh accents. I also saw for the first time in my life, at just seventeen, naked young women. To get from the main RADA building in Gower Street to the main rehearsal rooms and Vanburgh Theatre in Mallet Street you had to cross a long high walkway, and abutting this walkway was a very large building with many windows. It was a nurses' home. As we arrived at RADA all the night staff from various nearby hospitals would be getting ready to go to bed. It was heart-stopping. I knew from that first day at RADA I was without question a heterosexual. (I was invited back to RADA recently and noticed that a high brick screen had been built so the nurses' home was no longer visible.) More importantly it was while at RADA that I first fell deeply in love.

However, before that happened I had miraculously been awarded that first-term scholarship, although my mother, God bless her, insisted on continuing to work nights at a local hospital to help with my living expenses, and later passed exams to become a qualified auxiliary nurse. The one drawback to the scholarship was that it was reviewed every term. I would have to be a good boy, do as I was asked, and most certainly completely lose my Nottingham accent. At the end of my first year I took a Christmas job at the Nottingham post office sorting letters. I was fired after three days. 'The men won't work with you,' the manager told me rather sadly. 'You talk too posh.' Karel Reiz, who directed *Saturday Night and Sunday Morning*, set in the actual roads where I had lived in Nottingham, was to tell me at my audition, 'I'm afraid I can't cast you, Peter. You would be the only actor in it with a genuine Nottingham accent.' Albert Finney was to play the lead, of course, and he comes from Salford!

So after spending one year at RADA I had just reached the age of eighteen, and then I was called up. But I returned having unexpectedly failed my National Service medical. When I dropped my trousers in front of the Medical Board there was a sharp intake of breath. The chairman of the board pointed at my nether regions and asked me how I had received the long and livid scar. When I told him of my peritonitis and complications he said, 'I had that when I was about your age. We're both lucky to be alive. Do you want to go into the RAF?'

'No, sir,' I replied. 'I am in the middle of my studies at the Royal Academy of Dramatic Art.'

'Well in that case I'm going to fail you as being medically unfit,' he said. 'That's just a token of understanding of what you've been through.'

How lucky I was.

*

My first sight of Rachel was in the Markham Arms pub in Chelsea. At well over six feet in her high heels she stood head and shoulders above the other girls. She was an Amazon. She had the face of Ava Gardner, blue-black hair and an hourglass figure. As I discovered later, she had been a professional strong-woman in an Australian circus.

I'm not going to say much about the relationship except that when I met her I was a virgin and she most certainly wasn't. I witnessed the feats of strength – bending an iron bar, tearing up

London telephone directories and stretching open *all* the springs on a chest expander. We both fell deeply in love. Odd things happened while I was with Rachel – very odd things, extremely odd things – but at the time, not having had a relationship with a girl before, I thought somehow that perhaps this was how girls were. I was very innocent and travelled on an emotional roller coaster, and those memories and experiences troubled me for some years. One incident I will relate, because some people reading this will know and have an understanding, both of the sufferer and of those who love them.

I was living in a flatlet – one room, kitchen, bathroom – in Hornsey Rise, with Albert Finney. There were three beds, one double, one single and a single folding bed. The agreement was that should either of us have a girl with us for the night, that person would have the double bed and the other would unfold the 'zed' bed and sleep in the kitchen. Until this particular night Albert and I had never had a girl back at the flatlet. We had just been joined for a few days by another student who was not in our class but who was a friend, and at that time was homeless. He was an American, quite a bit older than us, Albert and I being eighteen then and Bud, who was built like an American football player, probably twenty-five. Albert was away visiting a girl this night. I knew only Bud would be at the flat so I invited Rachel to spend the night with me. We had, of course, by this time slept together but had never spent the whole night together.

Bud, who knew the sleeping arrangement, kindly took his zed bed into the kitchen. In the middle of the night, about three o'clock, I was awakened by a tremendous scream (the flatlet was a converted garage so no one was above or below). Rachel was shouting in a strong American accent and the word she was shouting was 'Murder'. I managed to get a light on. Rachel was naked in the middle of the room. She was frightened, she was serious and she was screaming murder! Big Bud came into the room. 'Christ, what's happening?'

The moment Bud spoke Rachel was on his side. He spoke American, she spoke American – no trace of her strong Australian accent. Bud was in a T-shirt and pyjama trousers. Rachel was naked and was holding onto Bud, telling him clearly and loudly that I had been trying to strangle her. Bud amazingly seemed to be reasonably calm. It was clear that he didn't think I was a potential murderer and agreed with me that I should call an ambulance. Rachel began to calm down a little as Bud talked to her, and said she wanted to go to a night-club. I lied, saying that I had just rung for a taxi to take us to one, and offered to help her to dress. She wouldn't let me near her. She wasn't capable of dressing herself. Bud would have to dress her. He managed to get her pants on and was pulling on her stockings when he began to visibly shake and pour with sweat. He was suddenly very stressed and upset – not surprising, I thought.

'Peter,' he said urgently. 'Come into the kitchen – now.' This was said in an odd quavering voice.

I left Rachel, who was by now smoking a cigarette, and went with Bud into the kitchen. He shut the door.

'Peter,' he said, 'she's mad. Rachel is mad – and Peter, it's catching.' He was sitting down now, looking up at me with a strange and pleading look on his face. 'Madness is catching, Peter. You've got to get her out of here, Peter.' Now Bud was really stressed. 'Get her out quickly because madness is catching, and what you don't know, Peter, is that I killed my brother with an axe.'

I decided to leave Bud alone in the kitchen. 'I'll be out of here as soon as possible, Bud. Please just stay in the kitchen. I can manage. I'll get her to hospital as quick as I can.'

And that's what I did. I managed to get some clothes on her and went out into the street with her as soon as decently possible. When the ambulance arrived I persuaded Rachel it was a taxi and that we were off to a London nightclub.

We went to the Whittington Hospital. Rachel was taken away by a nurse and I sat and waited in a deserted room. It was about 4 a.m. After about an hour a doctor appeared.

'Are you with the young woman?' he asked.

'Yes,' I said.

'What's your relationship?'

'She's my fiancée.' I said.

'Oh, you intend marrying her, do you?' he replied.

'Yes,' I said.

'She's Australian, isn't she?'

'Yes.'

'Well, here's some advice, young man. Do not marry her under any circumstance. Send her back to Australia. She is a schizophrenic.'

And I hit him. I didn't know what schizophrenic meant, I'd never heard the word before, but I did know he'd been very callous in his advice and in the manner that he'd delivered it. I don't think I hurt him, because he apologized to me, and before he went to fetch Rachel he advised me to take her to a psychiatrist. I did, but that's another story. A story that has, for me at least, no known ending.

It was because of my concerns about what had happened to Rachel that thirty years later I conceived a drama series called *First Loves Found* and nearly got it produced on TV. Ten scripts were commissioned and written. We were ready to go, and then they changed the head of drama. But that's TV for you.

*

To get back to the RADA side of my life. I was thrilled to win the same prize as John Turner, who had provided my original inspiration, and was lucky enough to be there at a golden time, with actors like Alan Bates, Peter O'Toole, Sian Phillips, Roy Kinnear, Richard Briers and, of course, Albert. But there was also another student there who was to influence my life fundamentally and completely. Her name was Susan Bennett. I was almost nineteen and in my last term, and was playing Hector in a newly commissioned verse play on the siege of Troy, called *The Face of Love*. The play required large crowd scenes which were provided by students in their first term. They were only put into their scenes for the final rehearsal. I immediately noticed a girl of extraordinary beauty and with a quality like no other. She had decided she would be a young mother and had concocted the impression of a baby, which she held in her shawl. I made a point of speaking to her as soon as I could. I found out her name, and that she liked to be called Sue, she was in her first term and that she was sixteen. I was playing a leading role and was a senior student and there was no question of a senior student dating a newcomer. It simply wasn't done, apart from the fact that I was very involved with Rachel. We always spoke when passing in corridors, or on the stairs. We knew each other, we were friendly, but unknown to us the forces of nature were brewing up a storm.

Apart from the few days at the Nottingham post office, I had a series of other jobs to help get me through RADA.

The first job was in my first term before I won the scholarship, and really needed extra cash. I washed dishes six nights a week at the Grosvenor House Hotel. I worked from about 7 p.m. until midnight. I think for 3s. 6d. an hour. The kitchens were huge and I should think ninety-five per cent of the staff were foreign, and about seventy per cent were living in the kitchens. That is, they all had bed rolls and slept under the long, long tables; they worked all day and evening, and sent most of the their money back to their families in Greece, Italy, Spain, Turkey or wherever. Food was brought round – all the uneaten bits from the restaurants – and we had our own tin mugs which we dipped into buckets containing the leftovers from the wine bottles and glasses.

The worst part of the job was the very hot water, because there were huge piles of dirty dishes and no rubber gloves. I've always loved those handcream and rubber glove adverts ever since.

We had six to eight weeks between terms, and during one of those breaks I took a job as a life guard/swimming pool attendant at Camden swimming baths. I got the job because I was a qualified lifesaving instructor.

On my very first day a boy of my age, eighteen or so, dived off the top board without using his arms and hands. I saw him go in and saw the blood rise to the surface. I immediately dived in and pulled him to the side. He was fully conscious and quite lucid, although shocked. He had hit his head on the bottom of the pool. As he was bleeding a lot through his hair I took him gingerly to the cold shower to see how bad the cut was. I didn't see a cut, but I did see pieces of broken bone and protruding brain tissue. I didn't tell him what I had seen, but asked him to sit quietly whilst I called an ambulance, saying that he needed hospital attention. He was taken away, and then the police arrived. I was heavily grilled as to whether I had been paying enough attention. Fortunately there were a number of witnesses to say I had done all I could. About five weeks later this young man came back to the baths to thank me. He had a steel plate in his skull, which he had been able to cover with his hair, and just seemed grateful to be alive. He had nearly frightened me to death, though.

I also worked as a film extra. The casting in that was reminiscent of On the Waterfront. I had first to join the union, the Film Artists Association, and then go to large casting calls. This was in a huge room somewhere, and depending on how you were dressed or how well you knew the 'Silver Fox', the man who did the casting, it was a pointing finger and 'You, you, you, Pinewood. You, you, you, Shepperton,' and so on. You didn't get cast every day, so it was either a depressed journey home or, if you did get cast, it was the first tube or train to the studios, arriving very early indeed. I enjoyed it, though. I didn't use my own name, after all I was really an ACTOR not an extra! I used the name of the director of my *Julius Caesar* at Nottingham Playhouse, John Harrison. We were paid at the end of the day in cash, and told if we were needed the following day. There were all sorts of wheezes to get extra money: running was extra, climbing was extra, reacting in close-up was extra. Some would even try to get extra danger money for stepping off a pavement.

But it paid good money. I saw for the first time the process of filming. I watched famous actors like Laurence Olivier, Richard Attenborough and Burt Lancaster act on film, and the 'real' extras were a very nice crowd of people. It's fun to see them today cropping up again and again in all sorts of old British movies on TV.

I also worked during two holidays in a hospital. The ward I was on was for incurable male patients. It was on the ground floor with large windows, which was just as well because, unbelievably, children under twelve were not allowed to visit in the ward. This meant there was often the harrowing sight of children waving to their dad or grandad through the windows. Thank God that has long been changed. I was a ward orderly which meant I cleaned and polished the ward, especially the floor, until it shone. It also meant cleaning and shining up all the bedpans, cleaning up the patients and even shaving them before operations. I enjoyed my work there tremendously, and because I was young and had a sense of humour the patients seemed to like me and enjoyed my fun and attention despite their terrible situation. I often think of the time I spent with those brave people.

I saw a modern prospectus for RADA in recent years and it made it quite clear that evening jobs in term time in order to earn money was not allowed, as 'it will make you too tired to attend to your lessons properly'. If that is the case today, how would the students have fared in the days of weekly and fort-nightly repertory theatre, rehearsing all day and playing at night, week after week, month after month, and still finding time to fall in love?

One of the students in my class offered me a job. This student was a friend and was extremely well built and handsome. In modern parlance, a real 'hunk'.

'Peter,' he said, 'would you like to earn five pounds this evening?' (£5 was a huge sum of money then, equivalent to at least £100 today, I'd say.)

'I most certainly would,' I gasped. 'How?'

'Well, Peter,' my friend said, 'not only will you earn five pounds but you'll be doing me a favour.'

'Yes? Oh good – go on.' I was eager to hear how anything I could do could be worth so much money in an evening.

'Well,' said my hunky friend, 'I have a date for dinner with—' (and he mentioned the name of a then famous male British film star) 'and I can't make it. Now there is nothing to be worried about, he will only want to fondle you under the dinner table and at the end of the meal he'll give you five pounds.'

At this point in my life, before Rachel, I had not been fon-dled anywhere, at any time, by anyone, but it didn't sound quite right to me, so I declined.

*

My first experience of television casting was in fact at RADA. As I have said, I shared a flat with Albert Finney, and we had been asked by the principal to come to RADA on this partic-ular day in our 'best' clothes, with hair brushed and shoes shining, because the bosses of a new independent television company (Rediffusion, I think) were coming to cast the first closed-circuit TV play (ITV had not started at this time). I think they may have used students from other drama schools, but we would play the leading parts, after all we were the Royal Academy of Dramatic Art.

'Bollocks,' said Albert that morning as he pulled on his usual holed jumper. 'Fuck 'em,' as he ran his fingers through his tousled hair. Albert never ever washed his hair as he believed nature's oils cleaned it 'like a dog's', he said. Albert still has a magnificent head of thick hair, whilst my once magnificent head of thick wavy, well-washed hair has all but disappeared! I got togged up as best I could, as I was on that best-behaviour scholarship. No 'bollocks' or 'fuck 'em's allowed.

The bosses of the new TV company, who all seemed to be ex-Royal Navy commanders, were to watch us enact scenes from *As You Like It* and I was playing Jaques. Poor Albert was only playing 'a Forester'. No wonder he said 'fuck 'em', I thought. The scenes were to be played in a large rehearsal room and the distinguished guests sat on a raised stage at one end of the room.

The scenes ended.

'Gather round, boys and girls,' said the principal. 'Sit cross-legged here in front of our guests whilst they decide who they would like to cast in their play.'

It was to be *She Stoops to Conquer*. We were all very excited, and I *knew* I had done the 'All the world's a stage' speech rather well.

'We would like to have that boy for a start,' said one of the men, pointing towards a figure who had not joined us cross-legged, but had gone into a corner at the far end of the room, and was standing in the position of a dunce with his back towards us.

'Albert, come here at once. What are you playing at?' said the principal.

'No, leave him where he is,' said the ex-Naval Commander. 'We want him to play the lead.'

I didn't get a part of any kind. Well, that's the mystique of star quality in an eighteen-year-old young man, who I think only had one line. I realized many years later, after I had acquired a certain amount of it, that confidence is almost 80 per cent of what is needed for 'star quality', plus a bit of talent of course. My teacher was Albert Finney.

One night in our room we were discussing what part we would most like to play. We both had the same ambition, that when we left RADA and became professional actors we would play Macbeth. Albert asked me how I would approach the part. I went on about Scottish history, the possibility of playing it with a Scottish accent, probably in a kilt, and of course I would study all the great scholars, including Granville Barker.

'How would you approach it, Albert?' I asked.

'I'd learn the fucking lines and walk on,' said Albert.

There's confidence – and from a boy of eighteen. You can't beat it!

CHAPTER 3

MY FIRST JOB

The Old Vic

Whilst at RADA Albert and I both received letters from Philip Pearman at MCA, the Musical Corporation of America, the most powerful agency in the world.

I cannot tell you the thrill of seeing the letter addressed to me with MCA emblazoned across it. It was in the B pigeonhole at RADA. I expect someone told me it was there. So the two room-mates, at eighteen and nineteen, were very excited when we went off to 139 Piccadilly at the appointed hour.

We were both signed up, with the following advice. Albert was advised to change his name.

'My dear,' said Mr Pearman, the nicest of nice men, 'first think for a moment of the poster: "Albert Finney as Hamlet". It sounds as though a footballer is trying his foot at acting.' (There was a famous footballer named Tom Finney playing at the time.) 'I really think you ought to change your name, Albert,' he said. Albert didn't, of course, and the poster saying 'Albert Finney as Hamlet' appeared at the National Theatre years later.

'Peter, dear,' said Mr Pearman, 'your good looks are spoilt by your crooked teeth. You will have to get them straightened.' I didn't. I looked into it but I couldn't afford the orthodontic fees. The camera might not like me in the future, but girls seemed to like me now, I thought, so I forgot about it.

We both joined MCA. Whilst still at RADA I was taken by Mr Pearman, rather grandly in a Humber Pullman, to be introduced to all the film casting directors. They were all men at that time, 1956. Now they are almost exclusively women. I was received at their offices at Pinewood, Shepperton, Elstree, MGM with great courtesy and a sherry and a dry biscuit. I had never drunk sherry before, I must have got quite drunk. I don't remember. What I do remember, however, is what they all said, without exception. 'Well, Peter, our advice to you is to go away and learn Spanish, Greek, Italian or even Arabic because you will never be cast as an Englishman.' This was a terrible shock – but to hell with it, I thought, all those great parts I want to play in Shakespeare aren't English. I want to be a classical actor. I may not get offered Henry V but there's Hamlet, Othello, Romeo, Don Adriano de Armado, Coriolanus, and even Macbeth is Scottish, for God's sake.

In the car on the way back to London my new agent said cheerily, 'Never mind, Peter, you will become a star, but not until you are over forty!' Now that was a real blow as we students at RADA at that time were all agreed that if you didn't 'make it' by the time you were thirty you never would. Perhaps I would end up as an estate agent, I thought gloomily.

Both predictions were correct as it turned out, and for many years on film and television I played foreigners, usually villains, and I didn't become a 'star' actor until I was forty-three, playing Richard de Vere in *To The Manor Born*, and even he was Czechoslovakian.

I graduated from RADA, and Philip Pearman got me my first job. It was to be with the Old Vic, the nearest thing to a National Theatre in 1956. I was thrilled. Yes thrilled, even though this scholarship-winning, 'best student of his term',

Kendall Prize-winning, 'most promising student of his year' was to be a spear-carrier! That is, someone who literally stands around with a spear or banner in his hand and occasionally makes what we dubbed a 'textless transversal of the stage'. Except, except I had a speaking part as well. It was Abraham the servant, at the beginning of *Romeo and Juliet*, and he had five lines. I know because I've just got up from writing and counted them. Oh, and I had a buckle and swash, and a swish too, as I had a sword fight. I also had to understudy various parts. The really, really exciting thing about this job, though, was that after a few performances in London we were to make a short tour in England and then fly direct to Canada and tour America before playing Broadway. WOW!

There were four plays: *Romeo and Juliet* directed by Robert Helpmann with John Neville and Claire Bloom; *Troilus and Cressida* with Jeremy Brett, Charles Gray and Rosemary Harris, directed by the great Tyrone Guthrie; *Richard II* with again John Neville and Charles Gray; and *Macbeth* with Paul Rogers and Coral Browne. These last two plays were directed by the boss of the Old Vic, Michael (Mick the Blink) Benthall. Coral Browne, who incidentally was married to Philip Pearman, played Lady Macbeth and I was actually sitting in the stalls when she came on for the costume parade and Michael Benthall asked her if she was happy with her wig. 'No, dear, I'm not,' replied Coral forcefully in her cutting Australian drawl. 'I feel as though I'm looking out of a yak's arse.' This is a famous 'Coralism' and it's true. I was there.

I had seen many of the leading actors on stage at the Vic in my years at RADA. Neville, of course, and Richard Burton, Claire Bloom and Paul Rogers, who was a truly wonderful Macbeth. I acted opposite Paul Rogers years later at the Royal Court. He is ninety-one years of age as I write this, bless him. I also starred opposite Claire Bloom just recently, and I felt thrilled and privileged (and told her so).

There weren't many young women in the shows and most of them were very attracted to a shortish stagehand, which we young actors, all well over six feet, could not understand. We felt miffed, in fact. The stagehand was named Jeffrey Bernard. He was not unwell then, I can tell you, and blisteringly handsome.

I arrived very nervous on my first day and was met by the London company manager at the side of the stage. 'My name is John Murphy,' he said, 'but you must call me Rosie. We all have girls' names here and we have decided you will be called Sally.' So Sally Bowles it was, John Neville was 'Nancy Neville', Charles Gray was 'Big Mother'. Yes, this was my introduction into the profession, and I felt grateful that the nurses' home had been built so very close to RADA. I met and made two lifelong friends at the Old Vic: Bryan Pringle and James Villiers. I also met a very pretty young Judi Dench, who was rehearsing for the London season. She asked me sweetly after a first-night party if she could borrow a pound, as she had no money for a taxi home.

When I starred opposite her fifty years later I jokingly reminded her that she still owed me a pound. She remembered the incident all right; she stopped the rehearsals and brilliantly embarrassed me by announcing to the whole company, 'Peter Bowles is so desperate he has just reminded me I owe him a pound he lent me fifty years ago. I want you all to witness I am now no longer in debt to him.' And she with a flourish and a swooping high held hand gave me a pound coin. I knew from that moment I was going to have great, great fun both on and off stage with Dame Judi Dench, and I did. Oh, the play was Coward's *Hay Fever*, directed by Sir Peter Hall at the Haymarket, and Dame Judi packed it out for six months.

As I said, after a short London season the Old Vic Company, before flying off to America, went on some dates in England. The one thing I remember of this is that at a matinee in

Manchester, during the sword fight between Macbeth and Macduff, which was played with real steel claymore swords so that sparks flew as they clashed, Macbeth's sword blade literally flew off its handle. I was on stage at the time and we all froze as we heard very clearly the swish, swish, swish as the steel blade spun into the darkened packed auditorium. It must have gone right to the back of the stalls, and after what seemed like a lifetime there was a horrible scream from someone 'out there'. The fight continued. Paul Rogers quickly pulled out his dirk and retreated with John Neville's Macduff into the wings.

Everyone was very worried and concerned as to the damage inflicted by the deadly blade. A man had been rushed to hospital with a cut head, we were told. But there was another performance that evening to take our minds off it. Paul Rogers must have felt awful, but at the end of that evening's performance, a gentleman turned up at the stage door smiling but heavily bandaged. Was he going to sue, and take the Old Vic for every penny it had, as would probably happen today? No, he just wanted permission to keep the sword blade that he had with him, as a memento, and would Mr Paul Rogers please give him his autograph. We were a lucky company, and he was a very lucky man, who it seemed had had the best theatrical experience of his life.

The company of about eighty, I suppose, including dressers and wardrobe assistants, flew in a chartered Stratocruiser from Liverpool, our last date. I remember there was a Guinness factory in Liverpool to which the company was invited. That evening the great, handsome John Neville played Richard II wonderfully, but he was often steadied quite firmly at the elbows by his devoted attendants.

It was such an exciting time for me as I'd never flown in an aeroplane before. We were to fly to Greenland first for refuelling, but had to divert quite quickly to Edinburgh as the cabin crew realized that they were already running out of drink and the actors needed refuelling first. So the plane was hastily restocked with alcohol and off we went. What a flight it was. The Stratocruiser had two levels; upstairs were the seats, but downstairs was quite a large lounge with tables, chairs and a bar. The pretty stewardess served drinks. The pretty stewardess served drinks for the next fourteen hours. We had an hilarious time and so did the pretty stewardess, judging from some of the photos I still have.

As I say, I had never flown before, never been abroad before, so being invited into the captain's flight deck as we flew up the mighty St Lawrence River into Canada was awesome and a beautiful sight. Toronto in 1956 had a very tall building, but I can't remember much else, apart from being befriended by a lovely woman who fronted a TV programme called the *How-de Do-de Show*, and staying in a hotel for the first time in my life.

Montreal was more fun – there was jazz and rock 'n' roll being played in the clubs. I noticed that a lot of the people doing the more menial jobs spoke French. We were a huge success. Niagara Falls, then Indiana University USA, where we played in its 6000-seat theatre and John Neville refused to wear make-up as there was no hot water.

Ah yes, make-up. In those days all the men wore thick make-up, except for Charles Gray, who wore thick, thick, thick make-up. Our lips were outlined, the nose straightened with a pale mark down its centre, eyes were hugely mascared with white on the inside of the line, there was heavy shading to make the cheekbones stand out, and most important of all (except I've never found out why) a red dot in the corner of the eyes. Did I say this was just the men?

Broadway was next, the Winter Garden Theatre, right opposite Radio City Music Hall. I saw the famous Rockets, the American equivalent to the Tiller Girls, and often had coffee with them in the local drugstore. I don't know if they still do it, but in those days before the films were shown this large troop of long-legged dancers would do a big high-stepping routine. It was a tradition left over from Variety days and the audience loved it. I wish we had it now in our local cinema.

I never really slept in New York. The adrenaline flow was too powerful. I felt as though I was in a film; all those huge finned cars and yellow taxis, and stick-swinging cops, 'Walk', 'Don't Walk' signs, the automat, drugstores and, yes, they spoke like they did in films with an American accent.

I remember waiting at the kerb and dropping a one cent coin just as the 'Walk' sign appeared. I decided to leave it and stepped into the road. A loud voice called out, 'Hey, bud, pick up the coin. Your Queen needs it more than we do.' It was a stick-swinging cop that spoke, how he knew I was English I don't know. Perhaps it was the way I walked.

Apart from that the Americans were tremendously polite and very welcoming. Quite different from the images in the English newspapers of the time, of gum-chewing, loud-mouthed, camera-carrying, fat, rich lords of the universe. The only thing that did disturb us was that many New Yorkers weren't sure quite where England was. They kept saying, 'You mean New England?' They would finally settle on it being somewhere in Europe. A fact that would be almost true today.

Once again we were a sensation. I remember, after the first night of *Romeo and Juliet*, sitting in Times Square reading the reviews that hit the streets about 1.30 a.m., and honestly expecting to read that my five-line performance had been picked out and my name mentioned. What a romantic. Although one notice was headed 'A Tall Company of Towering Talent, every actor could play a King'. I took that to include me as I am six feet two.

The Old Vic was such a sensation in the New York of 1956 that everyone wanted us at their parties. Almost every night and always on Fridays and Saturdays there would be a fleet of limousines, each with a capped chauffeur holding a card saying

'Mrs So and So's party, welcome.' We often took these limos to begin with, but of course the parties were always social and rather too grand for us spear-carriers.

I went around all the time with James Villiers and Bryan Pringle. James Villiers was the sort of person I had never really mixed with before. He was very tall, six feet four, very, very grand, an aristocrat with no title but a lot of blue blood and a very commanding manner. I loved him, he was good fun and he got me into all sorts of trouble. Bryan Pringle appeared to be the opposite; although public-school educated, he was from the north of England and affected a very 'working class' personality. He had more energy, more get up and go than anyone I had ever met. Both men had a really tremendous flashing sense of humour and of the ridiculous. And they loved drinking; I loved them, so I loved drinking with them, sometimes all night, catching up by sleeping in the dressing room until our cue was called, woken with a kick from a fellow actor. Actually all this drinking and late nights got me into a little trouble with the company manager, Douglas Morris. I was called to his office. 'Peter, dear,' he said kindly, 'as the Company Manager I feel like a father figure to someone as young as you.' (I was the youngest member of the company.) I wondered what was coming next. He went on, 'It is my job to warn you against James Villiers and Bryan Pringle.' (They were two or three years older.) 'They are very naughty young men and I think you are in great danger at your age, and in your first job, of being corrupted by them. Keep away from them.'

I said I would, but I didn't. Douglas Morris came back into my life, and later I will tell you of how he tried to 'corrupt' me. I am now writing this not sure whether I have been corrupted or not. Oh well.

Most of the company apart from the stars were booked into the Plymouth Hotel, a three-star place just off Broadway and near the Winter Garden Theater. Of course it was well known that this was where the company was staying. This, I'm afraid, had a bizarre and rather sad effect on some people aspiring to get into show business. Often, as we left the hotel, young men and women would launch into dances or speeches quite openly, loudly, right there on the sidewalk. There was nothing we could do to help them, and quite honestly we felt embarrassed. But not nearly as embarrassed as Ronnie Allen. Ronnie Allen, who later became a big star of the TV series *Crossroads*, was, as all *Crossroads* fans know, very handsome. One Sunday afternoon I heard a terrible commotion in the corridor outside my hotel room. I opened my door to see and hear just down the corridor a stark-naked girl shouting and banging at Ronnie's door. She was, I'm afraid, shouting, 'Rape.' Ronnie, it turned out, was inside the room calling for the hotel to get the police. The girl, who was clearly unwell, had stripped off her clothes outside Ronnie's room, then knocked and, when Ronnie answered, threw herself at him. Ronnie told me later that he'd only just managed to fend her off and lock the door when I saw her. The police took the girl away and took statements from us but we heard no more.

I used to listen to the rock 'n' roll radio stations all night. We'd never really heard rock 'n' roll in England but as we hit New York Elvis had just released 'Hound Dog' and 'Heartbreak Hotel', Frankie Lymon was 'not a teenage delinquent, No No No', Little Richard had just 'jumped back in the alley', and Fats Domino was on Blue Berry Hill. I've never slept properly since those nights of rock 'n' roll and I still keep the faith. The sexual power of the twenty-one-year-old Elvis Presley was brought home to me the night he appeared on the *Ed Sullivan Show*. There was a large bar right next to the Winter Garden Theater, in fact it had once been part of the theatre as Al Jolson's dressing room. Anyway, it was known that Elvis was to appear that night and the bar was packed with mostly young women. It may not have been a live performance, it may only have been happening on a TV screen in this bar, but when Elvis appeared and sang he caused sexual mayhem. When he began to gyrate and pump his hips and thighs, something no one had ever done before in a song, the women in the bar completely lost themselves. Some jumped onto the chairs, some jumped onto the tables, some just jumped up and down. They all screamed and many of them – believe me, I saw it – lifted their skirts and began unconsciously to play with themselves. But Elvis held my attention and he still does.

One night whilst listening to a rock 'n' roll station, an advert came on for the Arthur Murray School of Dancing. A very sexy female voice promised to give a free rock 'n' roll dance lesson if I rang this number. I did, and made a booking for the next afternoon; after all it was free and, my God, I wanted to learn how to rock 'n' roll.

It was quite a posh-looking place not too far from my hotel and the Theatre. I was greeted warmly by a beautiful young woman and taken to a desk. Yes, it would be so many hundreds of dollars for a course of lessons.

'No,' I said. 'I have come for one free lesson in rock 'n' roll. I booked last night.'

'Well, of course,' she said, looking at some papers. 'But we're sure you'll want to have more lessons especially after you have been shown some steps by the beautiful Dana.'

And I was introduced to a tall blonde woman of enormous sashaying charm and led away into an empty ballroom. She showed me the simple steps. I loved it. The lesson lasted about half an hour. I was ready to go.

Dana took me by the hand, looked into my eyes and told me in a whisper that she thought I was very sexy and looked forward to our next lesson. Well I won't go on. You can imagine. But I did manage to get away with my free lesson unscathed – I thought.

I had mentioned to her that I was an actor with the Old Vic, and that evening a note was left for me at the stage door from Dana. I wish I'd kept it. It was full of passion. She had fallen in love with me. Could I please, please meet her for a drink after the show? Well, she was beautiful and although a little older than me (that wasn't difficult, I'd only just turned twenty!) she was another New York adventure at the very least.

We went to a bar and the conversation quite quickly turned to me having more lessons with her at the Murray School of Dancing. It would be fun. I may have been only twenty but I cottoned on immediately and began to politely extricate myself from the situation. Then all emotional guns were brought to bear. She was a single mother. She had no money except what she earned at the dance school, and she had been told that if I didn't sign their papers (she pulled them out of her bag) for hundreds of dollars' worth of lessons she would be sacked. She then began to cry. I was polite, seemingly sympathetic to her obvious scam, and said I was sorry, but I couldn't sign. She said, suddenly dry-eyed, 'Fuck you, asshole,' and I said, 'Thank you and goodnight.' Welcome to New York!

*

I can't clearly remember where or when I met Maggie Smith in New York, but when I did meet her I fell for her. Maggie was one of many stars in an annual and famous review on Broadway called *New Faces*. I know everything went well between us that first evening, and I began to date her after her show. The Winter Gardens, where we were, was not far from her theatre and we seemed to 'come down' a little earlier.

Maggie would have been twenty-two, I suppose, and apart from her dazzling looks and figure she had, as you might imagine, a fizzing personality and a wicked sense of humour. I was well and truly hooked, but I had begun to suspect she wasn't. I discovered my suspicions were well founded in rather humiliating circumstances. For a poor but honest young lad, that is! Judy

Garland had made a huge comeback and was appearing at the apex of variety, the Palace Theatre, New York. She was giving a Midnight Matinee for the profession. I asked Maggie if she would like to go with me. Oh yes, she most certainly would.

'I'll book two seats in the stalls and come round after your show and pick you up.'

'Lovely,' she said.

The evening arrived. I hurried excitedly to her stage door, the tickets safely in my pocket.

The stage door keeper, who knew me well by now, said with awe in his voice, 'Bing Crosby has just gone up to Miss Smith's dressing room and he was carrying a large bunch of flowers.'

Yes, I was an Elvis fan but Bing was BIG TIME. I knocked, and on the 'come in' entered. Maggie was standing looking lovely with a large bouquet in her hands and there was the unmistakable figure of Bing Crosby, in a dinner jacket.

'Can I introduce you to Bing Crosby,' said Maggie. I said hello, and shook his hand.

Bing then said, 'Miss Smith, I would consider it an honour if you would join me in my box for the Judy Garland Midnight Matinee tonight.'

'Oh, I'd love to,' said Maggie without so much as a glance in my direction.

I made my excuses and left.

I enjoyed enormously the Judy Garland show (she brought on both her little girls), despite the empty seat beside me. I didn't see Dame Maggie Smith again for another fifty years, but when we did meet we were charming to each other. She looked just as beautiful as when I'd first met her.

My only regret is that I have never acted with her.

*

One of the great highlights of my time with the Old Vic on Broadway was when I 'went on'. That was because Ernest

'Bunny' Hare, who played one of the parts I understudied, fell ill. The part was Ajax in *Troilus and Cressida*. It was a terrific leading role and I played it for five performances. The company were so kind, so full of praise and Bunny, when he came back, gave me a lovely pigskin wallet with a $20 bill inside as a thank-you present. I've still got it.

*

Well, what with one thing and another, and all the corruption I was undergoing, I began to feel under the weather. It was a touch of tonsillitis, which I was prone to. The company sent me to a doctor. He frightened me almost to death. This New York doctor's surgery of fifty years ago had lots of machines where all sorts of tests were carried out on me. His verdict was that my heart had been affected by the poison from my tonsils and unless I had them out immediately I might die of a heart attack. Blimey, I was only twenty. I told the company manager, Douglas Morris.

'The Old Vic can't possibly afford to pay for your tonsil operation, Peter,' said Douglas. 'You will have to be sent back to London.'

This was devastating. I pleaded to stay, said I would cut out the drinking and smoking, walk up stairs, and perhaps if I could drag various dead bodies off stage instead of carrying them, I would be okay. I felt certain my tonsils would soon get better.

'All right, Peter,' said Douglas, 'I'll arrange the dead bodies, but you'll have to sign a form saying it's all your decision and responsibility.'

I signed willingly. But it slowed me down. It depressed me. It so happened we were going to take a short break from New York and play Boston for two weeks and I was advised by a responsible musician (female) who had befriended me that there was a top heart specialist in Boston. He happened to be her uncle. I went to see him. My corrupters, James and Bryan, who like me were very worried, took me there by the hand. This man had even more machines and took even more tests. I've still got his printed diagnosis. The gist of it said:

> This patient has nothing whatsoever wrong with his heart. What he has got is some debilitation due to too much worry over his New York doctor's diagnosis, too much drinking, too much smoking and not nearly enough sleep. What he is suffering from, however, is what is known as the Actors' Condition. That is, he listens to his body a lot of the time and expects to hear applause. Sometimes, however, such as now, he hears a boo and this causes him to panic. I have advised him to think outside of himself and take better care of his health.

Phew.

After a few more weeks in America – Boston, Chicago, Philadelphia and Broadway again – a few more weeks of drinking, smoking and going out with girls, we caught the plane for London, England.

We had been in America for six months and I honestly thought as the plane took off, 'If this plane crashes, I at least won't mind, because I have had the most wonderful life.'

CHAPTER 4

A SAD TALE OF TWO OVERCOATS

One of my strongest desires as a teenager was to one day own a 'British Warm' overcoat. The sort that John Mills and other actors playing army officers wore in the films. There was something so very English about them. When I joined the Old Vic and managed to make a little money, I saved up, and before we departed for America I had bought one. I always, or almost always, wore it over my shoulders like a cloak. I don't think any officer would have done that. That would have been too 'camp' but I was a bit camp. All good actors are a bit camp. Laurence Olivier was very camp.

When winter came in New York so came the excuse to wear my coat. After the plays, James Villiers, Bryan Pringle and I often used to go to drinking clubs. The sort that we had never seen in London. In fact I don't think we had ever been to any sort of drinking club before. I certainly had never heard of such a thing. Pub? Yes. Club? No.

Apart from the very late hours they kept, one of the main attractions of these clubs, which were always 'down town', were the beautiful girls who amazingly 'danced' on the bar. You could stand or sit at the bar with one drink and almost naked young women gyrated just in front of you. Commonplace now, absolutely unheard of in the England of 1956. It didn't cost anything to get into the clubs but the girls, after dancing, did expect you to buy them a drink. We didn't mind. They were fun and different to talk to. We were so young and very innocent, all three of us. The only thing I began to resent was checking in my lovely British Warm, because it always cost about $5 to get it back from the cloakroom. I took to 'cloaking', or wearing it on my shoulders at the bar. Jimmy and Bryan didn't seem to bother with coats at all.

One night at a club that we had not been to before, they were really keen for me to hand over my overcoat. I refused and grandly 'cloaked' it at the bar. We hadn't been there long, just bought a drink in fact, when I became very popular with the girls. They were very keen to talk to me and didn't seem to care whether I bought them a drink or not. Suddenly there was a tremendous smell of burning and I realized I was on fire, or at least my British Warm overcoat was. Flames were coming out of both my side pockets. I quickly slipped it off and drinks were thrown over it to douse the fire, but it was too late. The coat was ruined. There was a lot of laughter from the men who worked at the club, 'bouncers' I suppose you would call them today. My coat was on the floor having been stamped on and soaked and burnt. Of course the girls had been told to empty boxes of matches into my pockets whilst showing affection, and then drop in lighted cigarettes. I was very angry. Things turned really ugly. We three young English actors smashed bottles, and armed in a threatening manner, managed to escape unscathed, at least physically. We were very foolish, very drunk (I suppose) and very, very lucky. The overcoat never left the club.

On my return to England I once again began to save up for a British Warm. It took some time as they were very expensive for a struggling actor. Then finally I'd saved enough and bought one, cloaked it and went to the Salisbury pub, which was the actors' pub of the day in St Martin's Lane.

The Salisbury in those days was covered in photos of actors who were or had been customers. It was and still is a very beautiful Victorian pub with an exceptional amount of gilt decorations and engraved mirrors. In the old days actors from all over London would collect their dole and then meet at the Salisbury for a gossip and a pint and exchange news on possible jobs. I remember Peter O'Toole coming in one day and putting about £150 on the bar, said he'd just landed the role of Lawrence of Arabia, and that this was his expenses for the week; and bought drinks for everyone in the pub. When he was in *The Long and the Short and the Tall* in the theatre next door, the five-minute call was made in the pub, as the whole cast would be having a drink, including Michael Caine, who was O'Toole's understudy in that play.

On this particular lunchtime there was no O'Toole, no Caine, no Brendan Behan, no Kenneth Tynan or Micheál Mac Liammóir. I only remember a beautiful young girl who seemed keen to be in my company. I presumed it was because I looked so glamorous and arty with my brand-new British Warm overcoat slung over my shoulders.

Last orders were called at 2 p.m. in those days, and my charming drinking companion suggested we went on to an afternoon drinking club. I was still very green and unworldly-wise and said I didn't know where there was one. 'Oh,' she said, 'I hoped you might know one nearby. Never mind, if we get a taxi I'll take you to a lovely club in Knightsbridge.' I explained I wasn't sure I had enough money for a taxi ride and drinks. 'That's okay,' she said, 'I'll pay for the taxi if you get the drinks at the club.' And off we went. The club was just opposite the old Hyde Park Hotel, and was, strangely, up quite a flight of outside stairs. I have a feeling the steps were wooden.

We went in. There was a long bar with high-backed bar stools and my first impression was that it was empty apart from the barman. I slipped off my overcoat, put it over the bar stool and ordered our drinks. Until I put my hand in my pocket to pay I'd had my back to the entrance doors, but as I paid I noticed that in fact right by the doors was a group of about six or seven men. They were in a position where they could observe anyone entering without being seen. They were all smartly dressed in dark suits, ties and white shirts. One of the men had broken slightly away from the others and was beckoning me with his forefinger to join him. He was about 35 feet away and I returned his beckoning finger with mine in the same manner. He shook his head, pointed at me and again beckoned.

I turned to my new girlfriend and said, 'There's a chap over there wants me to go and talk to him.'

'Well go and talk to him,' she replied, then gave me a smile and took a sip of her drink.

I walked towards the man. 'What is it?' I said.

'Not here,' said the man gently and politely. 'Outside.' He flicked his head slightly towards the nearby door.

'Can't you tell me here?' I said.

'I want to tell you something very important that's to your advantage,' he replied. 'It won't take a moment.'

Thinking he didn't want his friends to hear what he had to say, I reluctantly agreed. I looked back at the girl and was about to call out to her what I was up to when I saw she was in deep conversation with the barman, who I'd already noticed she knew well.

I went outside. The man somehow managed to take a step above me. He was not tall but very stocky and certainly my height when he was on the higher step. He looked in his late thirties and had a cockney or east London accent. He spoke very quietly in a calm almost concerned manner.

'Listen, sonny,' he almost whispered. The 'sonny' although quiet had a sinister quality to it that I was aware of immediately. 'Listen, sonny, you don't know that girl, do you?'

'Of course I do. She's my girlfriend,' I replied with reasonable force.

'No, don't fuck about,' he said quietly. 'She's just picked you up and brought you here. She's a naughty girl.' From his general air of menace I decided to agree. I had met her that lunchtime and she'd suggested coming there. 'You seem like a nice lad, sonny,' he said, 'so I'm going to give you some advice. Fuck off.' He was smoking a cigarette and his eyes never wavered from mine.

'I'm not quite sure I understand,' I said weakly.

'You don't understand "fuck off"?' he said slowly and incredulously. He put one foot down onto my step so his face was now very close to mine. He smelt of cologne. 'Have you ever heard of the Krays?' he said. 'The Kray twins?' I had heard of the Kray twins and said so. 'Well,' said the man, 'this is their club and that girl is a special friend of Reggie Kray. He's going to be here,' he looked at his watch, 'in about five minutes. He's going to be cross with that girl and he's going to be very, very angry with you and I'm giving you the best advice you've ever had in your life, which you don't seem to understand. So I'll give it to you again. Fuck off.'

This time the 'fuck off' had a little more timbre to it. I suddenly understood everything absolutely and completely.

'Could I just say goodbye?' I said.

He shook his head. 'No.'

'Well,' I said, 'could I please just go in and get my coat? I only bought it this morning and—'

Before I could continue he brought his other foot onto my step, his chest knocking me down onto the one below. 'Christ,' he said. 'I thought you understood English. Fuck off.'

This time the 'fuck off', although not loud, had such a threatening edge that for the first time in my life I felt true fear. I managed to say, 'Thank you, sir,' and walked as calmly as I could down the stairs away from the beautiful girl, away from

Reggie Kray and away, once again, from my British Warm overcoat. The club, of course, was the now infamous Esmeralda's Barn.

This experience was a huge help to me when I came to play Gangster in *Gangster No. 1* by *Sexy Beast* writers David Scinto and Louis Mellis, at the Almeida Theatre in London. Incidentally they offered me the part because they thought I had a deeply menacing quality, and had frightened Loyd Grossman on *Masterchef*. It must have been because I'd been kept waiting in a dressing room for two hours! Anyway I got the reviews for the play that an actor only dreams of. If you will forgive me I will quote extracts from a couple because they directly relate to my time on the steps of Esmeralda's Barn.

'Peter Bowles as Gangster is truly frightening. A man of such menace that your flesh creeps.' Jack Tinker, *Mail*

'Bowles's performance has the icy power that will astound. There is a moment when he asks a thief he is terrorizing to look directly into his eyes; and I too believed, really believed, that they were black tunnels leading directly to hell.' Benedict Nightingale, *The Times*

You never know what having a drink with a pretty girl can lead to, do you!?

CHAPTER 5

EARLY THEATRES –
MORE DRAMAS

B ack in England the Old Vic decided for some reason they didn't want me, James or Bryan for their next season. Too corrupt, I suppose. The answer was to try to join a good repertory company. They don't really exist today but then, in the fifties, there were lots of them spread all over the country – weekly, fortnightly, three-weekly. There was only one monthly, but this was the apex of them all: the Bristol Old Vic. One of the best of the fortnightly reps was the Oxford Playhouse. The artistic director was the highly thought of Frank Hauser. I managed to get in for a season. I was twenty and the first part I was to play was a 'white wigged' old man in *The Man Who Came to Dinner*. Now I'm afraid that all actors (that is, the ones I knew) always considered the romantic side of joining a rep company. Unless you were going to be the leading man, the main concern was not so much the parts you would be offered, but who you were going to have an affair with! The very tricky part about this was that if you made your move too soon and it didn't work out, you had completely queered your pitch with all the other young women in the company. They would sympathize with the ex-girlfriend and certainly wouldn't want to be seen as having been a second choice. It's really quite a complicated life being young!

Anyway, playing a very old man didn't get me off to a very good start in the virility stakes, although, because it wasn't a big part, I had time for courting. There was a stunning juvenile actress that I was falling for, and I was about to declare my love when in early rehearsal I asked Frank Hauser, 'How do you think I should say this line, sir?'

'I'm paying you eight pounds ten shillings a week to know how to say that line,' he replied.

Well, that was me finished in the love stakes. I found that having my salary mentioned in front of the whole company humiliating. It also got a laugh. I didn't have any romance at Oxford. I did however make some lifelong friends: Ian Hendry, who went on to make many films including, of course, the villain in *Get Carter*, Prunella Scales and Gary Raymond. I also met several members of the Oxford University Dramatic Society (OUDS) – who all became good friends: Patrick Garland, Vernon Dobtcheff, and the playwright John McGrath. One of the happiest times at Oxford was when Ian Hendry and I were asked to perform cabaret for a May Ball. I had never seen so many beautiful young women in such lovely dresses. John McGrath promised to write his first play for me. He didn't. I saw *Why the Chicken* when it was put on at the Golders Green Empire. The young man who walked on in 'my' part was the astonishingly handsome Terence Stamp, and the whole audience, including me, gasped at his charismatic male beauty. I'll never forget it. No contest, I felt.

I saw Olivier in *Titus Andronicus* at this time, with Vivien Leigh and Anthony Quayle. I had never seen Olivier on stage before and I was thrilled. He was, I thought, awesome. Anthony Quayle was terrific too. I had occasion to meet Olivier many years later. After George Devine, the great innovator and director of the Royal Court Theatre, died a huge gala was arranged at the Old Vic in order to raise money to encourage new Writers. Actors who had played a leading role under George's reign at The Court were asked to do a turn, or enact a speech from whatever play they had been in.

I had played the lead in *The Happy Haven* (more of that later) by John Arden, so I was asked to do my big speech on the discovery of eternal youth! My two non-speaking assistants (I was conducting a scientific experiment) were James Bolam and Edward Fox. There were many great established stars including Peggy Ashcroft, Vanessa Redgrave, Geraldine McEwan, Robert Stephens, Albert Finney, Sir Alec Guinness and Sir Laurence Olivier. We all rehearsed on the stage of the Old Vic – just one day, I think. Anyway everyone watched each other. Guinness, who had just finished his piece from Ionesco's *Exit the King*, was watching me struggle to take a cigarette out of a packet during my solo.

'Excuse me,' he said. 'You might find that easier if you used a cigarette case.'

'I'm afraid I haven't got one, sir,' I replied.

'No, but I have,' said Guinness, and very kindly offered me his cigarette case.

I was very grateful. Olivier was standing on the other side of the stage about to come on as Archie Rice from *The Entertainer*.

'Dear boy,' he said as I exited, 'could I offer you some advice?' Thinking it was to be a note on my performance I shrank. 'Your exit, dear boy. Of course you will get a big round of applause when you exit there, but you will get an even bigger round of applause if you exit here.' Indicating a different opening in the wings.

'That's very kind of you, sir,' I replied, flattered and relieved it wasn't a note on my performance, 'but I am not exiting there because that is where you are about to come on.'

Olivier put a kindly arm around my shoulders, and his eyes went up to heaven as he said, 'My dear boy, don't worry about me. I can come on from anywhere.'

He meant it. He was invincible; he could do anything, anywhere, at any time. But all the same it was very, very kind of
him to help me in this way. I was still seemingly innocent or
stupid at this time. I had tea with a middle-aged lady who
asked me to join her at her little table in the Old Vic canteen
during a break. She was utterly charming. I was bewitched by
her. 'Who was that lovely lady?' I enquired of another table
after she had departed. 'Oh for God's sake, that's Dame Peggy
Ashcroft,' was the reply. One of the greatest moments of my life
was to happen at that rehearsal. Noël Coward, who was to be
acting a part in Wesker's *The Kitchen*, and who I had noticed sitting in the stalls watching us all, came up to me just before his
rehearsal began and said, 'I'm so sorry but what is your name,
dear boy?'

'Peter Bowles,' I replied.

The master looked at me for a long moment and then made
a humming noise and said, 'You're rather good.'

Perhaps I should have retired then – while I was at the top!
Back to reality. Back to the reps.

I had about ten weeks of a weekly rep after my season with
Oxford. A different play every week: farces, dramas. How did we
do it and drink and make love and learn our lines? Not a lot of
sleep and youth, youth, youth, I think is the answer. The rep was
Leatherhead, run by a very good woman called Hazel Vincent
Wallace, who I still see in Barnes where I now live, and although
she doesn't pat my bottom as she used to fifty years ago, she always
has time for a cheery chat.

I also did my first 'tour' (apart from the Old Vic) at around
this time. The extremely charming, dapper, and most friendly
Bill Owen had written, and was directing, a new play of his. It
was a thriller and he chose me to play the juvenile, and we
became at that time close friends. One of the 'dates' was Bath,
which in 1957/58 was a very different place to now. It was very
run-down after the bombing and the theatre still boasted the

old Victorian stage with the original Georgian stage under-
neath. All gone now.

I was haunted in Bath. I've never been haunted before or
since but I was haunted in Bath. It was particularly interesting
to me, because Albert Finney and I had looked into becoming
inspectors for the Society for Psychical Research during our
RADA holidays. I had digs with other members of the company at the Garrick's Head Pub, hard by the theatre. Directly
opposite was a large car park. (It is now a shopping complex but
in Georgian times it was open land.) There was a large room on
the first floor where we had our supper, and leading directly
from that was a long corridor with bedrooms off. My room was
at the very end. Two things to note: one, the corridor was carpeted until about ten feet before my bedroom door; and two, at
the end of the corridor outside my room you could still see
what had been a door long ago but was now completely
bricked up.

That first night in bed I heard footsteps coming down the
corridor, almost at a run, and the distinct change of sound as
the footfalls left the carpet and went onto the linoleum leading
to my door. The footsteps stopped outside my door. I waited
for the knock which didn't come, said, 'Who is it?' heard no
answer, got up and opened the door. There was no one there.
A few minutes later it happened again in exactly the same way.
I was again in bed, but as the footsteps came onto the lino I
called out, 'Who is it?' No answer. I got up and opened the
door; no one there. I thought it very strange, I tried to imagine
it was a member of the company fooling around, but didn't see
how it could be. I decided, although nervous by now, to stand
exactly by the door and wait. Sure enough I heard the hurry-
ing feet coming down the corridor, the footfalls came off the
carpeting onto the lino, one two three footsteps, and I opened
the door. There was no one there. I was awake most of the
night. Next morning I told the landlord; he wasn't surprised.

Apparently the pub had been investigated several times by the Psychical Research people.

The story was as follows. Sometime in the eighteenth century, at the time of Beau Nash, the large room used for supper had been a gaming room. A row had broken out over a game and one man challenged another to a duel. The car park opposite the pub was a duelling field in those days and the men repaired to the cloakroom to pick up their weapons. The cloakroom was now my bedroom, and the bricked-up door had led to a stairway straight to the street. The row flared again in the cloakroom and one man stabbed the other dead. There were men and women involved. The body was wrapped up in a woman's cloak and secretly carried to the nearby river. The cloak used in the wrapping was of a titled lady of the Churchill family. Some time in the 1930s a large clasp or brooch, such as would hold a cloak together, was found in the river. It had on it the Churchill coat of arms.

Well, my part in this story is absolutely true, that's all I can say.

I can also say we were paid on Fridays and we were paid by postal order. I think my wage was £9. We only played the theatre for a week, of course, and on the Friday I queued up with all the old age pensioners to cash in my postal order, which was attached in some way to indicate it was my theatre wages. There was a lovely girl at the serving hatch. I caught her eye whilst I was still queuing. She gave me a big smile, and I knew, it was on. Well you do, don't you, and it was Friday. We would have one night together before I had to leave Bath.

I arrived at the counter, she smiled again and said, 'I saw your play last night and I thought you were wonderful.'

'Thank you,' I said.

'It must be exciting being an actor,' she continued, as I slipped the postal order across the counter.

'I was wondering—' I didn't get any further. She had looked at the postal order.

'Oh, is that all you get paid?'

The smile had gone, my glamour as an actor had crumbled. Love was dead and bleeding on the post office floor. I hung my head and took my wages out into the grim war-torn Bath. Bill Owen thought it was very funny.

During this time my London digs were with James Villiers. By the way, they are called digs after an actor named Digs who, in Boswell's time, kept a list of good places for touring actors to stay. James had inherited a short lease of a very grand flat indeed in Notting Hill Gate. It was a luxury I had never known before. It was on two floors, close carpeted with five bedrooms and a huge drawing room. Apart from James and me there were three debs delights living at the flat. James sometimes took up one of the myriad 'stiffy' invitations that packed the drawing-room mantelpiece, but not as often as the other young men, who were all aristocratic and worked in the city. They seemed to go out every night in their dinner jackets and come back at three or four in the morning. They were always washed and stiff-collared and be-suited and off to the city by 7.30 a.m. the next morning. Youth, youth youth. James also had a maid, a charming old family retainer, who came into his flat, or 'my chambers' as James called them, every morning to prepare early breakfast, make the beds and brush and polish shoes. Alice was her name, and I always felt close to her because of the early profession of my parents. It was in this flat that I had my twenty-first birthday party. Apart from a good time being had by all, I remember Robert Helpmann performing his famous routine with a plate of sausages held close to his crotch – I leave the rest to your imagination – and the glowering presence of an uninvited American actor, Marc Lawrence, who you may remember always played gangsters, most memorably the Mafia man, Ziggy, who turns up for his counterfeit dollars at the end of *Key Largo*. He had been invited over to England to play Macbeth at the Nottingham rep, but was always drunk and couldn't learn his lines. He was fired and ended up at my party, *very drunk*.

Nottingham rep was my next engagement, run by the highly regarded director, Val May. It was good to be able to live at home. A man called Hugh Willatt, a local Nottingham solicitor, was the chairman of Nottingham Playhouse, and I remember walking along a street one day when a voice hailed me loudly: 'Aren't you a member of the Nottingham Playhouse Company?'

'Yes,' I replied proudly, 'I am.'

'Well, I'm the chairman of the Playhouse,' he shouted, 'and I don't want to see a member of my company wearing yellow socks. Make sure you don't wear them again in public.'

Hugh Willatt later became Sir Hugh Willatt, Chairman of the Arts Council, and lived near me and my wife in Hammersmith. He made a strong and unwelcome pass at my wife whilst I was away filming. My wife didn't tell me when I returned, as she knew only too well that I would have called on Sir Hugh wearing very yellow socks indeed!

Nottingham rep in those days was housed in a strange building. I think it had been converted from a furniture warehouse. The dressing rooms, such as they were, were directly under the stage (keep your voice down) and partitioned by thin asbestos sheets (keep your voice down!). Also housed under the stage was the old central heating boiler which was fuelled by coke (a sort of dried-out charcoal) and the fumes were terrible, both under the stage and on. In the winter we always had to have glasses of water on the stage. I suppose the audience must have thought the bluish haze was atmospheric effects. It was not good for the health, of course, and I remember a young Peter Gill (now a celebrated director and playwright) being taken to hospital with bad chest complaints.

The only panto I have ever done was at the Nottingham rep. It was Red Riding Hood and I was playing The Wolf. In the light of 'you'll never play an Englishman', I probably used a foreign accent. It was certainly a pointer to the many villains I was to play on television!

The wolf, of course, was to have a large tail as part of his costume. The general covering was a wolf's headdress with big ears and a woolly all-in-one sort of siren suit. Before the woolly suit was put on I had to strap on the tail. A belt went around my waist to which a pad and long wire-supported bushy tail was attached, flush against the bottom of my spine. The tail would then be gently pulled through the hole at the back of the costume as I dressed. We did two performances every day, and I think played for one month instead of the usual two weeks, Nottingham being what was known as 'fort-nightly rep'.

After about three weeks I became acutely aware of a growing discomfort at the base of my spine, just where the 'crack' of the buttocks starts, just where the pad that joined the tail was placed. It is properly called the coccyx. On investigation with my fingers I could feel a lump about the size of a hazelnut, or small walnut. It didn't bother me, but it was sore when I was wearing the tail. Because the tail was long it had to be stiffened, as I said, with wire, strong wire, so the tail stood out and bounced up and down as I prowled the stage.

I went to my doctor. He was mystified. 'I've never seen any-thing quite like it,' he said. 'I'd better send you to a specialist.' I don't know what specialists who look at the top of the crack of your bottom are called but anyway I was sent to one. 'Drop your trousers and underpants, young man,' he said, 'and bend over with your back towards me.' As I began to do as I was told, I was aware that he was dressed in a black jacket and waistcoat with something I'd not seen before: striped trousers.

Bare bummed, with my trousers and pants around my shoes, I turned and bent over.

'Good Lord!' he exclaimed. 'I haven't seen anything like that since I was in the war in Africa.'

'What? What is it?' I said. I was very worried, despite his rather delighted tone of voice.

'You've got Jeep Bottom,' he said. 'I never thought I'd see it in civilian life. Pull up your pants for a moment and I'll explain. But first, there's nothing to worry about. I'll cure you.'

He went on to tell me that in nature, in *On the Origin of Species*, the human was still near enough to the monkeys to be capable, under certain circumstances, of growing a tail. And I was growing one. Apparently at the base of the spine (he didn't say whether it applied to women but I suppose it does) there are the dormant roots of hair follicles. During the war jeep drivers, with the continual bumping up and down of the poorly sprung jeeps and the rough terrain, could begin to grow tails. That is, the hair would try to sprout through the skin, but in fact would be compressed and compacted, forming a lump. Did I drive a jeep?

'No,' I said, and explained to him about the wolf costume and the tail.

He roared with laughter. 'Who'd have thought it?' he said. 'I'm so glad you came to me. I'll be able to dine out on this for years. Now what I'm going to do is lance that lump, and squeeze out the matted hairs, put a plaster on and you'll be as right as rain. How much longer have you in the panto?'

'I finish tomorrow,' I said.

'Well put a big wad of cotton wool over the spot and you'll be fine. Oh and don't let anyone pat you on the bottom for a few days.'

Another memorable production by the director Val May was Chekhov's *Three Sisters* in which I played Andre. Sian Phillips, I remember, was one of the sisters. It was after this production that Val May called me to his little office, and gave me, in hindsight, profound professional advice. 'Peter', he said, 'I have been watching you closely over the past months and especially your performance as Andre. You have reached a crossroads in your career.' (I was twenty-one or twenty-two.) 'You have the ability to take the stony road which will lead you eventually to great classical heights or to take the smoother road that will lead you to great success as a popular actor. Both roads will be uphill but you have the talent to get to the top of either of them. The choice is up to you.' Looking back on it fifty-odd years later, it was a remarkably generous, kind, paternal thing to say to a young actor. I, of course, didn't fully understand, because I knew, I absolutely knew, I wanted to be a classical actor. That was the only reason to be an actor, I thought, jeep bottom or no jeep bottom. However, as I now know the stony path was blocked by huge boulders and by default I ended up on the other road. I am a very lucky man to have had any success at all, and all things have turned out for the best – unless you know of any theatre company that would like a 72-year-old Hamlet! As I write this, I have just been offered King Lear, which I have turned down in order to play Crocker Harris in Rattigan's *The Browning Version*, directed by Sir Peter Hall. Make of that what you will.

*

James's lease had expired on his Notting Hill chambers so on leaving Nottingham rep he and I took a lease on a tiny flat in Marylebone. A wonderful spot, as it turned out, for every actor who had got drunk in the pubs of the West End to beat a path to. James Villiers was, without my realizing it, to have an important influence on my life. Unlike Mum and Dad I had never really met, let alone lived with, anyone from the aristocratic classes. I discovered they were very, very different; and in later life when I did in fact play upper-class Englishmen, what I had observed from James automatically was 'there' in my skill if required. James was a great model for stoicism and cleanliness. Although not a great model in a number of other ways, as anyone who knew his towering personality will agree.

James, because the acting world of the day wanted 'street cred' working-class actors in the new wave of theatre, was out of work for long periods of time. Months and months and months out of work. Every day he would arise cheerfully, take his bath, which usually I had run for him, have his breakfast, which usually I had cooked for him (shades of my father), and then open his mail. Then he would repair to his bedroom, apply his various unguents and 'perfumes' and appear immaculate in the minuscule 'drawing room' in stiff collar, tie and beautifully cut suit, coloured handkerchief in his top pocket and always a white handkerchief just protruding from his left sleeve. He would then answer his mail, make a cup of coffee and light a cigarette. He would drink his coffee in a flat-armed leather armchair, putting his cup and saucer (never a mug) on one arm and his ashtray on the other. James would then remain all day in that chair waiting for the phone call that never came from his agent. He never complained, never admitted or showed depression and never moved, except for perhaps the loo or another cup of coffee. At six o'clock, when he knew his agent's office would have closed for the day, he would arise, have perhaps some toast and a boiled egg and then venture out to go drinking, and I mean drinking, the life and soul of the pub or party. James was to prove in later years that he was a very fine actor indeed.

I have many stories involving James Villiers but perhaps this one, which also gives me a chance to drop a few names, will suffice. It was Emlyn Williams's younger son Brook's twenty-first birthday. He had invited a few friends over to his father's house for a drink. The friends were James Villiers, Bryan Pringle, Peter O'Toole, Albert Finney and myself. Brookie's present from his father had been a new Ford Anglia. It was decided at around 4 am to continue drinking at a 'porters' pub' in Covent Garden. The mode of transport was obviously Brook's new car. The Williams's family house was in the middle of the curve of Pelham Crescent where the small car was parked. All six of us managed to squeeze in, with Brook of course driving, drink having been taken, to say the least. As he drove away there was a continual metallic sound of Brook clipping the wing mirrors of every other car parked in the crescent. All of them rather grand cars. The noise at 4 a.m. was alarming, and coming up the crescent towards us was a police car. We were stopped and asked to disembark.

Peter O'Toole, already famous, Albert Finney, already famous, Peter Bowles, unknown, James Villiers, Bryan Pringle and Brook Williams were lined up against the railings like naughty schoolboys.

"Ere, 'ere, 'ere,' said a policeman. 'What do you think you are a doing of?' (Or words to that effect.)

James Villiers spoke immediately. 'We are very sorry, officer, but the fact of the matter is that whilst travelling in an easterly direction Mr Albert Finney broke wind, and in the ensuing panic, which as you can imagine was quite considerable in such a confined space, Mr Brook Williams, in his endeavour to open a window, lost control momentarily and struck an Austin.'

The bemused policeman ignored our hysteria at James's explanation finishing with 'an Austin', took down Mr Brook Williams's particulars and told us to bugger off.

James Villiers has left the world of acting with a strange legacy: the expression and the word 'luvvie'. James always, from 1955, when I first met him, called everyone 'lovey', and he was famous in the profession for using the expression and when actors imitated him, as they often did, they always used his word 'lovey'. It is an unfair legacy because James was not in any way a 'luvvie' in the sense the word is used today. He never ever spoke of acting, never ever spoke about himself; he was camp, yes, theatrical, yes, but definitely and absolutely not a 'luvvie'. James died before the derogatory meaning came into modern journalistic vogue.

*

In between my seasons in rep I managed to get the odd part in television. Just enough money to pay my half of the rent. Then I auditioned for the Bristol Old Vic. I got the job. This was the big one for anyone hoping to follow a classical career. I was only to play as cast, of course, but the Bristol Old Vic had strong links with the Old Vic in London, the National Theatre of its day. Maybe I would make a triumphant return.

Just after I had given my audition, which had taken place in London, and was walking along Tottenham Court Road, I bumped into the beautiful young actress that I had spoken to in *The Face of Love* at RADA. You remember the sixteen-year-old who swaddled a pretend baby in the crowd scenes. Sue Bennett was with Dudley Sutton, who I knew well. We stopped and chatted. Sue was with Ipswich rep. Dudley was soon to be the young Mr Sloane in Joe Orton's play. As I exchanged a few pleasantries with Sue, including showing off, no doubt, that I had just got into the Bristol Old Vic, I could sense Cupid drawing back his bow.

My start at Bristol wasn't too auspicious in the classical sense. I was to play Prince Escalus in *Romeo and Juliet*. A very showy part in which Charles Gray (Big Mother) had been so magnificent at the Old Vic. This was good because I knew all the lines, having been in the play for nearly a year on the Old Vic tour. Leonard Rossiter, who was to become a good friend, was Friar Laurence, Annette Crosbie was Juliet and the part of Romeo was to be played by the young Canadian stage and film star Paul Massie. John Hale had recently taken over the Bristol Old Vic and this *Romeo* was to be his Big Production. It was fraught, mainly because Paul Massie, a dear sweet young man, was very nervous and couldn't learn his lines, even 'carrying the book' at the dress rehearsals. It was also proving to be very long. However I, in rehearsals, was magnificent; even more magnificent at the dress rehearsal in my gorgeous becloaked swaggering costume, bestriding the stage like a colossus as I delivered the last lines of the play: 'Never was a story of more woe, than this of Juliet and her Romeo.'

The first night, everyone nervous; Paul almost hysterical, Annette Crosbie fine, Leonard compelling, I as usual magnificent. Hours passed, the tragic couple finally died. Prince Escalus swept on and bestrode and dominated the stage. 'Never was a story of more woe, than this of Romeo' (pause) 'and his Juliet.' Curtain. Much bowing, much relief. It had taken about four hours. I walked off stage and was immediately slammed up against a wall by John Hale, his slamming hand actually around my throat. The throat that had issued forth the cocked-up last line. 'You've completely ruined the whole fucking production, you c**t. Four hours completely fucked up by you. You owe everyone an apology.' It wasn't a good start to my classical career. The cast didn't want an apology. They all thought it was an hysterical gaffe, and were just grateful to have got through it. I wasn't fired but I got much more lowly character parts after that!

One of the next plays was *The Long and the Short and the Tall* by Willis Hall and Keith Waterhouse. It had been a tremendous success in London with a cast that included many of my friends; Robert Shaw, Peter O'Toole, Ronnie Fraser, David Andrews, Edward Judd and Bryan Pringle. Bryan had played Smudger, the north country soldier. The play had been directed by Lindsay Anderson, a famous and greatly respected director. The Bristol Old Vic were to give the play its first 'out of town' production.

Bryan Pringle, who was really my closest friend, was coming down to see the production and to see me playing his part of Smudger. On St Pancras Station he bumped into Lindsay Anderson. After telling him where he was going and who he was going to see, Lindsay Anderson said, so Bryan told me, 'Peter Bowles in *The Long and the Short and the Tall*? There isn't a single part he could play.'

'Oh,' said Bryan. 'Why do you say that, Lindsay? Actually he's playing Smudger.'

'That's even more ridiculous,' said Lindsay. 'Peter Bowles, in my opinion, can't act. I know because I've seen him wearing a suit.'

Now this left-wing snobbery has haunted me all my life, although I felt much better when years later Michael Gambon, who was playing Lear at Stratford, and is, in my and many other people's opinion, probably England's finest actor, apologized to me at a party. Michael, who is a bit of a 'dresser', had arrived in denims and was embarrassed.

'Don't be silly Michael,' I said. 'It doesn't matter what you wear.'

'Well, I'd have liked to have worn a suit but I've just driven up from Stratford and I've got no decent clothes down there because if you don't dress like a fucking petrol pump attendant they don't think you can act,' replied Michael.

Also joining the cast of *The Long and the Short and the Tall* was Patrick Garland, who had just left Oxford and was to play Taffy, the Welsh soldier. Patrick, as we were to discover, had been the original Bamforth (the part O'Toole played in London) when it was done by OUDS at the Edinburgh Festival. Oddly enough O'Toole only got the part by chance because when it was in rehearsal with Albert Finney, Albert was struck down by appendicitis/peritonitis. Well, they say Bogart was fourth choice for Rick in *Casablanca* – and O'Toole's part went to Laurence Harvey in the film. That's show business. Leonard Rossiter was our Bamforth and he was of course brilliant.

The next play was to be *The Edwardians*, adapted from Vita Sackville-West's novel, and to play Vita Sackville-West John Hale had invited a twenty-one-year-old actress he had just directed at Ipswich. Yes, at the read-through, sitting in a yellow dress, showing just enough leg to drive any man wild, was Sue Bennett. Cupid released his arrow. My disadvantage was that I was to play Sue's eighty-five-year-old butler, stooped and again in a white wig. We broke for lunch. I asked Sue, who at this time didn't really know anyone else in the company, to come over the road for a drink and a sandwich. I ordered the drinks, but before Sue had decided on her sandwich, I asked her to marry me.

Well, here is a beautiful young actress who has just arrived to be the leading lady at England's greatest rep theatre, and this lunatic 'character' actor is asking her to marry him. I think I may have spoilt her lunch, because she knew I was serious from my tone, and she thought I was mad, hopefully not dangerously so. She kept well clear of me socially for some time and I discovered later that she also genuinely thought I was gay, which was even more confusing for her. The reason for this confusion was that she had seen me play Princess Grace very convincingly in Behan's *The Hostage*. I, however, was very much in love, the arrow having pierced my heart with tremendous force. Oh, by the way, Sue said, 'No.'

The season continued. I was persistent. I managed to persuade Sue I wasn't gay but that was as far as it went. She was too busy acting, having a good time. She was only just twenty-one and anyway she had a regular boyfriend at Oxford.

John Arden was the playwright in residence at Bristol University at that time and he had written a play for the students called *The Happy Haven*. It was to be directed by one of the new exciting directors from the Royal Court, London.

The Royal Court at this time was the absolute cutting edge of British drama. George Devine had created it. Its express purpose was to encourage and put on, come what may, new plays by new young writers. *Look Back in Anger* had been his first great success – but there were many more. Olivier had played Archie Rice in *The Entertainer* there in 1957. Every actor/actress wanted to be asked to play at the Royal Court.

The director from the Court who came to Bristol was

William (Bill) Gaskill, who was later to achieve enormous success at Olivier's National Theatre and elsewhere. Bill decided he wanted the leading role to be played by a professional actor and the Bristol Old Vic was approached. I got the part. I think Bristol was glad to be rid of me for a while, and after all it was semi-amateur and was only being done at the university. I had never worked with anyone of Bill Gaskill's talent before, and both I, and more importantly the play, were a huge success. George Devine came to see it. The play was to be presented at the Royal Court later that year with a full professional cast and I was to play the lead.

Meanwhile the Bristol Old Vic were invited to Baalbeck in the Lebanon. Apart from the heat, and the beauty of Baalbeck's ruins, I was struck by the tremendous class differences. You were either rich and spoke French and were probably Christian, or you were one of the vast majority of the very poor people who were Muslim. The rich ruled the poor. The girls had to be very careful what they wore. Once I was being driven around with an actress wearing shorts and I remember the car stopping at traffic lights and being surrounded by a mob of very angry men who shook the car alarmingly before we got away. This was on a day off in Beirut. Also, there were special beaches for the likes of us, that is 'the wealthy', and we saw horrible scenes of police whipping young men who strayed onto our part of the beach. We couldn't light the plays in the daytime, or rehearse them – too hot. So the first days there were in fact nights – all night rehearsing. Exhausting, but too much adrenaline to be able to sleep in the day.

Sue was having a wonderful time. She was a sensation in the Lebanon. Blonde, blonde, blonde and with the looks and figure to go with it. Although I was supposedly 'going out' with her I was having a terrible time. She was attracting very rich Lebanese like bears to a beehive. I couldn't even buy her any sort of present in the shops as she would be given the article. My protests were ignored. I was suddenly, it seemed, with a goddess. Sue basked in the attention. I was, through this and the fact I had almost no sleep, going quite literally mad. I'm afraid it ended up in a very dramatic and unfortunate way.

The hotel in Baalbeck was lovely. As I remember it had a very large landing where the cast collected if it was too hot outside. The bedrooms mostly led off this landing. Anyway Sue's did. I wanted to talk to Sue; she didn't want to talk to me. Fed up with me pestering her, she retired to her room. I followed and found the door locked, and my calling and knocking unanswered. I was suffused with jealousy, very confused from lack of sleep and only too aware I couldn't compete for Sue's attention against millionaire Lebanese men. I had a breakdown. Some things I remember, others I was told afterwards. Anyway, the sum of the parts was that I let out an enormous cry of anguish and kicked Sue's door until both door and doorframe were smashed. Sue, of course, was terrified. Members of the company held me. (I wasn't going to be violent to Sue, I only wanted her attention.) A doctor was called and it seems I was injected with something that calmed me down and I was put to bed. When I recovered I was naturally asked to report to the company manager, who, like in my Old Vic days, was Douglas Morris. On my way to his room I do remember the other company members being understanding. They knew, at least, that I was half mad with unrequited love. Douglas Morris was very understanding too. The trouble was, the main thrust of his understanding, if I may use that term, was that women were not to be relied on, that the love of a man was much more satisfactory in every way. He began to take his trousers down and gestured towards the bed. Yes, he who had warned me off the friendship of Bryan Pringle and James Villiers on the American tour, as they were a corrupting influence on me, was about to set me on the right path. I realized later that Douglas Morris was perhaps the first boulder I met on the rocky path to a classical career. Anyway I made my very strong excuses and left.

Sue had nothing more to do with me. I was subdued and ashamed until we got back to England when I once again tried to court her, to no avail. The contract with the Bristol Old Vic was finished. We were both back in London. Sue was living with her parents in Highgate; I had now moved into a flat owned by the painter Sidney Nolan, whose paintings were everywhere. My flatmates were the jolliest people in the world. They were all from the London Festival Ballet. Kenneth MacMillan was a constant visitor. Oh, I could write a whole chapter on the fun that went on with ballet dancers.

Sue wouldn't answer phone calls. Her parents threatened to inform the police if I didn't stop ringing. Sue did not want to have anything whatsoever to do with me. Please go away. I got the message. Then I had an idea. Before Sue had come to Bristol I had met a rich girl, my first and only rich girl. She was stunning in her beauty. She owned and drove a lovely convertible sports car, skied, shot, yachted – and she loved me. Then Sue came to Bristol.

I decided to contact stunning rich girl, who lived with her parents in a stately home, and ask her to come and live with me in London. She was delighted, thrilled, just give her a week or two to sort things out (and for me to find a room!) and she would be with me. Bryan Pringle who was rehearsing *Fings Ain't Wot They Used T' Be* with Joan Littlewood, rang me. Sue, who knew he was my best friend, had tracked him down (she didn't know where I was as I had gone away), and asked him to convey the message that she now realized that she was in love with me and wanted to meet. We did. I asked her immediately after we had kissed to marry me. She accepted. I was very, very happy, Sue was very, very happy, stunning rich girl was not. She was to express this unhappiness in a very surprising way on the day of our marriage.

CHAPTER 6

THE MARRIAGE AND THE LONDON DEBUT

I remember the resident stage carpenter at Bristol saying to me, not long after Sue had been acting there, 'Peter, I've been here since the theatre opened after the war. Susan Bennett is by far the best actress we've had here, and we have the pick. She is going to be a big star.' Peter Hall obviously thought so too, because when he became the artistic director of the RSC in 1960 he invited Sue to join his company; she accepted. Who wouldn't?

The trouble, and of course we discussed it, was that we had just agreed to get married. I had just won her love after a tremendous courtship. Sue had realized she loved me just as much. She is twenty-one and I am twenty-three. She is beautiful and will be in Stratford when we get married. I will be in London or wherever, certainly not Stratford. I know, and so does she, that there will be dozens and dozens of very randy actors in the romantic haven of Stratford upon Avon. I asked her to turn down Peter Hall and stay with me. She agreed and made a decision that as soon as we were married and started a family she would give up acting and look after the children – and me. Now I knew I had to succeed in my career.

I was contracted to do two plays at the Royal Court. *The Happy Haven* and then, immediately, *Platonov*, a play by Chekhov that had only been discovered in 1920, and I don't think had ever been performed before. It was to star Rex Harrison. Rex Harrison was a huge star at this time and this was to be his first stage play since *My Fair Lady*. I had seen his astonshing performance whilst in America.

The cast of *The Happy Haven* were all to wear masks. That is, all the patients in the Haven wore masks, but the doctor in charge, Dr Copperthwaite, me, didn't. At least if I was any good I would be recognized. The cast included Susan Engel (also from Bristol Old Vic), Frank Finlay, Rachel Roberts, Edward Fox and James Bolam. We had the read-through on stage on the set of Wesker's *I'm Talking About Jerusalem*. Immediately after the read-through I was summoned to the office of the general manager – Pieter Rogers was his name – and he was very angry.

I had been paid £16 a week at the Bristol Old Vic and I could remember moaning to my dressing-room companion in Bristol that the Court were only going to pay me £15. I was once again ignorant, stupid. I thought the great Royal Court in London would pay more. I didn't understand the ways of the world at all.

'I have been informed that you have been complaining to people about your salary,' said Mr Rogers.

'Well no, sir, well yes, sir, but only to my dressing-room friends.'

'It's all over London that you have been complaining about your salary here. We have had some of the greatest actors in the world, all being paid what you're being paid – Olivier, Guinness, Ashcroft and many, many more. Who do you think you are? You will promise me now that you will tell everyone you meet that you are being properly paid at the Royal Court, otherwise I will send you back to the provinces from whence you came.' Shrivelling stuff. Not a good start. I'd better be good.

'I'm very sorry, sir. I am a good actor but I've been stupid. I will do as you say,' I whimpered.

Bill Gaskill spent many, many hours teaching us, all of us, even the 'unmasked one', to wear and act in masks. It was wonderful, revealing, stimulating and the seeds and roots of what was to become the remarkable Royal Court Studio for Professional Actors, but more of that later. Oh, by the way, there were many songs in the play and the music was composed by a young Dudley Moore. The play got terrible notices. George Devine seemed to revel in this. 'The worse the notices, the better the play' was his expressed opinion. He loved his writers, backed them, supported them, encouraged them. A truly great man.

I got very good notices, however. 'Another star is born from the provinces' was the headline in one paper. I was very pleased with this because the other stars that had recently been born from the provinces were Albert Finney and Peter O'Toole, but the newspaper got it wrong this time. Once the play was on, we started to rehearse *Platonov* with Rex Harrison.

Platonov, which has been revived in recent years with Sir Ian McKellen, entitled *Wild Honey*, was to be directed by George Devine himself, which was just as well as it turned out because Mr Harrison required very strong handling.

I had the very good part of Kiril, a desperate young man who needs Platonov's help, and therefore I had an important scene with Rex Harrison. Immediate trouble. Not only was I the youngest member of the company – I was twenty-three – but I was also taller than Rex. I made my entrance at the first rehearsal (on stage at the Court) and approached Rex. He held out his arm at full length.

'What is your name, dear chap?' he enquired, as he would enquire for weeks.

'Peter Bowles, sir, Peter.' I replied.

'Oh yes, of course,' said Rex. 'Well, Peter, always keep a good arm's length from me while you are on stage.'

George Devine left us alone for a week or so, then I began to get into, and act the desperate side of my character.

'Dear boy, I'm so sorry what *is* your name?' asked Rex once again.

'Peter, sir.' I said.

'George,' Rex called out to George Devine sitting in the stalls, 'don't you think it would be a good idea if—' He turned towards me. 'I'm sorry, dear boy.'

'Peter,' I said again.

'If Peter sat down the moment he comes on stage?'

'No, Rex,' came the very firm reply from George. 'He is very agitated, he needs money and help from you, the last thing he would do is sit down. Now please just carry on, Rex.'

I thought Rex Harrison was absolutely brilliant during rehearsals; he was, I thought, the most talented actor I had ever worked with. I remember meeting Albert Finney on the underground whilst I was still in rehearsals.

'How is it going?' asked Albert.

'I'm working with Rex Harrison, Albert. I think he is a great actor.'

'Careful,' said Albert, who was soon to show us in *Luther* what a great actor he was. 'Don't use the word "great" unless you really, really mean it. There aren't many great actors about.' And on he rushed.

I did admire Rex, though, and watched him often during rehearsals standing in the wings while he made a long solo 'front cloth' speech. On the penultimate rehearsal he came off stage after this particular speech, and as usual found me standing there.

'Oh good, oh good,' said Rex. 'I am so glad you have been watching me, because I need your help, Peter.' He'd got my name by now. I expected to be sent on some errand, but no. 'Peter,' said Rex, putting an arm round me, 'I've been watching you too during these rehearsals. I think you're a very talented young actor.' What on earth was coming, I wondered, feeling very worried, but extremely flattered. 'And because you are so talented you've probably noticed I don't know how to say the last line of that speech I've just delivered. Have you noticed that, Peter?'

'Yes,' I replied as one professional actor to another, 'I have noticed, Rex.' Well I had, this fool had.

'I knew you would have noticed,' continued a seemingly benign Rex. 'Now please tell me, Peter, how you would say it, because I need help.' I told him. 'My God,' said Rex with an intake of breath. 'That's brilliant. I'd never have thought of saying it that way in a thousand years. Say it again.' I did. 'Let me try it,' said Rex, he tried it. 'Yes, that's it, that's it. I'm so grateful, Peter. I knew you would know how to say it,' and he squeezed me gently and walked off.

The next day, or actually the next night, was the early morning of the day we were to open. It was the dress rehearsal; it was about 3.30 a.m. and the stage was awash with blood. The blood of actors. A lot of it belonged to Graham Crowden, who was beside himself with grief. There had been massive cuts. Over an hour had been taken out of the play – re-jigs, new links, a classic nightmare of the theatre. When I came on for my scene with Rex, Rex called out to George, who was pipe-smoking furiously in the stalls, 'George, this scene with Peter seems an obvious scene to cut, don't you think?'

'No, Rex, I don't,' replied George in a very authoritative, 'I'm directing this play and running this theatre' sort of voice, and on we went.

About half an hour later Rex is performing his big front-cloth speech. I'm certainly not standing in the wings this time. I'm sitting rather collapsed with most of the company in the stalls.

Rex reaches the last line – doesn't say it, stops, puts one hand to shade his eyes and looks into the stalls. 'George, I'm so sorry to stop.' He looks at his watch. 'Good God, is that the time? I am so sorry to stop, George. Is Peter Bowles out there?' I raised a hand. 'Would you mind standing up for a moment, Peter, so I can see you?' Everyone is mystified, riveted but mystified. I'm not mystified; I have deep forebodings as I duly stand. 'Now, George, Peter Bowles has instructed me how I'm supposed to say this last line and I've forgotten his instructions. Would you mind giving me your instructions again, Peter?'

'FOR FUCK'S SAKE GET ON WITH IT, REX,' shouted George, who had had quite enough.

Rex continued, I was let off the hook, the incident was never mentioned again, and I loved George Devine very much indeed.

Platonov had a very distinguished cast which included Rachel Roberts, who of course was in *The Happy Haven*, and she often went over to Rex's flat – which was Vivien Leigh's flat – in Eton Square to 'help him with his lines'. I shared a dressing room with Ronnie Barker, who even then was buying and selling little antiques and postcards. I bought two 'old master' prints from him. The leading lady was Elvi Hale, a lovely young actress who was having serious trouble with Rex. We had opened and Rex, who had been quite brilliant in rehearsals, had reverted to a 'please like me, I'm charming Rex Harrison' performance – and Elvi Hale was having trouble.

At one point very near the end of the play, when all the cast are on stage, Rex comes on to tell Elvi's character that he, Platonov, has found her husband on the railway line and that he is dead. Elvi quite understandably always left a moment's pause while she took in this shocking news before she spoke her reply. Rex had taken to counting, yes counting, 'one, two, three, four,' during the pause before Elvi spoke. We could all hear it, and Elvi was going mad with unhappiness. The company rallied round her. 'You've got to say something, Elvi. You've simply got to tell him you're upset.' She agreed she would pluck up courage at the matinee next day. As usual the news of her husband's death came, then the pause and the counting and then a few minutes later the curtain, curtain calls, final curtain down.

'Rex, could I have a word?' said a tremulous young Elvi. The cast threw themselves behind sofas or slid around stage flats to listen and observe what was about to happen.

'Yes, dear,' said Rex. 'What is it?'

She told him amid floods of tears what had been happening, what he had been doing. We were all silently applauding her. Rex was absolutely aghast.

'I've been counting in your pause? My God, I must be losing my marbles,' said Rex, holding the sobbing Elvi in his arms. 'How long have I been doing it?'

'Since the first night,' sobbed Elvi.

'Well that's appalling,' said Rex. 'I'm so very, very sorry. Why didn't you tell me before? Perhaps I should see a doctor.' Elvi is now almost collapsing with relief and emotion. 'Please, Elvi darling, come to my dressing room and have a glass of champagne. You should have told me earlier. I'm so, so sorry.'

And off they went. We all danced onto the stage. It was all over, problem solved. Rex is all right really, we thought.

We were wrong on both counts. That evening's performance came and so eventually did the line informing Elvi's character of her husband's death. Pause, and from Rex Harrison as Platonov came a very loud, 'ONE, TWO, THREE, FOUR.' It was so loud the audience began to titter.

*

Many years later I was asked to do *The Admirable Crichton* opposite Rex. I declined. I believe Felicity Kendal's husband, Michael Rudman, who directed it, had 'fun'.

It was after the play at the Royal Court that a very important moment in my life occurred, although I didn't realize it at the time. The door to a classical career was opened to me. The Bristol Old Vic asked me to come back for their next season as the leading man. The first play was to be *Macbeth*. I turned down the offer. No, I thought, I'm a London actor now. No more rep for me. Little did I know that door was never to open again. Well not for many, many years, and only after I had great success on the other 'smoother' road that Val May had suggested was also open to me.

It was now the end of October 1960 and Sue and I were to be married in April 1961. We, of course, were not living together at this time. Sue was at home and I had left my jolly ballet dancers and was now renting a room from Mr and Mrs Bryan Pringle.

My next job was to be my first proper West End play. *J.B.* at the Phoenix Theatre, starring Paul Rogers, Donald Sinden, Constance Cummings and Sir John Clements. It couldn't miss, after all it had won the Pulitzer Prize in America. I auditioned for the part, the director was Laurier Lister. I was to play the role of a reporter and understudy Donald Sinden. The other reporter was to be played by my old friend from Oxford and Bristol, Patrick Garland. We were known as 'The Dolly Sisters'. Nothing camp about us dear.

Donald Sinden was very, very kind to me and treated me as an absolute equal. I learnt a great deal about how an actor should behave, both on and off stage, from Sir Donald Sinden. Bless him.

We rehearsed for four weeks and I never had a single note from Laurier Lister until the final dress rehearsal. After giving notes to everyone else he turned to me, pushed his glasses down his nose and said, 'Peter Bowles, you are a very naughty boy. I've been watching you for the past four weeks and you have been changing your performance. You got this job because of your very good audition. That's what I want, your audition per-formance.' I had of course completely forgotten what I'd done at my audition, but the show opened to terrible reviews and the notice went up immediately that the show would only play for two weeks so it didn't really matter. Except it did. Sue and I had planned our marriage around this play and the wages it would bring. Our wedding day was booked for Saturday 8 April, the day *J.B.* closed.

We were married at Highgate Church near where Sue lived, and the reception was to be at Sue's parents' house.

Bryan Pringle was my best man and my two ushers were to be James Villiers and Albert Finney. Albert arrived late. He was starring in the hugely successful *Billy Liar* and had overslept. He arrived with his raincoat hurriedly thrown over his pyjama jacket – but he did have proper trousers on. What he hadn't forgotten, though, was his wedding present: an envelope containing a cheque for £250. That is a sum equivalent to about £3,500 today. It set Sue and me up, kept us going, for I was to be often out of work over the coming months. Thank you again, Albert.

The biggest laugh I have ever got in my whole long career was at my wedding. It came from the congregation when I said, 'With all my worldly goods I thee endow.' It was a lovely reception, of course, so lovely that Albert decided that he couldn't make his matinee and rang his theatre with a very husky 'I've lost my voice' excuse. This was Trevor Bannister's first break because he was Albert's understudy and he was 'spotted' that afternoon. I had to get back to my matinee, though, so Sue and I left in the traditional hired Rolls-Royce for a quick lunch in Hampstead, where we had rented an extraordinary flat. As the Rolls turned into Hampstead High Street I heard a car hooting loudly. On looking out of the window I saw an open sports car had drawn up beside us. In the car was the stunning rich girl from Bristol, and when she saw she had attracted my attention she gave me a huge 'V' sign and zoomed off. I didn't mention this to Sue. I met stunning rich girl twenty-five years later when she came round to my dressing room after leaving a note at the stage door. We went for a drink. I could sense the embers were not quite cold. If I had blown they would have glowed, but when she told me what her husband did, my breath was sharply sucked in, and I made my polite excuses and we parted.

After my last show that Saturday, Sue met me at the stage door with our overnight bag packed. We were going straight on our honeymoon. Yes, we were going to Maidenhead for one night. I didn't realize the implication until much later.

Our little flat in Hampstead was divided by a staircase which went on to the next flat upstairs. We were above two shops and the only loo for us was at the bottom of the stairs. There was no letter box and all the deliveries, mail, milk and so on, were put through the little open window of the loo. Quite a shock when it happened, I can tell you. It had two rooms and a kitchen; no bathroom as such. The bath was in the kitchen, in a cupboard. It folded down on old hinges with a dangle of rubber pipes, and with an old door over it (with cloth), it also served as a table. What with eating and bathing it was in and out of that narrow cupboard like a cuckoo out of a cuckoo clock. We never opened the curtains in the bedroom because the room was so horrible for us to look at. The living room, which was across the divide of the communal stairs, was quite different.

We had rented the flat on a short lease from a concert pianist who was on a world tour, and in the living room were not one but two Blüthner grand pianos. The room had at some time been 'Tudorized', complete with wood panelled walls and an enormous open, working, Tudor stone fireplace, two chairs and an uncarpeted parquet floor. I never worked while we were in that flat, or learnt to play the piano.

After a few months we took over the lease of James Villiers's flat in Chiltern Street and an important part of my artistic life began.

George Devine and Bill Gaskill from the Royal Court

decided to set up a school for professional actors. It started at first with anyone who was interested signing up for evening classes at the City Lit. Then the newly built Jeanetta Cochrane Theatre in Bloomsbury was offered to us at a peppercorn rent and the real day school was established. There were movement classes, lectures on play construction from Royal Court dramatists, mask acting and improvisation classes. Really serious improvisation in the development of an actor's approach to the scene he/she was to play was in its infancy in 1961/62. The classes involving masks and improvisation were conducted by Bill Gaskill, with George dropping in when he had the time. The classes were held five days a week from about 10 a.m. until 4.30 p.m., and as I was out of work for about ten months during this period after our marriage, I was able to attend every day. There were about fifteen regulars, including a very young Michael Gambon (who never went to official drama school), Frank Finlay and Henry Woolf. Other actors such as Robert Stephens and Albert Finney would drop in from time to time.

I learnt far more from those days than I did from RADA. The main thing I learnt was a deep respect for other actors. Their bravery, watching their hidden talent being nurtured and exposed, and their ability to accept severe criticism coupled with encouragement from their teachers. You see, professional actors spend most of the time trying to please the director, (a) so they won't be fired and (b) so they might be employed by them again. The actual part they might be playing, so far as the actor's talent and instinct was concerned, came a poor weakened third. None of this applied at the George Devine School. All of us began to truly respect the uniqueness of each other and the importance, absolute importance, of the playwright's intentions. Our talents could be realized and released without fear of upsetting the director or losing a job. You would hope this would have been taught at drama schools. It wasn't, at least not then.

One of my first stage jobs after marriage was at the Arts Theatre in Anthony Powell's *The Afternoon Men*. It was directed by a young Roger Greif (now famous for his documentaries on crime and prisons) and the cast included the stunningly beautiful actress and painter Pauline Boty, the stunningly beautiful Imogen Hassall and the very beautiful Georgina Ward; the very handsome, shy Willie Fox, who held my hand in the wings every night as he was so nervous, but who was soon to emerge from his chrysalis as James Fox in the film *The Servant*; the powerful, soon to become famous in *The Blue Max*, Jeremy Kemp; the future superb classical actor Alan Howard; oh, and me. It failed, but my, we had such fun. Youth, beauty, and me: what a combination. Pity about the play.

What I didn't know at this happy time was that a big boulder was being pushed onto the edge of the mountain of ambition, and it was about to topple and completely block my pathway to classical acting. The hand that pushed it belonged to Bill Gaskill. Because of *The Happy Haven* at the Royal Court and the year working at the George Devine School I had completely given my artistic heart to Bill Gaskill. He was my mentor and absolute leader. I trusted him and loved him. I was so pleased to be asked to be in the York Mystery Plays in York the following year. Alan Dobie played Christ, Ian McShane, straight from drama school, played the Devil, and Peter Gill (ex-Nottingham rep days) was the assistant director. It was this experience at York which inspired Peter Gill's wonderful play *The York Realist*. Anyway the point, as far as my life is concerned, was that the National Theatre led by Sir Laurence Olivier had just been announced and two directors had been appointed. One was John Dexter and the other Bill Gaskill.

I asked Bill quietly during rehearsals if he would take me with him in any humble capacity whatever. The boulder was finally pushed over, and in a cloud of dust and rock chips I heard Bill answer, 'No, Peter, I won't.'

'Why?' I asked, truly mystified on all sorts of levels.

'Because,' said Bill, 'you know me too well.'

That was that. The path to a classical career was truly blocked, especially as John Dexter, the friend of my true friend Alan Bates, refused to accept that he had ever met me in his life, let alone drunk a thousand cups of coffee with me at the Kardomah Cafe in Nottingham. Such is life. Thank God there was another road, and I began fearfully and for some time unhappily to walk it.

CHAPTER 7

MY EARLY WORLD
IN TELEVISION

I did my very first television on film, playing the cockney villain in a series called *Dial 999* starring Robert Beatty. This was early 1957 and when it was shown, not possessing a TV, I watched it in a pub. I couldn't hear a word, but I was thrilled to see myself. However, I was too shy to mention it to my fellow drinkers.

I saw Robert Beatty many years later, again in a pub, funnily enough. He congratulated me on my success and said he hoped that I always put enough money away for the income tax. From the way he spoke I gathered he had not, and had left himself rather vulnerable in old age. He was a very nice man.

I did several live televisions in the late 1950s. They were always exciting because of the nervous tension that affected everyone. Changing clothes behind the sets; a prompter in case you forgot a line; the cameramen stripped to their vests and sweating with the tension and the labour of hauling the large TV cameras quickly across the studio floor for shot after shot after shot. If it was a television for ITV, which was in its infancy of course, when the commercial breaks came, they too were spoken or enacted by 'live' actors who were just as nervous as we were. We could see them because they were usually giving their spiel in a corner of the same studio.

One particular live television stands out, sadly for tragic reasons. It was called *Underground* and was about the aftermath of a nuclear bomb falling on London. As well as myself, the cast included Donald Houston, Andrew Cruickshank, Warren Mitchell and an up and coming young actor called Gareth Jones. We were all trapped in the underground and were trying to stagger over piles of rubble from one station to another whilst wondering what exactly had happened. Because of all the rubble, a fully qualified nurse was on hand in case anyone turned an ankle, easily done as we had only imagined the piles of bricks in rehearsal. Gareth Jones, a most talented actor who I think was only in his twenties, was probably cast as a man with heart trouble because he was rather plump. During the course of the drama his character was very distressed and kept needing his heart pills. I tell this because of the dreadful irony of what happened as he was climbing over some rubble towards a group of us, including myself, with some vital information. Suddenly he fell. The camera wasn't on him at that moment but on us, awaiting his arrival. We saw immediately it was something more than a trip. This was live television; we had to carry on as we saw Gareth being attended to, so we made up our lines to cover the situation, and somehow got to the end of the scene. The director called an early commercial break. The commercial actors hurried to their desk, and the director, Ted Kotcheff, and his young PA, Verity Lambert, rushed from the control room to find out how Gareth was. We, that is the actors, were told that Gareth was okay, he had fainted, and although he couldn't continue with the drama, he would be fine.

This was a great relief and none of us imagined anything more sinister. In fact poor Gareth Jones was dead of a heart attack. They knew that we, especially Donald Houston, who was a great friend of Gareth's, couldn't have continued to the end of the transmission had we known. We did continue, saying 'this is what—' (mentioning Gareth's character) 'would have said if he were here' and inserted his lines. The cast, including Gareth of course, had chipped in for a crate of beer to drink on the night train back to London (the drama was transmitted from Manchester). As we sat shocked and saddened, sipping our bottles, no one commented on the fact that Gareth's share was left untouched.

My first series for the BBC was in 1961. It was called *Magnolia Street* about mostly Jewish families living in the East End of London. The offer was nine guineas per episode. The BBC, unlike common, new ITV, paid in guineas for some rather snobbish reason! Anyway my grand agent at MCA got it up to twelve guineas. I was playing a young Jewish boy and many of my scenes were with older Jewish women – mother, grandmother, aunts and so on. After we had recorded two or three of the nine episodes, I was asked to have tea with the older actresses I was working with. There were about six of them at the tea table and me, no other male. They appeared very serious and rather concerned.

'We've asked you to tea,' they said, 'because we are a little worried that you are denying your Jewishness. You should be, must be, proud you are a Jew.' All this was said with enormous motherly love and tact.

'But I'm not Jewish,' I said, not quite understanding what was going on.

'That's what we mean. That's what concerns us, and we'd like to help you not to be afraid of people knowing you are a Jew.'

It was one of the most delicate and sweetly well-meaning situations I have ever been in and, of course, enormously flattering. I didn't win, though.

'No one could play a Jewish boy like you are unless they were Jewish. Acting doesn't begin to come into it,' they said.

Well, for whatever reason, I wasn't going to say I was Jewish if I wasn't, so I decided to accept their unmeant huge compliment, and put up with their slightly cold attitude towards me for the rest of the series.

I appeared in four *Avengers*, always the villain, and it was the night before I was to play the fight scene in 'Escape in Time' with Diana Rigg (fans will know the scene) that something strange, odd, and almost fatal, happened to me. I was driving along the Brompton Road towards Hammersmith. It was late and it was raining. Suddenly the driver of a cab a little way in front of me, who had just dropped a fare, did a U-turn without warning. I slammed on the brakes of my little TR3 and it went into an almighty skid, and hit the cab sideways right in the middle of the road. I was only saved from serious injury because I had the passenger seat forward, which left a great curved bruise to my side, and because I had a specially built steel racing steering wheel that I managed to bend double as I hung onto it.

I was very, very shaken but managed to get out of my totally wrecked car. Somebody must have called the police, but before they came I was approached by two male witnesses. After quickly checking I was not seriously injured, they pointed out that the cab driver, who incidentally never came near me, was reparking his cab at the spot he'd dropped his fare (who had disappeared). One man said, 'It was definitely the cabby's fault, but I can't wait for the police as I've got drugs on me, but here's my telephone number,' and off he went. The other man said to me, bruised and bewildered as I was, 'I'll tell the police it was the cabby's fault but only if you sleep with me tonight – I'm homosexual, you see, and I fancy you.' Just like that. Quite formal and polite he was really. I declined, and off he went. The police were terrific. The cab driver told them that he had been parked at the side of the road and I had run straight into him The police were quite aware from the skid marks and the position of my car that this couldn't be true; they arranged transport for me

and said they would call on me at home the following evening
when I got back from the studios.

I had to be at Elstree at seven o'clock the next morning. I
went by cab, shot most of the fight scene then collapsed in my
dressing room and phoned my doctor. He told me I was having
a shock reaction, not to worry and drink lots of sweet tea.

The police came, as promised, when I learnt several things.
One was that the accident and near death had happened outside
St Stephen's Hospital, where I had been born twenty-seven
years earlier, another was that the cab driver had given them the
names of four other cabbies who had been driving by at the
time and would bear witness that he had been parked. The
police assured me this was quite usual in such cases so it would
be a waste of time for them to prosecute him for dangerous
driving, but if I liked to make a civil case they would support
me with all their scene-of-accident measurements. I didn't
bother. However, I did ring the drug man's number and he did
send a witness letter, bless him. My car was a complete write-
off and I got £60 from a motor scrap dealer. About three
months later I saw my car gleamingly for sale on the forecourt
of a well-known sports car dealer. They were asking £595. I
went in and pointed out that I had sold the car with a very
twisted chassis for scrap, and they politely asked me to 'fuck
off'.

I have been obsessed with cars all my life because my father
had been a chauffeur. I recognized all makes of cars by the age
of about seven. I have spent a fortune on almost every make of
car and not regretted a penny of it. I have owned some of the
most powerful cars in the world, but I learnt to drive in a two-
seater NSU Prinz. Now this was a German car of 600cc with
no synchromesh to the gears. To change gears you had to
double-de-clutch, which required some skill, in a sort of tap
dance of the feet. My wife's mother said she had spoken to a
friend of hers who would be happy to teach me to drive. To my

home came this beautiful woman of about fifty. She was sweet, kind, very elegant and a very patient teacher. She was also the holder of the fastest-ever lap at the old Brooklands race track. She was the legendary Kay Petre, one of the greatest female racing drivers of her day. She could double-de-clutch all right!

My father had qualified as a very young man to be a Rolls-Royce chauffeur. This required full-time study for three months at the Rolls car factory school. They taught not just how to handle a large Rolls but more importantly how to strip down and rebuild the engine. Those grand motoring tours the rich made in the early thirties meant that, should the car break down, you were unlikely to be near a mechanic or garage. Your well-trained chauffeur, with his special Rolls tools, could fix it! As I mentioned earlier this training meant that when the war came my father, instead of being called into the services, was seconded to essential war work. He was sent to Hucknall in Nottinghamshire, the home of the Rolls-Royce Aero-engine factory. I remind you of this because when I was a little boy, I remember my father was driving someone else's Rolls. When I first made money, I went and bought a new Rolls, a Silver Shadow, in dark green. I wanted to drive Mum and Dad in it. It was my first symbol to them that I had 'made it'.

I bought the car from a leading Rolls dealer. I was thrilled and after a few weeks' driving, because I relished every part of the car, I read the manufacturer's leather-covered log book and for some reason, certainly not for suspicious reasons, I also had a look at the engine number. I had never looked under the bonnet of a Rolls before. It was mightily impressive. The only thing was, the engine number was not the engine number in the log book! I expect we have all heard the story of a couple who left their new Bentley at a garage in central London whilst they went to a matinee of a play; discovered their tickets were for the wrong week, and came back to the garage to discover their new Bentley engine hanging from a hoist above their

My future dad looking
for his true love.

My future mum waiting
to be found.

Mum and me.

Dad and me.

Me and my teddy.

Helping dad.

Grandad the
newscaster and
grandma.

My sister Patricia (6)
and me (14).

School play *Julius Caesar*. I'm
on the left and that's John Bird
in the middle as Brutus.

Susan Bennett at 16.
'I like to be called Sue'.

The first 'British Warm'
before the American tour.

Red Riding Hood and the Wolf. I grew my own tail.

At the crossroads. Andrey in *Three Sisters* holding Gillian Martell, that's Peter Gill kneeling, Sian Phillips in the white blouse.

Will you marry me?

No. (Anyway you're gay.)

Peter the Pole, my first gangster role. Have You Seen This Man? Poster for *The Informer.*

car – about to be exchanged. Well, I'd certainly heard this story so I was very disturbed.

I rang the dealers who were surprisingly unsympathetic. They had got their money (I'd paid cash) and suggested I rang Rolls-Royce direct. I did. They were more helpful.

'Oh yes,' they said, 'of course we know that car. Unfortunately whilst the engine was being tested here a mechanic made a mistake and damaged it. This I'm afraid, was after the log book had been made up, so we put in a new engine,' they said, 'a different one.'

'A brand-new different engine?' I asked, wondering anyway, why they hadn't issued a new log book.

'Oh no,' they said, 'a completely reconditioned engine which is just the same, just as good as a brand-new one. There is no difference.'

I was not happy, uncomfortable, mystified. I took the car back to the dealer. I had only clocked up about 1500 miles and they bought it back, without a murmur, for almost exactly what I had paid for it. Perhaps the next owner wouldn't look under the bonnet. I say this because many years later I took my then Bentley Continental for service at the Rolls-Royce factory, and the chief engineer told me that in all his years there he had never met an actual owner before, always the chauffeur.

Anyway I was glad to get rid of the Rolls as it had a profound effect on people's attitude towards me. It provoked envy and dislike, quite unlike the Bentley, which was okay. So was a convertible Aston Martin I once had, when lorry drivers would lean out of their cabs with their thumbs up and say, 'Lovely motor, Pete, fancy a swap?' and go cheerfully on their way.

A Rolls-Royce has a deep and lasting impression on people. I haven't owned a Rolls for thirty years and yet only recently a jolly man stopped me in the street and said, 'You naughty boy, you nearly ran me over in your Roller the other day, and I was on a zebra crossing too!' When I protested he said, 'Come off it, Peter. I'd recognize you anywhere and you do drive a Roller, don't you!'

I'm now going to tell you a Rolls-Royce secret and it's been hushed up for many many years. I don't know if it's true, but I did hear it from a very good source. The very first Silver Ghost that Mr Rolls and Mr Royce sold was to Mr Henry Ford in America. Quite soon after it had been delivered and parked in the large garage on Mr Ford's estate Mr Rolls and Mr Royce discovered, through further testing on the Silver Ghost, that a part on Mr Ford's Rolls was not as reliable as it might be. It had to be replaced. It had to be replaced as soon as possible. It had to be replaced before their part failed on Mr Henry Ford's car. Henry Ford was the most powerful car manufacturer in America. It had to be replaced secretly. Mr Henry Ford must never know the Best Car in the World didn't quite deserve its title!

It was decided to send out two men. One highly trained in espionage, which of course included secret travel and breaking and entering. The other was one of their top mechanics who could quickly and silently replace the small but important component. They would travel as tourists to Canada and enter America secretly. This they did, travelling incognito to Mr Ford's estate; they then broke into the garage, and without being disturbed or disturbing anyone else, completed their task and returned to England.

Mr Rolls and Mr Royce knew that had their car broken down on Mr Henry Ford, he would have had great pleasure in destroying the reputation of the Best Car in the World's manufacturers.

I've just remembered another interesting story regarding my TR3 sports car. We lived in a large block of Edwardian flats at the time I bought it, and I'd only had it a few days when the management of the flats decided to decorate the outside. One breezy day I found my car covered in little white spots. The decorators were sympathetic and said they would contact the insurers. They arrived, looked over the car, agreed I had a claim against them and about a week later I received in the post a cheque for about £5 for a tin or two of something called T-Cut. It was an abrasive substance that would take off the top layer of paint. The cheque and letter were from Norwich Union. I knew that the car really needed a respray so I got a quote – about £125, I think. It was now Saturday and I was so incensed at the T-Cut cheque I decided to ring the chairman of Norwich Union, whose name was on the letterhead, and I decided to ring him immediately. I rang directory enquiries and got his home number in Norwich. His delightful wife said he was at his golf club and gave me the number. The club said he was still on the links. I left a message asking if he would ring my number, as it was important. The dear man duly rang, understood my concern, thought the offer was insulting, asked what a respray would cost, and on being told said a cheque would be in the post on Monday. It was. It sometimes pays to go to the top!

*

Well, that was quite a diversion from my early televisions. Perhaps we could call it a form of commercial break, which were becoming all the rage, or even, for those reading this who are old enough to remember, the *Potter's Wheel*.

The most memorable part of acting in *The Avengers* was the grace, good manners and charm of Patrick Macnee. Despite working horrendous hours, continually working on the scripts, and suffering at times a difficult personal life, his standards both in friendship and acting never wavered. The series had started as *Police Surgeon* with Patrick and Ian Hendry, and when it moved on and became *The Avengers* Patrick invented the all-leather clad Cathy Gale – well, at least her clothes, and he designed all his own suits and clothing 'style'.

The only time I ever had a row with a director was on *The*

Avengers. The director was Don Sharp. It was at a time when the possibility of the director watching on a TV screen exactly what the camera saw, had just been introduced. The trouble was that instead of watching the scene live in front of him while it was being acted and shot, the director, after making suggestions about the scene, would disappear to a remote area of the studio, or inside a caravan, to watch after the first assistant called 'action'. The blazing row between me and Don Sharp happened because, on a retake, I had been asked to do something special with my hands. I had done it, but the camera had been too high to transmit it to Don Sharp's TV screen. Directors working under the pressure of TV shows like *The Avengers* don't like retakes in the first place and to have to go for a third take – well, if it was your fault, it put you into someone's little black book! Don Sharp exploded, and I don't like to be shouted at, especially if I have done nothing wrong, and I expressed my feelings clearly. I thought I would never work for Mr Sharp again. Three weeks after the episode was finished I had a call from Don Sharp asking if I would like to play a leading part in a film he was to make for six weeks in the south of France. It was a dark villain, of course, so perhaps my 'attitude' had been a useful audition.

Anyway although I haven't written about the film, it was heaven and I rented a boathouse right on the beach at Eze sur Mer for six glorious weeks. Part of the 'fun' I remember was that a huge villa was rented for filming on Cap Ferrat. Very, very luxurious with many bathrooms – but no loo paper. It was made very clear to all of us on the daily 'call sheets' that the screenwriter (who was with us) objected strongly to his script being used as lavatory paper. The same fate befell the 'call sheets', I expect.

New sheets of script were often pushed under the door at night so you were never quite sure if you would be called next day, or what you would say.

The screenwriter (a famous playwright) had his ten-year-old son to stay for a few days, and I remember this lad congratulating me after a scene. He thought I had played it very well. 'I should know,' said the boy, 'because I wrote that scene last night.' I was flattered.

*

But back to the making of filmed television. An example of the avoidance of retakes was brought home to me on an episode of *The Saint*. I was playing a villain – naturally, foreign – naturally, but this time I was a Russian in France speaking perfect French. I asked the director what he wanted in the first scene I had with my co-actor, who was playing a Frenchman.

'Well,' said the distinguished film director, who was 'slumming it' for the money, 'I think both of you must speak perfect English. Then we will presume you're speaking perfect French.'

Easy. We shot the master, during which the characters spoke to each other for some time. We then broke for lunch. I approached the director at the bar.

'That scene went well, Peter,' he said. 'I'll use most of the master shot, it was so good, with just a couple of close-ups.'

'What about the other actor?' I said.

'John? Oh he was perfect, I thought,' said the director. 'Considering he's only in this scene, we were lucky to get him.'

'Yes,' I said, 'I appreciate that, but he spoke English with a heavy French accent, which makes nonsense of my "cover" as a Russian spy pretending to be French.'

'Oh,' said the director, 'I didn't notice. I was so pleased we got through it. I'm certainly not reshooting. Don't worry, Peter, it's only television not a feature film. Have a drink.'

I did two *Saints* with Roger Moore and we got on very well. I think he beat me up or shot me in both of them. Roger has a wonderful sense of humour and we had lots of laughs together. I thought we got quite close, certainly in our sense of humour. I was wrong. A few years after the *Saint* series had finished I was asked to play the villain in an episode of *The Persuaders* starring Roger Moore and Tony Curtis. I was delighted to be working with Roger again and rather thrilled that I would also be working with Tony Curtis, who I had admired so much in his early films.

When I arrived on the location on my first day, Roger was leaning against a Rolls smoking his customary cigar. We greeted each other warmly.

'I hope you're good in this, Roger,' I said.

'Why?' said Roger, his eyes unexpectedly narrowing, and his handsome face darkening.

'Well,' I said, 'I hear Tony Curtis is brilliant.'

Joke over. No joke. Roger turned on his heel and walked away. Not long afterwards I was called to the production office; my agent was on the phone.

'What have you been saying to Roger Moore?' she said. 'He is terribly upset and has been talking to the producers about having you taken off the episode. They're not going to do that, I think, because they have already shot on you. But Peter, for God's sake behave yourself.'

Thirty years later I asked Roger what all that was about (I never mentioned it at the time – oh no!)

'Christ, Peter,' he said, 'you would remember that, wouldn't you? And you would bring it up again just as I'm trying to enjoy myself at this boring function.'

'Why did you try to get me sacked, Roger? Surely it wasn't because of my joke about you and Tony Curtis.'

'Yes, it was,' said Roger, suppressed memories stirring. 'What you didn't know was that I was having a tricky time with Mr Curtis, and I couldn't bear the thought of you teasing me in front of him.'

'I wouldn't have dreamt of that, Roger,' I said. 'But thank you for explaining. I understand.'

*

Patrick McGoohan and I became very friendly during the shooting of *Danger Man*. I played an Egyptian villain in one of those, I remember. I saw it recently. I was rather good. Anyway Pat and I hit it off and often went out together. He took me to nightclubs – places I had never been to, and have never been to since. Places where girls flock to your table, especially if you're a big TV star like Pat was, and you buy them drinks (at least Pat did; I had no money) and they chat. That's all. The man who turned down James Bond because of the sex scenes ('I only kiss my wife, Peter') never touched the girls. We enjoyed their company and they were our sort of age and just fun.

*

A number of years later I was asked to be a villain (I think) in an episode of the *Prisoner* entitled 'ABC'. When I arrived at make-up at 7.30 a.m., the make-up man, who I had known for years, said, 'Have you seen or worked with Pat recently?'

'No, sadly I haven't,' I said.

'Well, Peter, be very careful. Pat is not the man he used to be.'

'What do you mean?' I asked.

'I think I've said enough,' he replied mysteriously. 'Just be careful.'

I walked onto the set not knowing what to expect. Pat was delighted to see me, he threw his arms around me and lifted me off my feet.

'I'm so pleased you're doing this, Peter. We will have a great time together.'

Everything was normal, two old friends together again. What was the make-up man talking about? The first scene to be shot was quite a long two-handed scene between Pat and myself. I was introduced to the director – an American – and placed in position. Pat stood opposite me, and the director said that was fine, just play the scene now We did.

'Excellent,' said the director. 'You take a break while we light it and we'll go straight for a take.'

Pat took me away to a quiet corner of the studio. 'What do you think of the director, Peter?' he asked.

'He seems quite a nice man,' I replied.

'A nice man?' said Pat 'He is a complete prat, he has no idea how to direct. The way he has placed us in that scene is crap. Look, Peter, let's do the scene again just for ourselves, and I'd like you to express yourself, move around, instead of being stuck in one place.'

'That sounds a great idea, Pat,' I agreed. 'I do feel rather stuck in a position.'

'Of course you do,' said Pat. 'Let's go.'

We freewheeled through the scene.

'Wasn't that good?' said Pat sounding quite excited and elated. 'Isn't that the way the scene should be shot?'

'Yes,' I said, beginning to feel a bit elated myself, 'that is definitely how the scene should be shot.'

Pat's demeanour suddenly changed, he grabbed me hard by the arms and thrust his almost snarling face into mine. 'That is not how it's going to be shot. I'm not just the star, I'm the producer and to do it that way costs money.' There was a strange glint in his eye I'd never seen before. 'We will do it the way the director wants.'

'Okay, Pat, okay, that's fine by me,' I said and the moment was over.

The scene went well and afterwards Pat asked me to have lunch with him with a drink at the private bar first. There followed, to my mind, a silly sequence of events.

'What'll you have?' asked Pat.

'What are you having?' I enquired.

'A Guinness.'

'I'll have a Guinness too.' Pat then offered me a cigarette. I had been out of work for three months before this job and I had given up cigarettes two years before. I had just done a scene with Pat, and had undoubtedly held my own with him. I was aware as I stood next to him at the bar that I was taller than him. We were both drinking Guinness. He was a star and I wasn't. The only difference between us at that moment was he was about to smoke and I had stopped smoking.

'Thanks, Pat,' I said, 'I'd love one.'

I said it was silly, didn't I.

*

I loved doing *Rumpole of the Bailey* with Leo McKern. He was the most delightful friendly man and a magnificent and generous actor. After the series had been running for two or three years it was so successful and of such importance to Thames Television that a read-through of an episode usually consisted of about fifty people. On one occasion like this in a rehearsal room with everyone – cast, set designer, costume designer, director, producer, with their assistants, and their assistants' assistants – all sitting doubled-banked round a table, plus at the head of the table John Mortimer, playwright, barrister, lover, dandy, wit and raconteur, the guest star Emlyn Williams shuffled into our midst. I say shuffled because he was wearing carpet slippers. I presume he was having, like we all do, trouble with his feet.

We were thrilled to see the great and famous Emlyn Williams. I knew his work well, both as a writer and as an actor and speaker. He sat down and after introductions we started the read-through of the episode. We became quickly aware that Mr Emlyn Williams, distinguished actor, and more importantly distinguished writer, had rewritten his entire part. Not the sense or plot, but the words chosen, the very ebb and flow of the syntax and grammar. All eyes, when not on our script, were on

John Mortimer, whose face was beginning to go through many colours of the rainbow. Would he speak, stop the read-through, or just explode in a cloud of threads from his Savile Row suit?

The read-through finished and I, along with Leo McKern, was called into a little conference with John Mortimer, the director Rob Knight, and the producer. Everyone else had coffee. The powers that be, which really meant John Mortimer, decided what was to be done. John, against suggestions that Emlyn should be replaced, generously decided that he should be politely, discreetly but firmly 'reminded' that he should read and learn the part as written.

Rehearsals were broken for the day and next morning Emlyn Williams turned up jolly as a bean and played the part as written. I think he felt that he had made some sort of point – a bit like Pat McGoohan, perhaps!

*

My life in early television was about to change. I was offered and accepted the part of Balor, 'the most evil man in the universe' in an episode of *Space: 1999*. After playing him I knew that I could go no further in villains. I had played the ultimate. Perhaps I should turn my hand to comedy. The clouds parted and out of the blue I was offered the part of Hilary in the smash hit comedy series *Rising Damp*.

CHAPTER 8

WHERE DO FLIES GO IN WINTER?
OR
WHAT DO ACTORS DO WHEN
NOT WORKING?

One of the most difficult things for an actor is knowing what to do with yourself when you are not working. The best idea, that most of us had in my younger days, was drinking. Drinking and gossiping with other actors and, as the day wore on and evening approached, actresses. Things are different today, for a start there are no actresses only actors, and secondly there seems to be nowhere for actors/actresses to go, to meet, to gossip, to laugh, to exchange views, telephone numbers and, most important of all, information about possible jobs that are being cast. When I hear people say how wonderful it would be to win an Oscar, I think, 'Oh no, how wonderful to get a part that gives you a real chance to show your talent' – that's the only thing that matters really.

When I was a young actor there were quite a number of pubs and actors' clubs where everyone from the profession went, from film stars to chorus boys and girls. One was the now long closed but legendary Buckstone Club, named after a famous theatre manager of the past. It was right across the road from the

stage door of the Theatre Royal Haymarket, the theatre
Buckstone used to manage. It was a basement club, and you
were supposed to be a member or show your Equity card but
no one did. It had two small bars and a dining room. Booze,
steak and chips, gossip and actors of all sexes. It was heaven. I
can't remember now when I first met Sean Connery but I
remember him coming into the Buckstone one evening and sitting at my little table and telling me how he had that day been
to see 'Cubby' Broccoli and Harold Saltzman for the part of
James Bond.

The interview had not gone at all well, and I think Sean had
felt patronized; anyway it seems he had got fed up with the way
the interview was going, and expressed his feelings in a masculine way and walked out. He told me he was walking across the
car park when a window opened and he was persuaded to
come back. He had gone back, and was promptly offered the
part. I think once they had got over the shock of him walking
out, they had, as was said of Clark Gable, heard Sean's balls
clanking as he walked to his car. Oddly enough, although I
didn't mention this to Sean, of course, I had recently finished a
Danger Man with Pat McGoohan, who had told me that he had
just turned down James Bond because of the sex. I stopped
going to the Buckstone after many happy years when a heavily
tattooed sailor asked me for my autograph at the bar. I knew it
was time to move on.

The Salisbury pub in St Martin's Lane, which crops up here
and there in this book, was another great place for actors.
Everyone signed on for the dole in those days, and there was a
special place for actors in Victoria. You would see all sorts in
the queue, well-known film faces as well as theatre 'names', and
after signing on and getting our money most of us would head
for the Salisbury for a lunchtime drink and gossip.

One job I heard about at the Salisbury set me on quite an
adventure. The legendary and formidable Basil Dean was

casting a new play which he was to direct. Basil Dean, in the 1920s and 1930s, had ruled London theatre and also had his own film studios. He was famous for his temper and ruthless behaviour in dealing with actors – but he was also extremely talented as a director. I knew all of this when I was told that there was a wonderful leading role, of a partially disabled young man, in his new play. I tried through my agent to get an audition. Impossible, not a chance; they were looking for someone with a bit of a 'reputation' even at that young age. I was, I think, twenty-one. I couldn't get hold of a script, but I did get hold of a London telephone directory – and there was Basil Dean's phone number and, more importantly, his address! I decided to 'beard the lion in his den'. I called at his house in Regent's Park early that Sunday morning. His wife, I presumed, opened the door. I explained that I was an actor and that I was calling to see Basil Dean without an appointment. A huge voice bellowed, 'Who is it at the door?' It came from somewhere within the dim recesses, and although Dean would have been in his late sixties (ancient to me) it had tremendous power. His wife shouted my message, with the sadness of tone of someone who only expected one reply. Instead Basil Dean shouted, 'Show him in.' I was taken to Basil Dean's large study. He sat behind his desk and got straight down to business.

The first part of this was to give me a fierce ticking-off for my sheer cheek in cold calling on him, and on a Sunday too. Had I read the play? No. More harrumphing, and a script was offered but not a seat. I stood with the script in my hand, while he said, 'Turn to page seventeen, read the next ten pages, then read them out to me. I'll read the part of your mother and let me tell you now, you'd better be damned good.' I did as he asked and was offered the part on the spot, or on the carpet in this case. It was tried out in Birmingham and I became very friendly, not to say close, to Basil. I got rave reviews for my performance but on the last night I was told by Basil that my part was to be recast for London as they wanted a name. My verbal reaction to Mr Dean and his seeming disloyalty probably spoke for three generations of actors. I was recast. The play failed.

But the Salisbury hadn't let me down. Another meeting in the Salisbury was one lunchtime when I fell into conversation with a charming and handsome young man. We seemed to enjoy each other's company very much, and laughed a lot. That evening I went to see the first night of *The Birthday Party* at the Aldwych Theatre. I had two great friends in the company: Patrick Magee and Bryan Pringle. I went backstage to congratulate them and was wandering up a gloomy corridor looking for their dressing rooms, when my lunchtime drinking companion hove into view.

'Hello,' I said cheerily. 'What are you doing here?'

My new friend's face darkened. 'What am I doing here?' he replied, his eyes flashing. 'I wrote the play, you prat.'

Harold Pinter and I remained pleased to meet each other as companions over the next forty-five years, and I was lucky enough to be in the last play he ever directed, Simon Gray's *The Old Masters* at the Comedy Theatre, starring with my old friend Edward Fox.

When the Buckstone closed, Gerry Campion of Billy-Bunter fame opened Gerry's in Shaftesbury Avenue. Again everyone, on all levels of success, seemed to go there, including, and this was important, agents.

I stopped going there when, after finishing in Ayckbourn's *Absent Friends* at the Garrick Theatre, I popped in for a late evening drink. On leaving I noticed that wonderful actor Tom Bell sitting at a table with his brother. I had known Tom and his wife when we were in our twenties but hadn't seen him for years. That is to say I hadn't seen him since his truly tragic blacklisting. I don't know how true this story is but here is what I and others understood. Tom had just opened in the film *The L-Shaped Room* and received sensational reviews. It was going to make him a film star, of that there was no doubt. Then while the film was still in the West End, Tom was a guest at some very important showbiz gathering where all the heads of the industry were present and the guest speaker was the Duke of Edinburgh. It seems that HRH made a joke during his speech and after the laughter had died down, Tom said rather loudly, 'Why don't you tell us something funny?' or words to that effect. At least that was the rumour. But the fact was that whatever he said caused his career to be stopped in its tracks. But this incident and *The L-Shaped Room* had happened some years before I was leaving Gerry's Club and saw Tom. I called out a cheery, 'Goodnight, Tom'.

'Goodnight?' said Tom. 'Fuck off, you West End arsehole.'

The pain and understandable bitterness in Tom's response was such that I felt ashamed and upset that my profession had treated a hugely talented actor in such a way. I never went to Gerry's again. Of course Tom Bell did come back, and over the last years of his life he was once again recognized as a superb leading actor.

The afternoon drinking club was the Kismet, opposite the Arts Theatre. It was nicknamed Dancing under the Stars because it had once been a basement Indian restaurant and the décor, which included a dark blue ceiling decorated with silver stars, was still intact. This was strictly drinking, no food – well, there may have been a dried-bread sandwich with no filling, as required by law at that time. No drinks to be served after a certain time unless accompanied by food. The sandwiches were often the same ones that had been there days before. Again, all sorts came – we humble actors were always pleased to see well-known British film stars who obviously liked a drink, joining us as equals for a laugh and a joke.

Another wonderful pub that attracted many people from the

arts – actors and painters, writers, singers, film directors – was the now sadly closed Queen's Elm on Old Church Street, Chelsea. Julie Christie, with her astonishingly good-looking painter boyfriend, Don Bessant, Liz Frink, Helen Mirren, Francis Bacon, Laurie Lee, the cartoonist Jak, the gangster/actor John Bindon and many, many more were regulars – but many at that time were unknowns, including myself of course.

One unknown was the Man in Black, Bill Mitchell. Bill became a very famous deep, deep-voiced voice-over artist. He invented the sound now copied by so many today. I had first met Bill in New York in 1956 although he was in fact Canadian. He always dressed in black, always wore dark glasses and often a black hat. When I knew him, he also lived in the most extraordinary flat in Chelsea. It was a basement flat but could have been a series of caves lived in by the Flintstone family. Every room had been furbished to look like a roughly hewn cave, including the bathroom, which had a lavatory which looked like a large boulder with a flattish rough stone on the top for the seat, and the bath again was seemingly hewn out of stone. The water appeared as though from a split in the rock. All very weird and also very dark. Bill himself, though, was a charming man, and women absolutely adored him. His ladies were always beautiful, always rich and usually famous in their own profession, from film stars to opera divas – and always a little older than Bill. When I first knew Bill he had an 'ordinary' Canadian/American sounding voice but he trained his vocal cords for hours every day for many months to develop the lower registers. He recognized early on, in the late 1950s and 1960s, that there was huge money to be made in voice dubbing and commercial voice-overs, and he ended up making a fortune.

Another great friend from the Queen's Elm was John Bay, another Canadian actor, who almost never worked. I think he may have had a small allowance from his parents, but he lived in a small bedsit and also at the bar of the Elm. He was the sweetest of men, who after a drink or two would do quite brilliant imitations of Groucho Marx. I was always trying to persuade him to develop a one-man show based on Groucho, because John would get very depressed at his lack of recognition as an actor. Then one day, I don't know how, he met the great Elaine Stritch when she was doing a show in London. They fell madly in love and John left his bedsit and the Queen's Elm and lived in a suite at the Savoy, and drank in the Savoy cocktail bar. They married, of course, and I never saw John again, but many years after he had moved with his new wife to America, I received a letter thanking me for my encouragement to write and perform a Groucho Marx evening and he enclosed glowing reviews from newspapers in Los Angeles: 'John Bay Conquers the Town as Groucho'. I was very touched he'd remembered and had bothered to write.

One of the West End theatres had a very large stalls bar and someone had the idea of making this into a late-night club and rendezvous for actors and dancers in West End shows. All you had to do at the door was pay £1 and show your Equity card. It was wonderful. It opened about 11 p.m., I suppose, and served sausages, hamburgers and red wine, but seemingly hundreds of showbiz people would sit around on the floor (there were very few tables or chairs) and laugh, gossip and relax.

Many hours of being out of work were spent with my friends. Pat Magee, who I only mentioned briefly, was someone who was a great friend and also mentor. He was some years older, and was able to help me through various difficult, depressing times by (a) being a good listener, (b) having experienced everything I felt himself, and (c) being Irish, which meant he had a million diverting stories, including his days with Harold Pinter acting in Anew McMaster's touring company. He also had interesting tales of Stanley Kubrick as he had played large roles in two of his films, and of Samuel Beckett, who of course wrote *Krapp's Last Tape* especially for Pat. American actors have psychiatrists, I had Pat Magee. Although we lived near each other and met often, he actually wrote and posted a letter to me after *To The Manor Born*. It was a generous, kind letter, and a serious one. It said, 'You will now meet envy.'

Somewhere that I went during the day when out of work, and where I went for years, was an astonishing judo club run by Joe Robinson and his brother Doug. I say astonishing because this small dojo, below a once famous, but then still just open club called Jacks Club (the Duke of Edinburgh's favourite during the war), was owned and run by two of the greatest exponents of the martial arts, especially judo, anywhere in Europe. Joe Robinson was one of the stars of the film *Kid For Two Farthings*, which is often shown on TV today. Doug Robinson was a celebrated stuntman, who had taught and looked after every great fight scene that Honor Blackman, Diana Rigg and others ever did in *The Avengers*. Joe in particular would have won a gold medal in the Olympics if he'd been allowed to compete, but in those days any whiff of money received from your skill and you were not eligible. The Olympic and World Judo Champion in the heavyweight division came to give exhibitions at the famous Budokwai Club in Chelsea one year. Joe challenged him to a private contest, and there, on the walls of Joe and Doug's club, was a photo, simply framed, not large, of the World and Olympic Japanese Judo Champion caught in mid-air as Joe threw him for a perfect textbook ippon. Many showbiz people came to the club, which was open from lunchtime until early evening. The great Brian Jacks, as a sixteen-year-old black belt, was a regular, so was Terence Stamp and Jimmy Savile. Many of the British Olympic team would come to *randori* and learn from Joe and Doug. Apart from 'throwing' Brian Jacks with my ankle trip (he denied it when he came on my *This is Your Life!*), my greatest achievement was upending and beating the huge, muscular, fit and formidable Brian Blessed, in a brown belt grading. It surprised us both, I can tell you, and Joe and Doug laughed about this for years.

The training I received from these wonderful teachers and charming men, was to pay off many years later. Walking to get my car after a performance of *School for Wives*, I was, thank God, still alert and full of adrenaline after playing such a huge role. Suddenly out of nowhere, in a surprisingly deserted street behind the National Gallery, I was stopped by three young men, one of whom held a knife at my chest. I instinctively and immediately responded. There was violence, but it came from me; there was blood, but it wasn't mine. The two who were still standing chased me up the street, and I ran as fast as any sixty-year-old man has ever run, shouting, 'Help, murder.' I thought I would be killed. I ran around the corner to find two dismounted policemen having a fag. My two followers ran off. I'll stop there, except to say I am very, very careful at night now and realize I was lucky, and stupid not to have just handed over the money. I made sure I never spoke about this incident to the press as I was fearful that having hurt my attackers they would recognize me and track me down. I think thirteen years later is okay. I hope!

I'll just finish this rather historical sociological chapter with this. I worked with an old actor some years ago who told me that before the war actors 'below the title' would all join the Royal Zoological Society. Yes, the zoo in Regent's Park. It had a restaurant that stayed open until one in the morning. The parking was easy, the sound of the elephants trumpeting and the lions roaring added to the atmosphere, and sometimes stars like John Gielgud and Noël Coward would drop by. I envied him. It sounded better than Groucho's anyway.

Now some of you might ask, 'Why didn't you do another, temporary job?' Well, I found that once I had signed

'Profession – Actor' on my first passport, that was it. All I can say is that all the actors I knew who did do other work between acting jobs never seemed to make it as actors, although quite a few became very wealthy antique dealers or estate agents!

CHAPTER 9

EARLY FILMS I

The Informers

My very first film was a British gangster film called *The Informers*, starring Nigel Patrick, directed by Ken Annakin, known affectionately as panicking Annakin. Nigel Patrick was to be the chief of detectives investigating the mob, of which I had been cast as one, a rather lowly one with few lines. I had been cast, I gathered, because of my height. The lowly part required a tall actor, as I was called Peter the Pole. I thought of course that it was to be another foreign villain, but it was explained at the interview that Pole referred to bean pole or telegraph pole! I hadn't quite been cast, however, as I had to have a camera test, not so much for my acting but just to see how I looked. I was sent to Nathans, the big film costumiers, which then was in Leicester Square. The lady who was head of costumes for the film said after our introduction, 'Oh yes, you're playing one of the gangsters, so it will be the usual – black jacket, dark shirt and white necktie, and any trousers that fit.'

My 'difficult' gene immediately came into play. I felt I was just being treated as a cliché, a common or garden gangster type – based not on life but on other British film gangster types. On the spur of the moment I said, 'No, I don't want to wear the usual gangster-type clothes. I want to have a three-piece pinstripe suit, a striped shirt with stiff white collar and a bow tie.' The costume designer's mouth was beginning to fall open. 'Oh yes, and I'll wear a bowler hat and carry an umbrella.'

The costume lady was now beginning to get her breath back. 'You can't go for the camera test dressed like that, Peter,' she said. 'Ken Annakin will go mad and I will get into trouble.'

I'm afraid I was adamant but explained I would take all the blame, and say I had refused her suggestions. I was fitted out, and the costume sent off to the studios. My camera test was to be the following Monday. I was to be on set, made up and in costume, at Pinewood at 8.30 a.m.

On Sunday night my very pregnant wife felt our first baby was about to start coming into the world. The ambulance got us to the Old Charing Cross Hospital at about 2.30 a.m. We were put into a small labour room to await developments. Nothing happened until about 6.00 a.m., then Sue was quickly taken to the delivery room. In 1962 it was unheard of for fathers to be present at the birth of their child so I stayed where I was. Not for long. A young man appeared all gowned up, introduced himself as the doctor, and said as they were very short staffed could I assist in the delivery. I washed, was gowned, gloved and went very happily indeed to be with my wife. There was just the doctor and a midwife. No, I'm not going on to describe everything, suffice to say that when my son's head appeared the midwife said, 'Well, it's definitely a girl.' The doctor, who was doing the actual delivery, got into some sort of trouble and with quite a shout the midwife grabbed him by the back of his coat collar and pulled him away. I don't know what the trouble was but she safely delivered our son, Guy, and amidst the tears of joy the doctor apologized in a thrilled sort of way and said it was his first delivery. Kisses all round, then I looked at my watch. It was 8.10 a.m. Oh well, my wife was well and happy, the doctor and midwife were happy, my son was beautiful and healthy, and I was a dad – the film studio would share my joy at being late. Oh no, they didn't. I got a taxi and arrived at Pinewood at about 9.30 a.m. I was congratulated by the first assistant and then told to get changed as quickly as possible as I had kept a whole studio waiting and time was money. I didn't care. The proud father strode onto the set in my suit, bow tie, bowler hat and umbrella: Peter the Pole, a dangerous member of the East End gang of bank robbers.

I expected to get a bollocking. Instead Ken Annakin absolutely loved the costume and congratulated the costume designer on her originality of mind. I stayed mum. My photograph on large posters dominated billboards and tube stations all over London, advertising the film. I think the size of my part must have disappointed those who had rushed to see *The Informers* on the strength of my 'Have you seen this man?' poster.

Blow-Up

The film *Blow-Up*, directed and mostly written by Michelangelo Antonioni has become, and I'm sure will remain, an iconic and seminal film of England in the 1960s. I was lucky enough to get a part in the film and thus work with the great Antonioni. My interview with him, in a London office above where they eventually shot the opening scenes of the film, went very well. Antonioni was extremely polite and gently explained the role and directly told me I was his ideal for the part, that of the agent to the leading character, a photographer. There was enormous excitement amongst the acting world in Britain that Antonioni was to make a film in Britain; he was world famous and his film and direction were always out of the ordinary.

My first port of call after leaving his office was to go for a much needed pee at the nearest public loo, which was in Piccadilly underground. Standing in the next stall to me was an actor I recognized, not from his work, but from his jolly company in various drinking holes in London. As he stood there I blurted out my excitement at having been given a part in Antonioni's new film – title then absolutely unknown. The man was even more excited than me. 'I've just been offered the leading part,' he said. 'I can hardly believe it.' It was David Hemmings, then just twenty-four.

The part David was to play, that of the photographer (based so they say on David Bailey), was just about to be offered to Terence Stamp, but Antonioni had been the night before to see *Adventures in the Skin Trade*, a new play at the Hampstead Theatre. David played the lead and was now relieving himself in a public lavatory having been offered the most sought-after part for a young actor. I hope we remembered to wash our hands, but in the general air of excitement I doubt it.

The script arrived. 'The Antonioni film' was on the title cover. The money was arranged, and I had a very interesting part, for a particular reason, but more of that in a moment. I was also to be contracted for the whole sixteen weeks of the film. My first scenes to be shot were to be at night, when David comes looking for me after 'blowing up' his photos of the possible murder. I am at a drug-fuelled party and am partly stoned when he finds me.

The film unit had taken over two enormous houses in Cheyne Walk, one for shooting, the other for wardrobe, make-up. The scene I was to play with David that night was extremely important to the film as I had a speech to David that was absolutely crucial, the kingpin of the story. As I was being made up, Piers Haggard, a TV director who I had worked for and who was now acting as Antonioni's English assistant handed me a sheaf of rewrites of the scenes to be shot. In filming this is not unusual; that's why film actors never learn their lines too thoroughly the night before. I glanced through the pages, and saw to my utter disbelief that my main essential-to-the-film, speech had been cut.

'There has been a terrible mistake,' I said to Piers. 'Someone has cut my main speech to David.'

'That someone,' said Piers, 'is Antonioni.'

'But he's made a terrible mistake. Someone should tell him. I don't care about my part being trimmed as such, but this speech is the absolute crux of the story.'

'Please, Peter,' said a slightly irritated Piers, 'just get dressed and wait for your call.'

'But don't you see, Piers? A very serious mistake is being made. Someone must absolutely explain to Antonioni he has made a mistake.'

'For God's sake, Peter, this is Antonioni's picture, and he has written most of it, and he's cut it. Don't be so silly.' Piers was becoming exasperated.

'I must speak to him, Piers, and I must speak to him now before I get dressed or made up.'

Piers could see I was serious and after I had threatened to go home immediately he reluctantly took me next door. It was a huge house and the party was to be in the ballroom on the first floor. The stairs were packed with extras, all young and rather beautiful. The door of the ballroom was ajar; inside this huge room Piers and I could see Antonioni alone with his lighting men.

'Antonioni always clears his set completely after a shot, so he can think,' said Piers, who was by now very nervous indeed. 'However, I'll go in and tell him you must see him.' He went like a beaten man towards Antonioni. There was a brief exchange and he came back. 'Antonioni will see you,' said Piers. 'Go in.'

Antonioni received me with great grace and politeness,

something I was to learn was his absolute unwavering trade-mark. 'Peter, tell me what is worrying you,' he said in broken English, I told him as politely and forcefully as I could. He listened without an expression. I finally ran out of words. There was a silence. Still no reaction from Antonioni, except perhaps a slight smile.

'Thank you for listening to me, sir,' I said. 'Are you going to put the speech back in now?'

'No.'

'But why?' I pleaded, mystified.

Antonioni's smile became a friendly, warm smile. 'Because, Peter, you have explained to me so very well exactly why I am right to take the speech out. You see, Peter, if I leave the speech in everyone will know what the film is about. If I take it out they will say, "it's about this?" "No, it's about this," someone else will say. It will be a mystery, enigmatic, controversial, everyone will talk about it, everyone will have an opinion. If I leave it in, the best I can hope for is, "I enjoyed that film." Do you understand, Peter?'

I did understand. I understood I was in the presence of, and was going to be directed by, someone completely out of my known experience. And I hadn't started yet.

When we came to shoot the scene that involved me, Veruschka and later David Hemmings, the ballroom was full of beautiful 1960s people. The air was full of smoke; we were all supposed to be stoned on marijuana. I acted it, perhaps others didn't. That is, I can remember Antonioni rejecting some actual marijuana to be used in the scene because it was the wrong colour. Antonioni was very, very particular about colour. He was very particular about everything, as I was quickly to discover.

We started to shoot a close-up on my first scene. I had a little speech (I can't remember what about – it may have been stoned ramblings) and Antonioni gave me an inflection. That is, he himself said my line, and wanted me to imitate him. This was after my first take. I didn't understand why my character should say the line the way he wanted, but I was damned well certain I would do my best. Now, I had come from a world of TV filming where if you went to more than two takes you would probably never work again. We went on take after take after take. After the word 'cut' Antonioni would say quietly something like, 'Yes, Peter, that was good but not as good as take five, although better than take nine.' Then as always he would give me this strange inflection on a word. Eventually it was take thirteen, and I was really trying. It wasn't that I couldn't just copy his inflection parrot fashion, of course I could, but my instinct wouldn't let me. But I was trying, my God I was trying, and I had to find it in my character to say it his way. I may never be asked to work on a feature film again, I was thinking. 'Cut. Good. Print.'

'Peter, thank you, come with me.' Antonioni put his arm around me and led me a little away from the busy technicians. 'I understand, Peter,' he said gently. 'You wish to show the world what a fine actor you are, I know, I understand.' He is speaking very intimately and quietly. 'But Peter, I have chosen you because I know you are a good actor. I have chosen your clothes, I have chosen the words you say. You are not in the scene before this one, and you are not in the scene after.' I am riveted. 'Peter, when you speak I am interested not in your character but in the mood you create on the screen.' He seemed to have moved even closer to me. 'You see, Peter, if I had moved my camera just six inches to one side −' he made a gesture with his forefinger and thumb − 'I would ask you to do the line in a different way.' Then he took me in both his arms and drew me closer to him, almost like a lover. 'Peter, believe in me. Trust me.' His cheek is touching mine as he continued his voice taking on a whole new rising timbre. 'I am not God, but I am MICHELANGELO ANTONIONI.'

I'll walk through fire for you, I thought, and I felt a very privileged actor.

Yes, I was on the film sixteen weeks because Antonioni might change his mind, might invent a new scene, and as all my scenes were inside I was good weather cover. We came to my next big scene. This was to be with David Hemmings to discuss the book of photographs David's character is to have published. I was playing his agent. It was to be shot in a little Italian restaurant behind Peter Jones in Chelsea. (It is still there under a different name.) David and I sit at a small table next to the window. We rehearse the scene all day. The table has a blue tablecloth and blue napkins. I am colour blind so I didn't notice their colour. I only discovered they were blue later.

David and I were very friendly by this time, because often I had been called but not used and had laughed and chatted to David a lot. David told me that he didn't really know how his character looked or how it was developing as Antonioni never ever let an actor watch 'rushes', that is, film that has been shot but not edited, and is usually viewed at the end of the day. The 'rushes' being the previous day's work. Although being David, with his enormous charm, he did manage, unknown to Antonioni, to see some key scenes.

During our rehearsal I always, on action, took the folded napkin from the table, shook it and placed it out of sight on my lap. Everything was ready, but we had run out of time. We would shoot the scene first thing tomorrow. Camera 'turnover' at exactly 8.30 a.m., a quick last rehearsal at 8 a.m.

The next day, David, who had seemed his usual laughing joking self in make-up, arrived on the set looking very pale, despite the make-up. David used a 'Chinese Eye' convertible Rolls in the film, and I knew he would often use it at night for going around London and was also on occasion spending what was left of the night in it. David, of course, was in every scene, and he was very, very tired. On action for the quick last rehearsal, David fainted, fell right off his chair onto the floor. Attention is immediately given to him and he comes round but is obviously not in a condition to continue. A doctor is called and David is taken to the small hotel across the road where we dressed and made up. After what must have been several hours, David returns, bright eyed and bushy tailed. He has had an injection and he has had some sleep. He is fine. Okay, we will go for this last rehearsal. 'Action.' I do everything as I have done in all the rehearsals the day before: that is I pick up the napkin and place it quickly out of sight on my knees before the dialogue. Now we are going for the first real take. 'Action.' I pick up my napkin, and instead of putting it on my knee, I put it in my collar, forming a bib on my chest.

'Cut! What is this, what is this?' The voice is Antonioni's and he is very agitated. I have not seen him like this before. He is angry. 'What is this?' And he begins to flick my napkin bib up and down.

'I'm so sorry, Michelangelo' (nobody called him Mick – well, you wouldn't, would you?) 'I won't do that again, I just did it for a change.'

'No, no,' said Antonioni, his voice changing politely as he spoke to me. 'No, Peter, I like what you do but I can see now that the napkin is a different shade of blue to the tablecloth.'

I tried to help, feeling very guilty there is consternation on the set, we've already lost time. 'Perhaps, if I put the napkin straight onto my lap no one will notice,' I said.

Antonioni put a kindly hand on my shoulder. 'Peter, I have noticed and also I like what you are doing with the napkin, but we must either change the napkin or the tablecloth.'

Antonioni really, really cares about colour, about tones, about mood. The first assistant asks for the art director and 'buyer'. Carlo Ponti, the producer, is hovering. Time is passing.

Well, in the event, the shop where the tablecloth and napkins were bought had a half day that day, and by the time the manager

was found and had opened up, and new linen had been brought
to the set, it was too late to shoot. We did the scene the following day.

Yes, Antonioni was very, very particular about colour, but at
least he approved of my inflections!

The Charge of the Light Brigade

The start of this strange eventful history couldn't have been
more perfect in the classic Hollywood style. My wife and I were
on our first holiday abroad together, and were in the swimming
pool of a hotel in Tenerife when the poolside-bar telephone
rang. It was my agent phoning from London to tell me, as I
stood dripping in the scorching winter sun, that I had landed a
major feature role in Tony Richardson's film *The Charge of the
Light Brigade*. Unfortunately, before I left England I had gratefully signed a contract to play the villain, Meres, in a new thriller
series for ABC TV to be called *Callan*. I knew straight away that
I must do the film, and after threats of 'You'll never work for us
again!' (I didn't) I was released from the contract.

I had met the extraordinary and brilliant director and co-
founder of Woodfall Films during my hurly-burly days at the
Royal Court a few years earlier, and knew, having read Cecil
Woodham-Smith's *The Reason Why*, that this was going to be a
very important film.

Things didn't get off to a perfect start, however, as Laurence
Harvey had bought the film rights of *The Reason Why* and felt
that John Osborne's script, supposedly from historical sources,
was based too closely on the book. The courts agreed and he
managed to get an injunction on Tony's film. This was resolved
by getting a new script written by Charles Wood and a payment
of reputedly £70,000 to Harvey. Also, Harvey insisted on playing the part that was to have gone to John Osborne, which

seemed rather vindictive, as it was only a cameo part and not one that a big star, as he then was, would ordinarily have dreamt of playing. The part was that of Prince Radziwill – but more of that later.

My part was to be Captain Duberley, Paymaster of the 10th Hussars. Trevor Howard, as Cardigan, says in the film, on being introduced to me, 'Paymaster? Paymaster? That ain't a rank, it's a trade!'

I, who had never before been on a horse, spent the hiatus caused by Harvey and the courts, riding horses everyday bare backed. At first on a lead, then with a saddle but no stirrups, and finally with the very long stirrups in the straight-legged cavalry style. I did this every day for about six weeks and ended up galloping and jumping and with a very strong leg grip. Which was just as well because our Turkish soldier friends liked nothing more than to stick mustard up our horses' bums just as we were about to set off. All of this was paid for by the company, so they must have really wanted me!

Then I got mumps. It was only a week or so before we were to fly to Turkey, our location for the next four months of filming. I kept quiet however and, having been told by my friendly doctor that I probably wasn't infectious any more, joined the excited flight, which included Trevor Howard, Harry Andrews, Sir John Gielgud, David Hemmings and my screen wife, Jill Bennett.

We were to be based for the first three months in Ankara with the filming location being about one and a half hours away by road, on the Anatolian plain. We were housed in a five-star hotel; a large unit of about ninety, including cast and crew. I quite quickly noticed that some of our people were signing drink and food chits with the wrong name and room number, so I decided I would pay my bill every week, just in case.

At the end of the first week I duly asked to see my bill, and realizing that something was wrong, asked to see the chits.

Quite a wad was brought by the pretty young cashier. I soon saw the signature was not actually mine on quite a few of them. While I was pointing this out, the cashier was joined by a smart-looking dark-jacketed man who enquired what the trouble was. This was all taking place, of course, in the very busy lobby of the hotel. When I explained my problem he asked if he could have the chits. I handed them over to him, and without looking at them he said calmly, 'This should solve your problem.' He tore them up and threw them straight into my face. My instinctive reaction was to immediately grab him by his lapels and pull him over the counter. 'Get me the manger,' I said. 'I am the manger,' he replied, just like the old vicar joke. So I dropped him, walked through the astonished crowd in the lobby and went to my room, where I phoned the production manager and explained what had happened. He, of course, was shocked and said he would remove the whole unit to another hotel as soon as possible.

While I was packing there was a knock on my door. A waiter entered carrying a huge bowl of fruit, on which was a note. It said, 'I witnessed the appalling incident in the lobby. The man who said he was the manager, isn't. I am. Come to suite 516 and I will explain. This is most urgent.' The 'urgent' was underlined. I was received in suite 516 by a tall blond man in rimless glasses, who explained to me that the hotel was built and owned by a Swedish company, that he was Swedish, and was, in fact, the real manager. He went on to explain that this was Turkey and things were complicated here. The man, who said he was the manager, he told me, was in fact a major in the Turkish secret police, and he had great power. 'I can absolutely assure you,' he said, 'that if, because of what happened, the film unit leave this hotel, your film will be placed in great jeopardy. Indeed you may find that permission to continue filming will be cancelled.' He then said, in a phrase I've never forgotten, 'I speak to you and apologize to you as one civilized man to

another.' I was convinced. I got the point; the production manager got the point, but everyone understood that I was going to
leave. Little did I know that what would happen at my new
living quarters would be worse. Much much worse! But more
of that later.

*

'What are you going to do in this scene, Peter? I mean, are you
going to be absolutely brilliant?' Tony Richardson said to me
on my first day of shooting.

Everyone was there – all the crew, of course, and the various
stars who would also be in the scene, but no one else was
paying any attention to Tony's little chat with me.

'Yes,' I replied positively, not really knowing how I was going
to play my role at that stage.

Tony laughed a loud neighing, delighted laugh, and shouted,
'Quiet everybody.' Everyone stopped what they were doing,
and paid attention to the director. Tony went on, 'Peter Bowles
has just told me he is going to be absolutely brilliant in this
scene, so we are going to rehearse it now, and we are all going
to watch him.'

This was and remains one of the most exciting pieces of
'direction' I have ever had. Simple really: I had no choice but to
be brilliant! I loved Tony Richardson from that moment, and
never stopped loving him until the day he tragically died not
long after I had finished my third film with him.

The making of *The Charge of the Light Brigade* was enormously
exciting and riven with incident off the screen as well as on. This
is one of them. The film would have been impossible without the
help and employment of the Turkish cavalry, which I believe was
unique in the world at that time. It consisted of about 450 men and
horses. Woodfall Films, as part of the permission to film on Turkish
soil, and use all the cavalry, had had to drain a large section of land
not too far from our main locations, and build long-lasting, that is

to say permanent, barracks to house all the men and horses of the Turkish cavalry. A very expensive operation.

We had been shooting a few weeks, when, on turning up at the location at 6.30 one Monday morning (we used to film from about 7.30 a.m. to 2.30 p.m. because of the heat), we discovered that the cavalry had been confined to barracks. They were withdrawing their labour. We were told that a diplomatic and very serious personal incident had occurred the day before, Sunday. It transpired that Mark Burns, one of our leading actors, who played an officer in the 17th Lancers, had gone for a walk in Ankara's public park and had seen a man in a raincoat throwing stones at a frog, with the intention of killing it, or so it seemed to Mark. Mark had asked him to stop, the English having an empathy for animals that is not shared by all nationalities. (I was to be clearly reminded of this by Rudolf Nureyev some years later – more of that anon!) The raincoated man ignored Mark's request and continued stoning the frog. Mark, who was an ex-English cavalry officer, and had been equerry to Prince Philip no less, was most incensed at being ignored and shouted, 'Stop throwing stones at that frog, you bastard,' whereupon the man did stop stoning and without a word calmly walked away. Sometime later, when Mark was having a cup of tea in the park tea rooms, the raincoated man reappeared accompanied by two policemen. Mark was arrested on a charge of insulting the raincoated man's family and legitimacy, and was taken to the police station. What went on that Sunday night I don't know, but we discovered on Monday morning that the raincoated man Mark had called a bastard was in fact the Colonel in Chief of the Turkish cavalry.

There was no filming that day and we were led to believe that the Turkish troops would be withdrawn until Mark's case came to court, which in Turkey of 1967 could have taken months. We were told that discussions were taking place at the very highest level and we were sent home with instructions to keep near a phone. That night we were told that the matter had been resolved and would be explained in detail the next morning on location.

We arrived to discover that the Turkish cavalry were all 'out' and mounted in serried ranks in their modern Turkish uniforms. It had been agreed that the Colonel would drop charges and release his troops for the film if he received a public apology from Mark Burns. However, and this has to be imagined, he would only accept this apology if it was made to him in front of all his modern uniformed troops by Mark Burns dressed in the uniform of an officer of the British 17th Lancers circa 1854. Also the apology would be made in front of all the British actors, stars and crowd alike, dressed in their officer and rank uniforms circa 1854. So various earls, lords and field marshals, generals, colonels, captains, including a certain Captain Duberley, and other ranks of the British Crimean army stood to attention as Mark Burns gamely strode forward, boots, spurs and sword gleaming, and made a fulsome saluting apology. Apology accepted – on with the film.

*

Before leaving the hotel I had managed to rent, along with some other actors, a large house on the outskirts of Ankara. It was quite grand, standing in large gardens, and had been at one time the Chilean consulate. The rent was reasonable and was taken off our *per diem* or location expenses and paid monthly in advance by the production office. The importance of this will become clear later. It turned out, we were to discover, that the landlord had mistaken one of the actors, T. P. McKenna, for Sir John Gielgud. We could only imagine that some press photo had been wrongly captioned. I mention this because we were big, big news in Turkey at this time. The newspapers were full of the importance of the film, and of course the currency and work we were bringing to the country. I, we, all of us, were very high profile, as I was quite quickly to discover.

I was just thirty at this time. It was a very masculine cast, apart from Jill Bennett (Vanessa Redgrave's scenes were shot later in England). I liked the company of women and there was a young and beautiful production secretary who, although surprisingly blonde, was in fact Turkish. I asked her to have supper with me one Friday evening at one of Ankara's smartest restaurants, and that's how I discovered I too was high profile. My photo with my dining companion was splashed over the front pages of Ankara's Sunday papers. The accompanying story was not complimentary, especially regarding my companion!

The Sunday photos had dire consequences for my Turkish date. She was from an upper-class family who took great exception to her behaviour and withdrew her from her job on the film, which she had told me she just loved. I was visited that Sunday evening by her two elder brothers who made it clear by the sudden appearance of a knife that I was never to contact her again. I felt very sorry for the girl and of course terribly guilty.

It was not the only time I was made to feel guilty in my relationship with a Turkish girl, but in this case at least I was able to apologize and say how sorry I was. I was browsing around the huge department of antiquities in Ankara's National Museum when I became acutely aware that I was being watched, followed, then positively stalked by a most beautiful raven-haired young woman. I felt extremely uncomfortable. The young woman seemed extremely uncomfortable. It definitely was not sexual attraction on her part, although under different circumstances it most certainly could have been on mine. Suddenly she stepped close to me and said in a nervous whisper, 'I need to speak to you. I am the curator of this department. Would you please come with me to my office?' She seemed so agitated I didn't ask why, but followed her. Once inside her office, she quickly shut and locked the door and before I could utter a word, broke down. This tall, obviously intelligent young woman began to sob, and sat in the office chair with her head in her hands. I stood there not knowing quite what to do except ask as gently as I could what the matter was. Quite quickly she pulled herself together, managed a smile and said, 'I'm sorry,' and then went on to say something like the following.

'I am the curator of antiquities. It is a very responsible position. I am very proud to have this position, but I am most desperate and beg you to help me.' I was transfixed. 'I have recently discovered that my parents promised me in marriage when I was six years old to a distant cousin. We have arranged marriages in this country. It is not unusual but I do not want to marry this man. I want to have a career, which would be impossible if I were married to this man. I have to leave Turkey as soon as possible, but in this country a woman is not automatically allowed a passport. I can only obtain one if I can prove I am going abroad to work for someone, be their personal assistant, that sort of thing. I know from looking at you that you are from the film *The Charge of the Light Brigade*. I feel sure that if you, a British film star, were to come and sign papers at the appropriate government offices, I would be granted a passport and be able to come to England with you as your assistant. Please do this for me or my whole life will be ruined.'

What could I say? What could I do? I'm afraid I simply didn't have enough courage, didn't understand enough about this country's customs to offer to help. I was in Turkey to act in a film. A film which had only just started. What would I be getting myself into? I made my excuses, bitterly inadequate, but in my view practical, and left. I have never forgotten her. She haunts me still.

*

Tony called us all together one day and said, 'Tomorrow Laurence Harvey will be here to shoot his big scene as Prince Radziwill, and although quite a number of you will be in the scene, I want you to know that there will be no film in the camera. Otherwise, everything will be quite normal.' They did resent the £70,000 that Harvey had demanded. £70,000 was an awful lot of money in 1967. I was paid £100 per week and Mark Burns, who had a huge leading role in the film, told me he was on £50 per week. We didn't care too much. We were just thrilled to be in the film.

Sir John Gielgud was a tremendous leader of the company. He often took us out for dinner and told us the most amazing, funniest stories. We wept with laughter, and I can't remember any of them now! Trevor Howard, who we knew had a bit of a reputation as a drinker, was very careful. He had an enormously demanding role, and as the world now knows, was absolutely brilliant as Lord Cardigan (why he didn't get an Oscar I don't know). Anyway, he always ate dinner in his room, and if he came down to the bar of the hotel before we set off somewhere, he would always wear his carpet slippers. It meant he couldn't be persuaded to join us; the perfect polite excuse. Trevor was always bright eyed and bushy tailed in the make-up truck at 6.30 a.m.

Finally, after twelve weeks or so, the main battles, including the great charge, had been put in the can as they say, and we were off to Istanbul to film the landings of the British Army at Sebastopol. By this time Sue had come to join me, thank God. We had three small children by this time who were cared for by saintly grandparents. David Hemmings and his extraordinarily beautiful Texan girlfriend, Gayle Hunnicutt (incidentally, she had come to Turkey with us and had immediately gone down with the mumps – I kept mum) asked Sue and me if we would like to drive with them in David's huge chauffeured Cadillac limo to Istanbul, instead of flying with the main unit. David was to go later as there was another day's shooting with the 2nd unit. The main unit wouldn't be ready to shoot on the coast for several more days.

Most of my housemates left for the coast, except one, who went off to shoot on the 2nd unit, leaving his girlfriend, who like Sue had recently flown out, and myself at the house. David was to pick up Sue and me for the Istanbul trip that afternoon. The two girls were preparing lunch when suddenly the landlord arrived in a rather aggressive mood saying that he was owed a month's rent. We had had trouble with this man before; a rich, large rather formidable German who had become a Turkish citizen. The trouble being, that he had let himself into the house on occasion in order to spy through keyholes – and had been caught. However, this time it was about money, and I knew that the money, the rent, had, or should have been, paid in advance by the production office. I rang the skeleton staff at the office, and was assured that the money had been paid. In fact we were paid up for another week! The landlord denied this, became agitated, shouted at me and left the house. All this, of course, was very disturbing for the two young women who had recently arrived full of joy and excitement.

After quite a short time our landlord reappeared in the garden of the house accompanied by a number of burly men carrying various garden tools such as forks, spades, hoes and wooden stakes. They were being held like weapons and were clearly meant to intimidate. He did not however come to the door, but we felt very menaced. Suddenly the girls were aware that the electric cooker was not working and we quickly discovered that all the electricity in the house had been cut off. Also the water mains had been turned off. We began to get really worried. We had a Turkish houseboy who lived in the garden flat. He came upstairs and told us that we were not under any circumstances to let anyone in, as it was against Turkish law for anyone to come into your house unless invited. He then began to cry and said he knew he was going to be beaten by our landlord, who of course employed him as part of the lease. The young man, whose name was Ihan, was so very disturbed that my wife and the actor's girl became frightened and distressed also.

I knew that I needed to do something. I again rang the production office. This time to my surprise the phone was answered by David Hemmings. I explained to David what was happening, and he said he would come straight over to see if he could help to sort things out. This seemed a good idea because David was very much a public figure in Ankara at this time. His photograph was everywhere in the papers and magazines. He was the big new young and extremely handsome film star of the day – he would carry some weight. He would impress our landlord. He would sort things out. I was very mistaken!

Through the windows I saw David arrive, come into the garden and start talking to our landlord knowing from his size and dress he was obviously the boss. Suddenly I saw our landlord turn a garden hose on David, drenching him at close quarters. David, in shock and self-defence, pushed the man away and ran to our front door. 'The man is absolutely mad,' he said as we let him in. 'I had only just been introducing myself when he soaked me.' I felt a mixture of great guilt and foreboding. I was right about the foreboding. Before David had had time to dry himself, two police cars arrived with sirens screaming and out jumped about six policemen. Then began much pointing and shouting directed at the house. We couldn't understand what was being said but we knew it concerned us, and it was serious.

A few days earlier, the British Embassy had thrown a lavish party for the film company to say goodbye before we departed to Istanbul, and as we now had police hammering at our door, and quite a large crowd of onlookers beginning to gather in the road outside, I decided that we needed the help of the British Government, or at least its embassy. I rang them. They were most helpful, told me that under no circumstances to open the door and repeated the Turkish law on uninvited entry.

The crowd had now grown quite large and we felt surrounded and pretty scared. Then nosing through the crowd appeared the British Union flag flying at the front of a Rolls-Royce Phantom – the cavalry, so to speak, had arrived. Out of the car appeared two beautifully suited and quite obviously Turkish gentlemen carrying briefcases, who we quickly learnt were diplomatic lawyers.

We watched them talk to the police and landlord, then one of them came to our door. We let him in. Help was at hand, everything would be sorted out, we were saved. We were very wrong.

'This is a very serious matter,' said 'our' lawyer in perfect English. 'Your landlord has accused this man –' pointing at the still wet David Hemmings – 'of attempting to murder him with a knife whilst drunk.'

Pardon?

'Yes.' he said, 'He saw this gentleman drink a bottle of whisky, then come out of this house and attack him. He resisted, then called the police. The charge is attempted murder. I'm afraid there is nothing we can do. Mr Hemmings will be arrested and will be held in jail until his trial, which could be months or years away.'

We were absolutely aghast. 'But this is utter lies,' and we started to tell our lawyer the truth.

'It's no good,' he said. 'You will have to explain all this at the trial.'

'Oh this is ridiculous,' said David. 'I'm going out there to speak to the landlord.' He rushed out of the door and we suddenly saw him pushed to the ground, and a gun was held to his temple. David began screaming, 'Help me, help me!'

The lawyer, with us went outside and began, with his companion, to speak to the police and landlord. During this time David was quite clearly under armed arrest. Our lawyer returned. 'This can only be resolved in one way,' he said. 'All charges will be dropped if Mr Hemmings will kneel in front of your landlord, confess his crime and beg forgiveness.'

Poor David. He, who had done nothing but come to help, knelt on the rough pathway at the feet of the landlord, watched by a large crowd and begged forgiveness. It was given. The embassy lawyers then told us we would all have to leave the house immediately, grab what we could – clothes, passports etc., including those of the absent actor – and go. Now. David had come by taxi so we were all bundled into the Rolls-Royce with Union Jack flying and left the ex-Chilean consulate for ever.

*

The trip to Istanbul was wonderful. The scenery magnificent, the laughter endless, and the sight that greeted us as we approached this timeless Byzantine/Roman city is something never to be forgotten. As it turned out it was not the only thing never to be forgotten during our stay in Istanbul!

We were to be in this astonishing city for almost three weeks and David had asked Sue and me to live with him and Gayle on his yacht. It was beautiful: all gleaming mahogany and brass, and masts and furling sails. David was renting it, and it had been, according to David, the ex-president's schooner. Anyway it was magnificent, with a state room and beautiful bedrooms and a crew plus cook. A film star's life for someone who had not long before been on Social Security.

The army landing was a stupendous affair with ships, landing craft, or their Victorian equivalent, and many dozens of horses and hundreds of extras – all coming from the sea onto the beach. The location was about an hour's drive from Istanbul across and over some spectacular scenery. Because of the enormity and scale of the scenes to be shot, Tony Richardson had done a 'blanket' call every day. That is to say every actor and extra on the payroll had to be on set every day at around 6.30.

David and I were always driven in David's huge limo whilst David played the very latest hits he had sent out from London. The ladies stayed in Istanbul, sightseeing and shopping – except for one fateful day.

The shot on this particular day was to be the never-to-be-repeated one shot, with many cameras; a panorama of the complete invasion landing. It wasn't something that they could rehearse properly, but just plan, work out in detail, guess, and really hope for the best. But at least all the ships could be put in the right position before everything and everyone, horses and all, were launched over the side.

David and I set off as usual at about 5.30 a.m. but after forty-five minutes the car broke down on some mountain track. It was absolutely essential that we were on location on time, especially David, who was to be in the thick of the action on this day. We literally flagged down a donkey and cart, which took us to a nearby village where we hitched a lift in an old bread van. We were late. Tony was not pleased. Cameras were set up, actors and extras were sent out to the ships and by about eleven o'clock we were ready to start shooting – when into view hove a three-masted schooner with full sails unfurled. Horror, horror, horror! Two excited and lovely ladies had sailed the schooner from the sea of Marmora, right into the most expensive shot of the film. I have never known such anger. Tony was almost speechless with rage as the girls were now happily phutting towards us in the schooner's bumboat, approaching a huge crowd of screaming assistant directors and two frightened and shocked and angry actors. Tony requested the ladies to 'get the fucking boat out of shot'. A relationship and a marriage tottered – and eventually filming was able to take place.

*

We also had an earthquake! David and I were sitting in a harbour-side hotel bar in Istanbul late one evening when everything began to shake, glasses fell and people suddenly began to rush downstairs in a scramble to get out of the tall hotel – quite a number had been in bed or having a bath. The quake was so strong all the bath water shot out of their baths. We were all very frightened. All the myriad lights of Istanbul went out as the hotel guests rushed into the road. David and I managed to scramble to our little bumboat and motor quickly to our schooner, which we could see with its oil lamps lit, heaving in the disturbed water. Anyway, we got aboard safely and survived, although a number of people were killed in collapsing buildings in outlying villages. Our families in London were very worried as it was world news. We finished the film in London without further incident, but that was not quite the end of *The Charge of the Light Brigade*.

Charles Wood, who as I said had written the script for *The Charge*, was with us at all times during the shoot and whilst with us he was writing something else – a play. A play about the making of a period war film located in Turkey, inspired by *The Charge*, with many of the actors and crew, including the director, seemingly becoming characters in his play. It was called *Veterans* and was produced at the Royal Court Theatre sometime after the film had come and gone. My wife and I went to see it on the first night, and we went with Trevor Howard and his wife, Helen Cherry, both of whom had become friends.

The part that seemed to be the part Sir John Gielgud played in the film was in fact played by Sir John Gielgud. He had taken the part, it was said, because he didn't want another actor 'guying' him. Sir John, not surprisingly, played himself to perfection. The other main role in the film was taken by Sir John Mills. James Bolam played the director, and just to make it quite clear he copied the very distinctive camp cadences of Tony Richardson's voice. The John Mills character was portrayed as someone who had a drink problem and been fired from some previous films. His early successes were either war or railway station films, and during the play the character exposed himself and was referred to as Flasher. This was in the first act.

At the interval, Trevor, Helen, Sue and I went to the pub next door, and even before we had managed to buy drinks, Trevor clutched me fiercely by the shoulders and, with a look on his face that I would never like to see on the face of anyone again, said, 'Peter, tell me, please tell me, that that is not supposed to be me on the stage.' And then he broke down and cried. I did my best to reassure him that it wasn't, but we didn't return for the second half.

For myself, I was so proud and pleased to have been part of what I thought was a great film, I turned down a huge advertising campaign using the theme of *The Charge of the Light Brigade* for Courage Light Ale. I met the long-since-retired head of the advertising company quite recently. He reminded me that I had turned down the equivalent of £80,000 in today's money. Another actor in the film, Howard Marion-Crawford, did the campaign and I remained an almost penniless moral fool.

CHAPTER 10

EARLY FILMS II

Laughter in the Dark Take 1

The next film I did with Tony Richardson after *The Charge of the Light Brigade* was *Laughter in the Dark* by Nabokov, scripted by Edward Bond. This was also Tony's next film and it was to star Richard Burton.

Richard Burton and Elizabeth Taylor were at this time, 1968, at the absolute zenith of their public fame. The film was to be shot on location in England and Majorca. I had a really good feature part with important two-handed scenes with Burton. I was very excited, as were the rest of the cast, especially Anna Karina, who was to play the love interest opposite him. Burton had come to London with Elizabeth, but because they had two dogs and there was a quarantine law then, they lived aboard a yacht on the Thames.

Burton looked magnificent. Only forty-two, he still had that great male beauty coupled with tremendous 'presence'. He could also act, and I knew because I had seen him as Hamlet and Henry V at the Old Vic when I'd been at RADA. The first scenes were shot at the exquisite Grade I Farringdon House in Oxfordshire, once the home of Lord Berners of Mitford fame and renowned apart from its beauty for its dozens of doves, dyed all colours, which fluttered from a large dove-cote.

We were shooting in the gardens of the house that first morning, and were just between takes, when suddenly the whole unit began to clap. Turning, I saw that Elizabeth Taylor had just come into view. Here was true cinema royalty and immediately the English crew had responded. It was really touching. Elizabeth wore a little hat, I remember, and a very short skirt. Later Richard, Elizabeth, Sian Phillips (who was playing Burton's wife), Tony Richardson and myself (I was the brother-in-law) all had lunch with our hosts in the beautifully furnished and 'pictured' dining room of the house. I mention this because it was all to be repeated in very different circum-stances a week or two later.

We shot at Farringdon for a few days, and then moved to London, where we were to shoot a scene in Wildenstein's Art Gallery in Bond Street. Richard and I had got on very well from the start. He was very easy to talk to about anything under the sun. He did, however, have quite an entourage, made up of companions, bodyguards, a dresser, make-up artist, driver, and one particular man whose job, it seemed, was to continuously keep Richard's glass fresh. Richard would be handed a glass of vodka very early in the day but never at any time showed the slightest hint of its effect, either in his acting, charm, voice or manner. He was a big STAR and everyone, including Tony, seemed to adore him and be very pleased to be working with him.

On the very first day of our scene in Wildenstein's, Richard said to me quickly during a break, 'I saw a sweet little pub just round the corner. It's exactly ten fifty-nine and if we nip out now we will catch it as it opens at eleven.' Richard, a minder and myself walked the few yards to the pub, which indeed had just slid its bolts and was completely empty of customers. The minder, who knew what Richard wanted – apart from the atmosphere of a pub, which was what he really wanted – asked me what I would have and moved to the bar, leaving Richard and me at a little table. Before the minder was able to pay for the drinks, the pub was absolutely heaving, packed, people struggling to get in. I had never experienced anything like it. Richard had been spotted by the office girls, the shop girls, the passers-by and it was absolute pandemonium. We had quite a job to get out onto the street. Richard was at all times polite and cheerful as he tucked in behind his huge minder and headed for the door. Our drinks never left the bar.

We shot inside the art gallery for two or three days quite normally. Richard, I think, had a room at the Dorchester where he was made up, but changed with me in a room at the gallery. Dark-suited, sweating and rather nervous men were always coming to see Richard with samples of jewellery or catalogues of paintings – it was like being near a potentate. They knew he had money and he liked to spend it, usually on Elizabeth.

It was the last scene at the end of a normal day. Richard, amiable, topping up and acting as only he could. 'Cut,' said Tony. 'I'd like to go again, Richard.' Burton made no comment. We went to the top of the scene and did it again. 'Cut. That was lovely, Richard, thank you. Thank you, everybody,' said Tony, and then suddenly Burton exploded, expletives firing like shrapnel. The windows shook, pictures flapped in their frames. Burton's anger, which was ear-splitting, was directed straight at Tony. Now, Tony was the 'guvnor'. It was his film company and the crew adored him. They had worked on all his films. Everyone was flabbergasted. I had never seen Tony Richardson so helpless. It was as if someone had suddenly opened the door of a blast furnace in Tony's face. Burton then left us and went to the dressing room.

'I take it that's a wrap then, guvnor,' said the first assistant, which broke the tension.

'Yes,' said Tony. 'Thank you again, everybody. I'll see you all tomorrow.' And he moved to talk to his producer. I went to the dressing room.

Richard was changing and quite calm. 'I expect you wonder why I did that, Peter,' he said.

'Well, yes, Richard. But I wasn't going to ask.'

'I'll tell you,' he said. 'I like Tony. He's an old chum. As you know we did *Look Back in Anger* together, but I felt he was beginning to overstep the mark.'

'In what way?' I asked, rather lamely, still feeling shell-shocked.

'Well,' said Richard, 'when I started in the film business I had a seven-year contract with 20th Century Fox and they treated me like shit. They worked me like a dog. I swore that that would never happen again. So now when I do a film, I have a team of lawyers dot every i and cross every t, especially, and I mean especially, as to when my day finishes. My contract on this film says I finish at five o'clock, not one minute past five, and I felt that Tony was beginning to forget that. So when we went for that extra take I knew it would take us past five and I decided to remind Tony, because we still have several weeks to go. It was nothing personal. I wasn't even angry, it was just a gentle reminder,' he said, his eyes twinkling.

'Oh, I think he'll remember now all right, Richard,' I said. 'I know I'll never forget it.'

'See you tomorrow then,' said Richard, and he left with his hovering team for the Rolls Phantom and the arms of Elizabeth.

We were called as usual to start shooting at 8.30 the next morning, rehearsed, dressed and made up. Richard was late, then later. At 11.30 or so the producer called everyone together and told us that Richard was on his way, he would be here in a few minutes, and would we all mind stepping out onto the pavement as Tony wanted to have a private chat with Richard when he arrived. We all went outside, crew and actors. The

Rolls Phantom glided up. The entourage alighted, then Richard, and he had brought Elizabeth's young daughter with him. His entourage broke aside to let Richard and family through the door, but the moment they were through two enormous members of the film crew barred the way. Richard and his stepdaughter were alone with Tony. It was only for a few moments, then Richard stormed out, gave a gesture with his arm that I had only seen John Wayne do in the movies, and all his team clambered into the Rolls and away it went. The producer went inside alone. After quite a long time, he came out. 'Ladies and gentlemen,' he said, 'I'm sorry to keep you waiting on the pavement so long. Mr Burton has left the picture so would you all please go home now and keep close to your phones. Thank you.'

Within a few days we had started reshooting the film with the young, but great, Nicol Williamson.

Many years later, and while I was doing another film with Tony Richardson, he told me what had happened before and after the firing of Richard Burton. He told me with great sadness in his voice that when he was alone with Burton, he had asked him to apologize, not to him, not at all to him, about anything, but to his fellow cast members he had kept waiting for three hours. (The scene had included Sian Phillips, and other actors besides myself.) Burton had pointedly refused. 'Fuck off' I think Tony told me he'd replied and Tony therefore felt he had to tell Burton he was no longer on the picture – otherwise his position would have been totally undermined.

However, Tony told me he had gone to see Burton that evening on the boat to patch things up and felt he had succeeded then Richard changed his mind and that was that. I learnt after Tony had died that Burton's fee of £1,000,000 was coming out of Tony's personal pocket and he was still paying off the debt when he died. What a brave, remarkable man Tony was, and as I say, I loved him.

Laughter in the Dark Take 2

Nicol Williamson, who was considered by his contemporaries, including me, to be the most exciting actor of his generation, took the part on very, very short notice. He can hardly have had time to read the script let alone the book on which it was based (sometimes that's a good idea!). He was taking over from Richard Burton and was arriving to make love to a very disappointed Anna Karina, who I honestly doubt had ever heard of Nicol. I knew Nicol from various carousals in pubs and parties, and liked him, and by the end of the film we became close friends.

On the way back to London after his first day shooting he asked me if he was going to be okay in the part. Being Scots he was particularly worried that he wasn't managing Queen's English. I reassured him in every way, and was flattered that he had sought my opinion.

The first day of shooting had in fact been the reshooting of the scenes at Farringdon House in Oxfordshire, and once again our splendid hosts gave us a wonderful lunch, served by their staff. The lunch hadn't been going very long when Nicol, to everyone's horror, suddenly said with tremendous venom, 'Tony, why do you speak with that ridiculous false whining camp accent? It's very affected. I want to know why you do it, because I think it's silly.'

We all received it like a blow in the face, especially Tony. But he gave one of his neighing laughs.

'Oh come along, Nicol. I don't know what you mean and I certainly don't know why you're saying it. It's very embarrassing for everyone.'

As far as I remember, Nicol got up and left the room. I think what Nicol was up to was domination, driven by insecurity. He was going to deliver the first blow by insulting and embarrassing

Tony now, up front, straight away, full frontal, with everyone to hear and witness it. He felt he couldn't be fired, I suppose, and he wanted us all to know he was not to be trifled with, that he was dangerous – and he was. However, we proceeded filming happily. Of course I don't know what happened in the scenes I wasn't in, but all my London scenes went well and off we went to Majorca.

Tony had a lovely habit when filming. At about eleven a.m., six bottles of Dom Perignon would be brought onto the set and everyone would be given a glass or cup, every day without fail. Another rather charming habit was that after a shot had been completed, he would suddenly turn to a sparks or carpenter or any member of the crew and ask if, in their opinion, the scene worked, if it was convincing. The actors didn't seem to mind – though I can't remember him doing it with Burton! He didn't always do it; just occasionally. Just enough to make sure that everyone on that set, thirty people or so, would be absolutely quiet and intently watching the scene. The actors were well aware of this, and actors love to have the undivided attention of an audience.

I remember one hot day when Anna Karina had to be nude at a swimming pool. Tony got the whole crew to take their clothes off. Much laughter, much relaxation and Anna was much less embarrassed.

Because Nicol is such an exciting actor, he could at times be unexpectedly volatile, and I had a personal experience of this in a two-handed scene we had together. Nicol's character is blind at this point in the film, and he was using a walking stick to help him get around. The scene was outside and it was a tracking shot, which means the camera was following us on rails. It was the first take. We had rehearsed the dialogue but not the unexpected improvised attack. On action, and after the first few lines of dialogue, Nicol attacked me. It was an explosion of maddened violence with his heavy walking stick. Fortunately I was an expert in judo and immediately and instinctively defended myself by parrying the blow and throwing Nicol. As I turned him into the air I realized that I must somehow break his fall or he would be hurt as I landed on him. I aborted the perfect Tai Otoshi and screwed around so that he fell partly on top of me. It saved him from what would probably have been serious harm, as his violence had been so propelled. I was okay and the film still had a leading man. Tony thought it was the funniest thing he'd ever seen. 'Oh Nicol, you are naughty. Now we will have to do it again.' After we had brushed ourselves off, Nicol looked at me with unblind eyes and I knew he would never try anything like that again – at least not with me.

It was a very happy time in Majorca. Robert Graves would occasionally visit, surrounded by adoring young female fans from all over the world, it seemed. There was lots of swimming, tennis and of course late-night drinking. Yes, filming on sunny locations is any actor's dream.

Nicol was to go on to become one of the truly great Hamlets of his generation in a production directed by Tony Richardson at the Round House, Kentish Town. I saw the production as I had become a close friend of Nicol's. He spoke the lines as if he were saying them newly minted, straight from his mind. Claudius was a young and, I later learnt, an unhappy Anthony Hopkins; Ophelia was a young and happy Marianne Faithfull.

The Dog Picture
'For the Love of Benji'

It didn't start too auspiciously. I had been asked to meet the producer and director, a nice man called Joe Camp, at a huge hotel in Hammersmith that had, as it turned out, an underground car park. I duly parked my car and took a lift to the director's suite for the interview. I soon discovered that they were both Texans and had had a huge hit with their first and only picture, called *Benji*. Joe Camp had been a successful commercials' director in America and having shot a commercial for dog food had been so impressed with the cuteness of the little mongrel dog and the brilliance and skill of the owner/trainer that he had the idea to devise and write a film around and starring the dog. This, it seemed, was proposed to Disney. They declined, so he decided to produce the film himself, and with the help of his usual commercial film crew and friends he raised the money and together they made the film. It took about $70 million in America alone (around $350 million in today's terms), and as everyone from the clapper boy to the cameraman to the electrician had a share in the film, everyone made a great deal of money. They were, I discovered later, all dollar millionaires.

This film was called *For the Love of Benji*. They were all going to get even richer. My interview seemed to go okay but nothing was offered or indicated, although it was clear that the part was the villain of the piece (therefore they wanted an Englishman!) and it was to be shot in Greece – sunny Greece. Every actor loves a good location no matter what the part.

I got into my car and discovered that I couldn't have the car park barrier lifted until I paid £1. I had no money at all.

'You can put it on your room,' said the attendant.

'I'm not resident.' I said.

'Then I'm afraid you'll have to leave your car here,' he said.

Well, I wasn't going to be offered the part anyway – it was such a good part they would want a star – so I decided to clinch their rejection by using the hotel phone to call the director and ask him to put my car parking on his bill. Joe Camp thought it was the funniest request he'd ever had and graciously agreed, and I suddenly felt I might get the part after all. I did.

I arrived in Athens to discover my wife was to be played by a very distinguished and beautiful English actress. We were booked into the Hilton Hotel in Athens, the whole unit was there on several floors. We drove out to the location the next day in a large bus. It was packed with the whole American crew. The director was standing strap-hanging right beside me. I offered him my seat, he declined. Country and western music was playing somewhere and I decided to be sociable and feature-film wise.

'Have you seen the new Altman film, *Nashville?*' I asked the director.

Suddenly the whole bus went quiet – conversations stopped, the music was turned down.

'Yep,' said Joe Camp, 'we saw that film.'

'Wasn't it wonderful?' I said.

The music was turned off. The atmosphere was electric. All you could hear was the swish of the tyres.

'Nope,' said Joe Camp, his voice becoming a little louder, his drawl becoming more pronounced. 'We're all Texans and we found that film kind of patronizing.'

There was a soft growling sound from the crew on the bus. I kept very quiet for the rest of the journey.

The scene we were to shoot that day was between the distinguished actress and myself and the dog. We were introduced to the star of the film, Benji, and also his trainer/owner, a very big fat man wearing a Stetson. In fact, most of the crew wore Stetsons and beautiful tooled cowboy boots and very expensive Native American jewellery. 'What's that?' said my 'wife to be', indicating a cat in a small cage. 'Oh, that's what we use to fire up the star,' said the trainer. He led Benji towards the cat in the cage. Benji began to bark fiercely and strain on his leash, his hackles rising. He really wanted to get at that cat. He was certainly fired up. The cat arched its back; its hackles also rose and it fired back with loud hissing noises. The actress was very upset. 'But this is terrible. You're being very cruel to this cat. Does the Greek RSPCA or its equivalent know about this?' she said, or words to that effect. This was all observed and heard by many members of the crew. They couldn't believe their ears.

Suddenly a kindly, non-Stetson-hatted, well-dressed man stepped forward, took the actress gently by the arm, said something quietly in her ear and led her away. In fact, she, poor, delightful woman was led all the way back to the hotel, and then led on to the airport. She was fired. They didn't want trouble. They had made millions from that cat and dog and they were going to make more. But there was no filming that day as I didn't have a wife – but as the man said, you ain't heard nothing yet.

The director asked me if I could recommend a replacement actress as a matter of urgency. I had recently finished a television and suggested the young actress who had played opposite me. 'I'll get onto it straight away,' he said, 'as I'd like to start shooting this scene tomorrow.'

Later I was told the actress had been booked and would be flying out that evening to start work the next morning. It was quite a big scene and the actress must have been faxed her lines. This is how it works in the film business sometimes. But when you're offered a good part in a film, in Greece for God's sake, unless you are a movie star you jump at it.

At about 2.00 a.m. that night my bedside phone rang. My actress friend had arrived and she was desperate and crying – could she come to my room? She arrived in a hotel dressing gown. In the scene the next day we were to be in evening dress, me black tie, she low-cut, sleeveless evening dress. She had been fitted for it in London and brought it out with her.

'What am I going to do,' she said, throwing open her gown. She stood there trembling in her underwear and she was covered in bruises on her arms and shoulders.

'My God,' I said, 'what happened?'

'Someone didn't want me to come.'

Not wanting to go too far into her private life I said, 'Don't worry. Let's see what make-up can do.'

I had a unit list which gave the room number of the two make-up girls. I rang them and explained the situation.

'We'll come straight down,' they said.

The make-up girls were wonderful. They stood there in their nightwear and reassured the crying, trembling actress that everything could be covered, no one would know a thing. In fact they would come to her room early and do the major work before anyone else saw her. We all went back to bed. So that was all right then. Oh no, it wasn't.

Does anyone know how those dogs in dog films do those wonderful intelligent cute things that they do? I don't think anyone who hasn't done a dog film knows. In this context I even include *Thin Man* films, never mind *Lassies*. Anyway, I certainly didn't, nor did my alabaster-armed and pink-shouldered wife! As I said, we were the villains. We had kidnapped the star, Benji, who we were holding in our house. The scene to be filmed was the kidnappers having a discussion on what to do next, how to arrange the ransom and suchlike. An intimate and concentrated discussion. So concentrated that we don't see Benji come into the room, listen to our conversation, decide he's heard enough, then notice an open window and jump out of it to freedom, carrying in his clever head important over-heard information.

Before we rehearsed the dialogue in the middle of the room, the director explained that Benji's understudy would be brought in on a lead and placed quietly in a couple of positions on the carpet, then placed on the sofa in front of the window, and we then had to imagine that he had jumped out of the window for our exclamation of despairing horror. We rehearsed it a couple of times, it was lit, and we were ready to shoot. 'Bring on the star,' shouted the first assistant. On came a very down-at-heel, bored, tired-looking Benji. 'Okay, fire him up,' said the assistant, and onto the set is brought the cat in the cage. Immediately Benji is very alert. Indeed, he seems to grow to twice his size. His eyes are ablaze and his hair is on end as he yanks at his lead. He really, really wants to get at that cat. Gradually the cat man moves away from Benji, and while Benji growls and whines in anticipation he slowly, in Benji's full view, kneels on the sofa and places the cat and cage on the other side of the window, just out of sight. Benji is really fired up. He knows where the cat is. We are ready to shoot. We are ready to play our scene and Benji is taken out of the room with the door left ajar. Action! We start our dialogue.

What we don't know, but are about to discover, is that there are about eight men around the edges of the set, opposite the sofa and window, with very powerful whistles. We start speaking. Benji bounds into the room and immediately all the whistles whistle. The cacophony is so loud, so piercing, we cannot actually hear what we are saying to each other, and rely on lip reading, speaking only when the other one stops. We don't complain, we do not hesitate, we do not forget our lines. We are pros.

This is how it works. The dog, whose only thought is to get at the cat out of the window is distracted by the blasting of all the whistles, stops and turns, supposedly towards us. Then strong blasting from one side alone. The dog cocks his head towards this sound, ears twitching, cute. He's listening to the humans speaking. Then that side stops and the other side explodes. The dog's head whips around towards this noise, more ear twitching. Yes, he understands what we are saying. All whistling stops. The dog remembers his main purpose, the cat, and jumps onto the sofa. Another tremendous, almost deafening blast from all the whistles. The dog stops again, turns, cocks his head, and flicks his ears up and down. Yes, he's got the vital information. The whistling stops. The dog remembers the cat, and jumps out of the window! What an intelligent dog; what a great scene; the audience can't wait to see what will happen next. Cut!

The whole crew burst into whoops of congratulations, clapping and cheering. No, not for the star, but for the two English actors who they deliberately hadn't told what would happen and are amazed and indeed very grateful that we have got through it without a hitch, in one take!

'Don't worry,' said the director, 'we'll record all your dialogue when the filming is finished.' And that's how they make a dog picture. (Oh and by the way, quite a number of the Texan crew bought small primus stoves, obtained raw hamburgers from the American embassy canteen and cooked up in the corridors. What with the campfire smoke haze and country music, they were back in the old corral.)

The Offence

This film remains a mystery to me. Not the story in the film but what happened to me and why. I can't quite make it add up. If you can perhaps you'll drop me a line, especially if your name is Sean Connery. The film *The Offence* was based on the play *The Story of Yours*, written by John Hopkins.

The film was to star Sean Connery, who was still making *Bond* pictures, Trevor Howard and Ian Bannen, and was to be directed by the great American director, Sidney Lumet. Sean Connery was playing a policeman and I was to play his superior officer. It was a terrific part and I was thrilled. It was a terrific part not only because I went through the film but because I had a major scene with Sean Connery where I tore him off a very severe strip.

Sidney Lumet called a two-week rehearsal period before we started shooting. I had known Sean before his starring days and had teased him that I had his photo as Mr Junior Scotland on the front of a 1952 *Health and Strength* magazine. I liked Sean very much and I also liked and admired Sidney Lumet. It was a very happy atmosphere in rehearsal despite the harrowing story of child molesting.

The only problem was that whenever we came to the scene where I had Sean before me in my office and I gave him a severe dressing-down, Sean would begin to laugh. That is, while I was speaking Sean would be suppressing laughter, then not suppressing laughter. Sidney Lumet was always saying, 'Sean, pull yourself together,' or 'What's so funny, Sean? You're making it very difficult for Peter.' Sean, with tears running down his face, would always apologize profusely. On one rehearsal, which was unfortunately being filmed by some TV channel, Sean laughed so much he actually lay on the floor, helpless. I, of course, was very anxious, bemused and troubled. Sean made it clear he couldn't understand why he couldn't control himself, and Sidney Lumet made it extremely clear to me when I questioned him closely in private that he was very happy indeed with my performance.

When we came to shoot this scene in the studio – master shot and close-ups – Sean was masculine and very serious. He took his ticking-off well.

'Cut, print. Well done, Sean. Well done, Peter. Next set-up, please,' said Sidney Lumet. I was very relieved and very pleased that the scene had gone well. 'Peter,' said Mr Lumet 'would you like to socialize with me while they are doing the next set-up?' I had never been asked to socialize with anyone before, but I was very pleased to be asked to socialize with this wonderful film director. Sidney Lumet put his arm around me and walked me away from the film set. 'Peter, I am enjoying working with you very much,' said Mr Lumet, 'and I'd like to ask you a question.' What was coming, I thought, is he going to ask me to be in his next film? He seemed so friendly and serious.

'Yes, Sidney,' I said. Sidney Lumet asked his question.

'Peter, have you ever thought of playing comedy?'

All the walls came tumbling down, Sean's rehearsal laughter rang loudly in my head.

'You didn't like the way I played that scene,' I said.

Sidney Lumet was offended. 'Peter, for God's sake, I'm socializing with you. Of course I liked the scene. You were terrific. If I hadn't liked what you did I'd have said so and we would have done the scene again. Peter, when I say print I mean print.' I was still nervously confused. 'Peter, the reason I asked you if you had ever thought of playing comedy is because I am interested in you, both as a person and an actor, that's all.'

'We're ready, guvnor,' said a voice and Sidney left my side.

*

Months later, Sue and I were invited to the big gala opening at the Leicester Square Odeon. For some reason Sue couldn't come and I went on my own. Very grand, black tie, a special room set aside for the leading actors, stars and producer to have champagne before the showing. We took our seats. The film starts, something is odd, not quite right. My big scene with Sean arrives twenty-five-foot high on the screen. Got it. My stomach reeled, my anger and shock were such that I stood up. I had been dubbed, re-voiced. I had been invited to the film and champagne reception and no one had mentioned or warned me I had been re-voiced. I must mention it is not at all unheard of for an actor/actress to be re-voiced, that is show business. I would have been disappointed, would like to have known why, but I would not have been angry. I was angry because no one had told me, warned me. I felt a fool and I was going to speak to my co-actor about it. I was going to speak to Sean Connery, and I was going to speak (if I could stop myself shouting) right this minute; in the middle of the film. I couldn't find him. I left the cinema, phoned my wife, bought a half bottle of whisky, found a quiet spot away from Leicester Square and drank it.

Complaints about the massive discourtesy were made by my agent who was also at the film, and who also knew nothing.

The answer came by letter. I have it before me now. It was from the producer, who expressed shock, shame and sorrow. He was surprised I had turned up for the showing. He understood, at that time, that Sean Connery as a fellow actor and star of the film had warned me. He had now discovered that Sean thought that Sidney Lumet had contacted me. On contacting Sidney Lumet he now knew that Sidney had thought that he, the producer, had written me. A cock-up. Profuse apologies.

The mystery remains. Why, apart from the take, couldn't Sean get through the scene without uncontrollable laughter? Why did Sidney Lumet ask me after such a serious scene if I'd ever thought of playing comedy? Why did he praise my performance during rehearsals and shooting if he was not pleased? And of course the big question: why was I re-voiced? Just to let you know what an interesting world the actor occupies, the most powerful casting director of the day, Maud Spector, told me soon after *The Offence* opened that I had given 'the best performance' of my career.

She also said to me many years later, when I had achieved 'star' status, 'I'm so pleased, Peter, that you are at last having such a success. I always thought you were a marvellous actor, but I never cast you in any of my films, because I didn't think you had any character in your face.'

What's a poor boy to do?

*

I am reminded on mentioning Maud Spector of some strange auditions I have had for films. A very early one was for Michael Winner. It came at a time when I was in the middle of filming *Three Hats for Lisa*, a musical film starring Joe Brown and his Bruvvers. I was playing his manager and it was fun and quite funny.

My agent called to say Michael Winner was very keen to see me for a film. I duly arrived at what I now presume was Michael's house and was shown into an anteroom. A very bored-looking Sloane of about twenty sat reading a magazine. 'Name?' she enquired in an upper-class drawl. I told her. 'Mr Winner will see you when this phone tinkles,' she said. It tinkled and I went to meet, for the first time, Mr Michael Winner.

It was a large room with, I seem to remember, two desks, one at each end of the room. Mr Winner rose from one desk and extended an arm with a slightly clenched fist at the end of it. He wasn't about to shake my hand, which had started to come forward in anticipation. Oh no, he then opened his fist to reveal a piece of paper which he invited me to take from him. I did. I was confused.

'What's this?' I enquired as politely as an actor looking for a job could enquire.

'What does it look like?' barked Mr Winner, who at all times has a slight smile on his face.

'A piece of paper with something written on it,' I replied. 'Possibly a phone number.'

'Well done,' said Mr Winner, 'Now I want you to go to that phone –' he pointed to the desk at the other end of the room – 'and dial that number.'

'Why?' I bravely asked.

'Because,' said Mr Winner, his smile becoming broader and a twinkle appearing in his eyes, 'at the other end of that phone there will be a man who has seen some of your rushes' (early prints of *Three Hats for Lisa* scenes) 'from the film you are making at Shepperton Studios and said I ought to see you. I want you to thank him very much and tell him that you are now in the presence of Mr Winner and phoning from his office. Go on,' he said, pointing towards the other end of the room.

I cannot remember ever feeling quite so embarrassed, so

The Avengers. Escape in Time with me, Dame Diana Rigg and me with a beard.

Blow-Up with David Hemmings. David taught me life is fun and games.

Captain and Mrs Duberley (Jill Bennett) in *The Charge of the Light Brigade*.

A break from the Charge. Lunch at the Chilean Consulate including T.P. McKenna (in glasses), Trevor Howard and Harry Andrews in middle. Me far right.

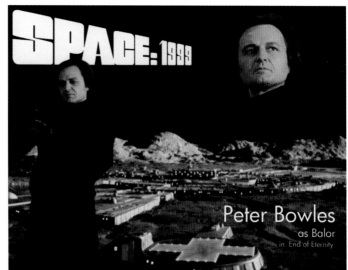

The most evil man in the universe.

Peter Bowles
as Balor
in End of Eternity

Who is this John Gielgud? Sir John and me in a Tale of the Unexpected.

We were ill for four years. *Only When I Laugh* with Richard Wilson, James Bolam, Christopher Strauli.

'The Sisters Dream'
by Elizabeth Oakley.

The only people fooled
were the *Sunday People*
(and the British
Museum).

I can't act, I wear a suit.

No need to act 'I look just like him'. *Born in the Gardens* with Barry Foster.

I can't act, I don't have a car! Sheila Gish, me Janet Suzman, Peter Medak and Alan Bates – *A Day in the Death of Joe Egg*.

The very first publicity shot of Penelope Keith, Angela Thorne and myself in *To The Manor Born*.

Richard de Vere.

Sue, me and Sam in our very first press photo.

Carry your bag ma–am?
Sue keeps her distance.

His story makes the front page
(again). Neville Lytton –
Lytton's Diary.

stupid, so helpless and emasculated. To my shame I did as I was told. The man who answered the phone was extremely surprised and embarrassed to receive my call and the conversation was awkward and short. The next thing I actually remember was finding myself passing the receptionist in the anteroom.

'What did you think of Mr Winner?' she enquired without looking up from her reading. I sensed danger.

'Oh he seemed very nice,' I replied weakly, still dazed by what I'd been through.

'Nice? Nice?' she said poshly and then used an expression that surprised me coming from such beautiful bow-shaped lips. I didn't get the job.

Many, many years later at some reception I bumped into Mr Winner and tried to remind him of our meeting. He had no recollection of it. I then made the mistake of telling him of my exchange of words with his Sloaney receptionist. I thought he would roar with laughter. He roared all right. 'Who was it, what was her name, what exactly did she look like?' Mr Winner was not amused. 'Michael,' I said, 'you can't fire her, it was forty years ago.' I'm not sure he heard my last words as he was backing swiftly away from me. Perhaps he thought I was deranged.

Mr Winner was to show how truly nice he was when, many years after my 'audition', he gently reprimanded me for being so rude as not to thank Marlon Brando for his lunch invitation. 'I'm sorry, Michael. I don't know what you are talking about.' He told me. Brando was a friend of Mr Winner's and on being in England, and it being his birthday, Michael had asked him if there was any particular English actor he would like to meet at a little birthday lunch Michael was throwing for him. Brando told him that he would like to meet me, as I was his favourite English actor. Someone had phoned my agents, and presumably spoken merely to a receptionist or 'temp'. Whoever phoned was told I was not available, and the message was never passed on to me. I learnt from Mr Winner the date of the lunch – I could have been available – and will regret this missed chance all my life. Just to underline the truth of this, a year or two later I was presenting the *TV Times* Awards, when the young attractive hostess who brought over the statuettes asked if she could have a private word with me during rehearsal. She told me that she was Marlon Brando's girlfriend when he came to London, and did I know that he was a huge fan of mine and had all my tapes of *To The Manor Born*, *Only When I Laugh* and *The Irish RM*, and often watched them in his hotel suite. I noticed that some of these tapes were among his effects when he died. I tell you all this because obviously I am humbled, flattered and extremely grateful to have discovered that this greatest of all film actors liked my work.

Another film audition I had was arranged by Maud Spector and was for a film to be directed by John Frankenheimer. It was held at the Mayfair Hotel. In the corridor directly opposite Mr Frankenheimer's suite was a sofa, on which I was to wait. Also waiting on the sofa was an old friend from RADA, the distinguished actor Dudley Sutton. We were very pleased to see each other. Maud Spector appeared. 'Mr Frankenheimer would like to see you together,' she said. In we went. Mr Frankenheimer was leaning back from a huge desk with his booted feet crossed on the top of it. He viewed us through the V of his crossed boots. I also seem to remember he was wearing a Stetson. Anyway it was all very American and very exciting. He didn't get up but warmly indicated we should sit opposite his desk on a little sofa. Dudley and I perched side by side, our bodies touching. 'Now, boys,' said Mr Frankenheimer, 'I know you haven't seen the script so I am going to tell you the story and during the telling you will notice I emphasize and dwell on a certain part. That is the part you are both up for. So when I have finished, I am going to sit back' (he would have fallen over if he'd sat back further) 'and watch you guys fight for that part.' Dudley and I looked at each other, rose as one man, told Mr

Frankenheimer what he could do with his film, and left the room. The part went to David Warner. I'm not sure that he enjoyed it.

I subsequently learnt that Mr Frankenheimer was not being rude. That was how auditions were often conducted in America.

Another audition was for the film *Frenzy* directed by Alfred Hitchcock. Here my innocence and naivety came into full play. I was received warmly by Mr Hitchcock at the offices of my grand agents, MCA. Again I hadn't seen a script. Mr Hitchcock handed me one. 'Peter,' he said, 'if you turn to page twenty-seven you will find a good long scene which concerns the part you are up for. I'd like you to go into the next room for a while and read it. Then when you come back I will not ask you to read the scene but I will be asking for your help. You see, Peter, that is a difficult and long scene and, to be honest with you, I don't know how to direct it. I would be extremely grateful when you return if you could help me by telling me how you think I should direct the scene.'

I went out. I read the scene. I came back. I told him how he should direct the scene. I didn't get the part. No, Mr Alfred Hitchcock, the most meticulous auteur director in the world was, I think, playing games, don't you?

A few years ago I went up for a very good part of a very grand upper-class man. The company and casting were American although the director was not.

I decided to wear a suit as the character was an ex-general and would probably have worn one on all formal occasions.

On entering the room I was confronted by three people, the director, the casting lady and the producer. They were all laughing as I entered the room. I instinctively checked my fly buttons, as all actors do. They were seated. 'Why are you laughing?' I asked. A reasonable request, as I was obviously the cause of it. 'Well,' they almost said in unison, 'we have been in this business for some years now and this is the first time we have ever seen an actor arrive for an audition in a suit.' I immediately dropped my trousers. They asked me to read the part. I insisted on reading it bare legged. They were impressed, not by my legs but by my reading, at least that's what I gathered. 'Mr Bowles, that reading was so good, that we can see you are so talented you could play any part in this film, including that of the leading lady.' Perhaps my terrific legs were impressing them after all. I never heard from them again.

*

A little rider to the Hitchcock story. Many years ago I played opposite Yolande Donlan, the actress wife of the old-time film director Val Guest. He always picked up his wife after the show and on my telling him of the encounter with Hitchcock he told me the following story.

Sometime in the 1930s, when Hitchcock was making films over here, Val Guest was also making films and had offices in the same studios. He had not, however, met Mr Hitchcock, who was already making quite a reputation for himself. One day, a minion of Mr Hitchcock's called on him. It was a Friday, the weekend beckoned and the minion explained that Mr Hitchcock was embarrassingly out of money for the weekend, and as the banks didn't open on Saturdays could Mr Guest possibly loan him £25. Twenty-five pounds was a lot of money in those days, but Val Guest found enough money in his safe to cover it and gave it willingly to the minion. 'Mr Hitchcock said you will definitely be paid back on Monday, and thank you.'

Monday came and went and so did three weeks. There was no money. Mr Guest sent a polite but terse note of reminder to Hitchcock's offices.

The next day the Hitchcock minion arrived with a very large bag, and poured onto Mr Guest's desk and floor £25 in farthings.

There were four farthings to a penny, twelve pennies to a shilling and twenty shillings to a pound, which makes 960 farthings to a pound. Multiplied by twenty-five, that meant 24,000 farthings. It was a lot of farthings, the smallest coin of the realm.

Mr Guest, who obviously had the most wicked sense of humour and of revenge, thanked the minion politely, sent his regards and thanks to Mr Hitchcock, and then spent the next few weeks searching for old discarded keys, which as you know can be found all over the place. He collected over two hundred of these and on each one he tied a label which said, 'If the finder of this key takes it to—' and he gave Hitchcock's address in the Cromwell Road 'he will be given a reward in cash.' Val Guest then, that weekend, took several buses around London and threw the keys out of the bus windows in almost every borough of London.

Later that week a very distraught Mr Hitchcock himself burst into Mr Guest's office having deduced he was the culprit, pleaded with Val Guest to stop the joke as he, Hitchcock, couldn't cope with the queues that had formed outside his door every day when he got back from the studios.

I have a feeling that if I had known that story before my audition I might have been stupid enough to have reminded him of it.

CHAPTER 11

ON BEING DIFFICULT

At an early point in my career I seemed to develop a reputation of being 'a bit difficult'. This is okay if you are a star
but can hold you back from becoming a star if you start before
you are, if you see what I mean.

I remember after the read-through of one of my early televisions, in which I had a small part, a number of cuts were made
as the reading had been too long. None of these affected my
part, but I couldn't help pointing out to the director as everyone happily applied the blue pencil, that if certain of the cuts
were made, the story wouldn't actually make sense. The director was very, very angry. Actually, because he saw I was right,
but he certainly wasn't going to admit it. When we all got up
from the table, the leading actor, a much more experienced
older man, kindly took me aside. 'Peter,' he said, 'listen, this is
only television. Nobody cares. The viewers certainly won't
care, even if they notice, which I doubt. I have a mushroom
farm. That's what I care about. But as far as television is concerned I just take the money and run, and that's my advice to
you, old chap.' I hope you agree I didn't take his advice. My
kindly advisor ended his career playing in a well-known soap
for about twenty years. He must have been a very contented

mushroom farmer. It's all a matter of choice – if you're lucky enough to get it.

I think often it's a case of where angels fear to tread. Fools, that is. In an early *Armchair Theatre* TV play, after rehearsing the part of a top art connoisseur in a rehearsal room for three weeks, I arrived at the studio to discover that the 'set' of my home was totally kitsch, appalling paintings, terrible furniture. I felt strongly I couldn't act in it and said so! The director was almost speechless. 'Look,' I said, 'I have spent three weeks trying to be as believable as I can. That's my job. It will all be destroyed the moment I walk on that set.' I'm afraid they didn't record my scenes that day. The set was refurnished that night and the scenes shot the next day at, I suppose, great expense to the TV company. I would have made a terrible mushroom farmer anyway, but I did get a reputation for being 'a bit difficult'. I have worked quite often with actors who I have been warned are 'a bit difficult'. They invariably turn out to be the ones who actually want to get things as near 100 per cent right as possible. Not 98 per cent but 100 per cent, and none of them as far as I know were particularly keen on mushrooms.

The only exception to that I have come across was Michael Crawford, who seemed to want to get things 100 per cent right for him and not necessarily for the scene. Anyway this was my experience of Mr Crawford.

I had been asked by my very long-standing friend Patrick Garland to play the part of the undertaker (Shadrack) in the musical version of Keith Waterhouse's *Billy Liar*, music by John Barry, lyrics by Don Black. I had done a musical for Patrick before, *The Stiffkey Scandals of 1932*, which I had adored doing, mainly because of Annie Ross and the lovely dance group the Go Jos. Unfortunately it only lasted two weeks at the Queens Theatre! I don't think either Patrick or I put it in our CVs now!

Billy was quite different. It had huge money behind it, a big American producer and it was going into Drury Lane. As

Patrick Garland said to me, 'It's First Division, love.' I was penniless at the time and although it was a small part it did have a song and it paid £250 a week – and it was going to have lots and lots of dancing girls. Heaven! Elaine Paige, who went on to greater things, was also in it; also Diana Quick, ditto. But it starred, and I do mean STARRED, Michael Crawford as Billy.

I'd met Michael now and then with other actors in pubs and he appeared charming. It was going to be fun, and I did need that money. The rehearsal period was to be six weeks and the very first scene to be rehearsed was between Michael and myself. Billy is working in the funeral parlour and has a speech to the audience, thinking he's alone in the 'shop', it's all about how awful his boss is (me). During the speech I come in unbeknownst to Billy and stand just behind him. He finishes his speech. I speak. Billy turns and sees me. Panic from Billy, laughter from the audience and on with the scene. We started the rehearsal, Michael started his speech, finished his speech, I spoke, he turned, and on we went, everything's fine. I then made a suggestion to Patrick and Michael about something we might try in the scene. Immediately Michael looked at his watch and declared he was sorry but he had to go for a dancing lesson. I finished the scene with the director. I don't think I rehearsed with Michael again. Patrick Garland always played Billy instead. The not unreasonable excuse being that Michael was having singing or tap dancing rehearsals elsewhere.

After five weeks came the first run-through of the whole show. It was to be held in the huge rehearsal rooms and it was going to be watched by the show's main backers. I had never seen big-show backers, or Angels, before. They were very fur-coated and bejewelled. They looked rich. All the management were there, the big American producer, the famous choreographer, John Barry, Keith Waterhouse, Don Black, and of course my friend and director of the show, Patrick Garland. Overture, opening dance number and then straight into the first acting scene in the undertaker's parlour.

Michael began his speech – I'd never heard it before – and from the look on the faces of the management, nor had anyone else. It was a long shaggy-dog story about an American bomber pilot. There was no reference to my character whatsoever. I decided I must enter the scene, go through the pretend door and take my overhearing position. Michael finally finished his speech, which had a punchline finish, and just as his laugh started to die I boldly said my line as written.

Michael, in full STAR mode, turned on me – no panic, no surprise – and said, as Michael (not Billy), 'No, not yet. When I want you to speak I'll give you a nod!'

For just a moment time seemed to stop, and then I said, 'Michael, of course you are a star as far as the public is concerned, but as far as I'm concerned you're a fellow actor and a fellow actor doesn't speak to another like that. I think you should apologize.' Some applause from the chorus boys and girls and suddenly the required panic from Michael, although much more than scripted. He moved quickly to the side of the rehearsal room. I didn't think my tone had been threatening. In fact in the circumstances it had been well modulated and calm. Perhaps that gave it a deadly quality. Anyway, Patrick Garland bounded onto the acting area and pinned down my arms in his embrace and pulled me as far away from Michael as possible.

'Peter,' he said, 'for God's sake.'

'I wasn't going to hit him,' I said, 'but I couldn't take that from anyone. He was very, very rude to me.'

'I know,' said Patrick 'I know, but I can't help you, Peter, dear. Michael is the STAR.'

I told Patrick I quite understood his position and stepped forward again and announced I would be leaving the show. This time it was the big American producer who came up to me. He put a big friendly arm around me, and he too drew me aside.

'Listen, Peter,' he said, 'I quite understand that you cannot stay with us after the way Michael spoke to you, but after watching you in rehearsal I'm sure you've got a big future. Just one favour, Peter. Could you please stay until we find a replacement for you?' I agreed. He was so nice, so pragmatic and after all it was really his show.

We went to Manchester for the pre-London opening. Michael in his personal dealings with me was charm itself, there seemed to be no hard feelings on his side whatsoever, and I, knowing I was going to be leaving his show, felt okay too. However, before we opened there was another moment when I felt humiliated by Michael in rehearsal. I am sure he wasn't even aware of it, but I was. I spent the night in torment. I couldn't continue like this. I rang my sweet and understanding new agent, Joy Jameson, at about six in the morning at home.

'Don't worry,' she said. 'I will have you out of the show by eight-thirty breakfast.'

My dear friend Bryan Pringle, with whom I was sharing a flat, was most upset at my leaving and was in tears. Michael made a point of finding me to express great regret I was leaving and to say how much he'd enjoyed working with me. When not in star mode Michael was quite charming, but I hope you'll agree it was a good example of it being okay to be 'difficult' if you were a star. The one thing I did gain from the experience was the certain knowledge that Michael Crawford didn't have a secret mushroom farm.

Another early memory of my being 'difficult', which actually is often just standing up for yourself when you are being bullied by someone of a higher status – either the star or the director, was when I did *Bonne Soupe* in 1962 in the West End. It starred Coral Browne, who, as I mentioned earlier, was quite a character. The play couldn't have come at a better time as Sue and I now had our first child. Funnily enough, I took over during rehearsals from the superb actor Peter Sallis. For some reason they had decided he wasn't right for the part and replaced him with me. The play was about Coral Browne's character's 'love life'. She sat on a bar stool at the side of the stage and spoke about her life whilst several actors and an actress enacted her amours. Her character also told jokes about her life. There was young Coral and her three lovers; I was the first and Nigel Davenport was the third. I can't remember who was the second. My first surprise came when the pretty actress Erica Rogers, playing the young Coral, wouldn't look at me during our love scene. I stopped the rehearsal.

'Forgive me, darling,' I said, 'but could you please look at me occasionally whilst you're talking to me, or even better when I'm making love to you?'

'No,' she replied without any irritation whatsoever. 'You see, I've already been in rehearsal for a week' (with Peter Sallis) 'and I'm all "out front" now.' This was said as a simple way of explaining and expecting me to be completely understanding.

It didn't get us off to a good start. The director, a peculiar man called Milo Sperber, sympathized entirely with the actress, and oddly enough, though I'm sure for other reasons, was fired the next day. He was replaced by the wonderful Eleanor Fazan, a lovely woman with whom Nigel Davenport promptly fell in love, but that's his life not mine!

Coral, as I say, spoke jokes, some scripted, some not. The ones that were not were quite often at my expense. The show was a huge hit. We had been running several months by now and the rather bored Coral Browne, who was and is still remembered by all the profession for being outrageous, generous and altogether quite wonderful, began to step up her jokes at my expense.

They were said out of the side of her mouth in that deadly Australian drawl. Quite often they were deliberately meant to be heard by the audience. After all she was watching the past being enacted, it was her life. 'You missed your laugh there, dear.' 'I think you should get on with it now, dear.' 'That didn't sound too good, dear.' That sort of thing. Rather off-putting for a young actor who took himself and his acting very, very seriously indeed. I was becoming very unhappy and dreaded going on stage. My actress companion, who was quite full frontal in every way by now, didn't seem to notice. Then one night as I was about to rush on stage with my young Coral (we made our entrance together), she held me back, blocked my entrance, plucking my sleeve. With a sharp whisper of 'What are you doing, darling?' I managed to get on stage. Coral was ready and waiting. She belted out to the audience, 'He's missed his entrance again,' getting a huge laugh. Then there was no stopping her!

I managed to get through the scene and as soon as we were off stage I said to Erica, who seemed rather amused by what had happened, 'What were you doing? Why did you stop me from going on, on cue?'

'Oh, it was Coral,' she replied, giggling. 'She put me up to it. She wanted you to be late on.'

Loveable legendary character, or no, married to my agent or not, I 'who took my acting very, very seriously indeed', knocked on Coral's Number One dressing-room door in the interval. 'Come in.' I entered. She sat there in all her considerable sexual glory. High heels glinting, skirt gaping, stocking tops darkening and suspenders beckoning. 'Oh how lovely, dear,' she said, pulling on her cigarette. 'Sit down, have a gin.' She seemed to have no idea in the world that I had been upset, or indeed that I was upset. She was genuinely pleased to see me. After all, we had toured America together when I was nineteen and her lovely husband was my agent.

'Coral,' I said, not sitting, certainly not 'ginning', 'I understand you put Erica up to it – my late entrance, I mean.'

'Yes dear,' she said. 'It was fun, wasn't it? Got me the biggest laugh I've had in ages. We should keep it in.'

'Coral,' I replied, 'that was a terrible thing to do to me. It made me look a complete prat. I warn you, Coral, if you do anything like that again, in fact if you make any more side-mouthed comments on my performance, I shall walk off.'

Coral immediately broke down sobbing and said, quite obviously deeply hurt, 'You wouldn't talk like that to me if I was Dame Edith Evans.'

'Oh yes, I would,' I said. I meant it, but was actually rather charmed by this woman who had suddenly become a little girl.

Coral and I got on famously after that and she never made any more comments or tried any tricks. Years later we talked of the incident. I said I felt rather ashamed I'd made her cry.

'Perhaps you'll understand one day, dear,' she said, 'when you get a big starring role that you have to do night after night, month after month, and you are so bored you could scream.'

A very nice woman, Coral Browne, and really unique in her generation.

*

I've discovered that as I've got older I am literally unable to act in a production if I am unhappy or at least haven't unburdened my unhappiness in the hope it can be resolved. My first manifestation of this that I can remember was during the filming of Peter Nichols's *A Day in the Death of Joe Egg*. It was a small cast and quite a lot of it was shot in the studio. We had been shooting for several days at Boreham Wood. Alan Bates, Janet Suzman, Sheila Gish and me, directed by the utterly charming Hungarian Peter Medak.

Suddenly, during a scene in the middle of the afternoon, I stopped. I couldn't continue. My ability to act had simply gone. I stood there quite helpless.

'Whatever is the matter, darlink?' asked Peter Medak.

'I'm sorry, Peter. I'm sorry, everyone. Please forgive me. Peter, could I talk to you off set?'

Peter put his arm around me and took me aside. 'What is it, darlink?'

'Peter,' I said, 'I can't continue, because at six o'clock Alan, Janet, Sheila and you are going to have a studio car to take you home. I'm going to have to go to a bus stop. I feel an outsider and I know it's ridiculous but I somehow feel I'm second class and I can't continue.'

'Well, darlink,' said Peter, 'I quite understand. You had better speak to the producer.'

David Deutsch was a nice man with a huge voice. I went to his office and explained that I couldn't act unless I had a car like the other actors. He went ballistic, shouted that it was up to my agent to have contracted me a car, that I couldn't have a car, he couldn't afford it, and basically to get back on set. I said I quite understood his position and why he was shouting at me but if I went back onto the set I wouldn't be able to act because I still didn't have a car. There was a terrible silence. He looked at me very fiercely, then he began to laugh just as loudly as he'd been shouting. 'Okay, Peter, you will have a car. I will drive you home tonight and you will have a studio car every night from now on. Now get back on the fucking set. You're costing me money.'

A nice man, David Deutsch; a nice man, Peter Medak; and a very happy film to work on despite its rather harrowing story.

One 'being difficult' trait could have landed me in a lot of trouble. It was in an American film shot abroad. I was playing the foreign Chief of Detectives. My most important scene was in my Chief of Detectives office with the two American stars. I had shot several scenes in outside locations, when the director came up to me one night and said, 'Peter, I'm afraid the producers have decided that they want to save money by shooting your big office scene tomorrow in a corridor instead.'

'Then I won't be in it,' I said. 'I'll explain to the producers that I will reimburse them to reshoot the scenes on me with a new actor, and they can put *him* in the corridor.'

'My God, you're serious,' said the director.

'Yes,' I said, 'I am.'

'Well I'll take you to see the producers in their suite in the hotel,' he said.

I sat down with two men in dark suits I had never met before, and explained my proposition. The bottom line being that my part would be considerably diminished if shot in a corridor.

The producers were for a moment open mouthed. Then one said, 'If you care that much about the part and therefore the film, Mr Bowles, you've got your office.'

Phew! That bluff could have meant me selling my house, because I had meant what I said – I think.

*

When I starred with Sir John Gielgud, Joan Collins and Michael Aldridge in 'Neck', one of Roald Dahl's *Tales of the Unexpected*, Michael Aldridge had told me before filming began what he was being paid. He told me only because he imagined I was being paid the equivalent, and was very pleased for both of us. I made no particular comment.

One sunny day on location, the producer saw me sitting reading my script and said, 'Are you happy?'

'No,' I said, 'I'm not.'

'Oh dear,' said the producer. 'Why not?'

'Have you seen the rushes?' I said.

'Of course,' he replied. 'You are wonderful.'

'Am I as good as Michael Aldridge?' I enquired.

'Don't be silly,' he said, 'of course you are.'

'Then why are you paying me five hundred pounds and paying one thousand five hundred to Michael?'

I've never seen anyone so flabbergasted, angry, absolutely furious.

'How dare you speak to me like that?'

'Well,' I said, 'you asked me why I wasn't happy and I'm telling you, that's all. I'm just being honest.'

'My job as a producer is to get you as cheaply as possible,' he managed to splutter.

'Then please don't ask me if I'm happy.'

Impasse.

The producer disappeared. He returned after a while, sat next to me and said, 'Out of the goodness of my heart I have spoken to your agent and you are now being paid one thousand five hundred pounds.'

'Ask me if I'm happy,' I said, as pleasantly as possible.

CHAPTER 12

HOW ONE THING
LED TO ANOTHER

It was around 1970 that I was fortunate to land the role of Byron in a BBC television film about the life of Shelley and his relationship with Lord Byron. It was to be directed by the film director Alan Bridges. It was called *Shelley*. Robert Powell was to play Shelley and the very young and beautiful Jenny Agutter was to play Mary Shelley. Apart from the excitement of playing one of the sexiest, most heroic, handsome, dangerous English poets, the whole film was to be shot on location in the actual houses they had lived in and was to use, from letters and diaries, the words they had written. The only slightly odd thing was that it was in 'hippie' dress to give it a sort of timeless romantic look – hopefully.

The film almost never happened. The director had driven to the first location in Switzerland and his passenger was Jenny Agutter. On a motorway somewhere on the continent they suddenly saw a car wheel bowling along at great speed in front of them. When their car gave a sudden lurch they realized that the wheel was theirs and it was only through great skill and luck that Alan Bridges avoided a deadly accident.

The first thing I decided to do on getting the part was to read as much as I could about Byron and of course research his affliction, his lameness, his well-documented limp. I was brought up in Nottingham and had been to Newstead Abbey and had also seen the quite small house he had lived in as a small boy on Castle Hill in Nottingham. My first port of call was the Wellcome Institute in the Euston Road, London. That huge American-funded home of all medical papers and medical research. To my great excitement I found the actual notes made by the surgeon who had operated on Byron's leg when he was a little boy.

Now it was, and still is, believed and assumed that Byron had a club foot, and before I went to the Wellcome Institute I believed that too. I discovered, however, that this was not the case. He had an underdeveloped Achilles tendon and withered calf to one leg. This meant he had no power to rotate his foot in the normal way of walking. I took extensive copies of the surgeon's notes, with names, dates and other details. I then went to his publishers, Murray, who I knew had some relics of Byron including one of his boots – and what I understood from the surgeon's notes was confirmed.

The boot at Murray's, which would have covered his calf, had, in order to simulate the curve of the muscle, straw wadding; indication, of course, that Byron's own calf was indeed withered. Just as interesting, the sole of the boot was made of iron, giving it quite a weight. It was obvious that this extra weight allowed him to swing his leg forward into his steps rather than turn his ankle. Again I took notes. I had discovered something quite unknown, and I would show it in the way I walked.

I arrived on the evening before my first day's shooting in Venice. I had all my research papers with me and there, sitting at the bar was Alan Bridges. I approached him, glowing with excitement, and quickly began to give him news of my research, offering him my sheaf of notes. He was immediately annoyed. 'I don't want to see your notes,' he said. 'I come from a family of doctors and I know exactly what was wrong with Byron. True, he didn't have a club foot, but he had suffered some kind of cerebral palsy when young which had affected that part of his brain used in walking. No, I don't want to see your surgeon's notes. I know what was wrong with him and that's how I will expect you to play the part as far as his walking is concerned.' There then ensued what could have been a rather ugly debate but noticing the time and knowing I had to be up at 6.30 a.m. I bid Mr Bridges goodnight and slunk, mystified, towards the door. As I reached it Mr Bridges called out to me in a most charming voice, 'I absolutely realize that as you are playing Byron you must play him exactly as you wish. I'll just make sure that there won't be a single shot of you walking!'

I staggered off to bed. Of course, in the film there are lots of shots of me walking, Mr Bridges convinced I'm doing it his way, me knowing I'm doing it my way. It was never discussed or returned to again during the four weeks of shooting. One reviewer said of my performance, 'Peter Bowles devoured the part of Byron with the relish of a hungry man faced with a plate of roast beef.' No mention by any one at anytime of my way of walking.

I became very friendly with everyone in the cast. It was a very happy and exciting time. One actor who I particularly liked and admired was Simon Gough, son of the wonderful Michael Gough. Simon seemed to have had early childhood connections with Portofino. We were filming along the Italian coast at Lerici, and some of us had taken the day off to drive to Portofino. We were all sunning ourselves at a café overlooking the bay when Simon got up and made a phone call. He came back to say a friend had invited us to tea. This friend lived at the top of a small mountain or high rugged hill overlooking Portofino. Off we set. We arrived at a door set into a sheer rock face which ascended into the sky. Simon rang a bell, a voice answered, the door opened and we entered another world. The world of James Bond, or at least one of his locations. Before us, inside the mountain, stretched a well lit, beautifully decorated passageway, the sides of which had long glass fishtanks full of tropical fish. At the end of this long passageway was a lift. The lift took the four of us straight to the top of the mountain. As the lift doors opened at the end of its journey, and we stepped out, I was amazed at the sight I saw. There, a few feet away, was a huge, probably fifteen-foot high, Henry Moore bronze of Mother and Child. An enormous architectural wonder of a house, tennis courts, a swimming pool and luxurious tropical gardens. There was also a helicopter pad with a helicopter sitting on it. Our hosts, who I think may have been German Swiss, were enchanting. After tea we were offered costumes for a swim and invited to stay on for supper. We couldn't resist. As the evening came, our host gave us thick jumpers and insisted we kept them for our journey home.

Inside the beautifully furnished house the walls were adorned with many Impressionist, and post-Impressionist paintings, Picasso, Cézanne, Modigliani, Matisse among them. Everything, all the furniture and building materials, had been brought up the mountain by donkeys and mules. Our most gracious host seemed to be the head of a very famous luxury-car manufacturer. I think even Elton John would have been impressed by his eyrie.

Simon was quite heroic at the funeral pyre of Shelley's body, in Lerici. The BBC, at quite some expense, got a real human skeleton and dressed it up and filled it out to look like the drowned body of Shelley, which for some reason, I forget now, had to be cremated on the shore. A large bonfire was built and the 'body of Shelley' placed on the top of it. Petrol was poured around it. History relates that Trelawny, the part that Simon Gough played, snatched the heart from the burning body and smuggled it back to England where it is now buried in

Westminster Abbey. The 'heart' had been placed in the body. It was a pig's heart.

The various friends, including of course Byron, had been having a wake with large jugs of wine around the pyre. This part of the scene had been shot – now came the scene where the bonfire is lit and the shirt-clad Trelawny suddenly reaches in and snatches out the heart. It was something that couldn't be rehearsed. It had to be done in one take, otherwise the expensive skeleton would have to be replaced. A match was struck, and whoosh – too much petrol had been poured. The firewood was very dry and suddenly, in the fearsome heat and amidst the crackling flame, the 'corpse' began to sit up, the skull beginning to appear grinning. Simon leapt towards the fire and was beaten back by the heat. Immediately and with amazing instinct, Simon tore off his shirt, picked up a large jug of wine and poured it over his head and body, hands and arms, and dived into the flames. With a great shout he held aloft the heart of Shelley, his body glistening from the still leaping flames. Cut. Simon had done it. It was triumphant, and a scene I will never forget.

Simon Gough led me onto a really big adventure a few years later. I'll call it 'The Elizabeth Oakley Story' or as one Sunday newspaper called it 'The Great Art Hoax'.

*

Around 1972 I got a phone call from Simon. He knew of my great interest in paintings and he had something to show me. I went over to his house, where Simon explained he had bought from Bermondsey market, some little time before, a portfolio of early Victorian watercolours. He was short of money. Would I like to buy them? There were, I think, thirty paintings in the artist's original ribbon-tied portfolio, and they were quite beautiful and to my mind unique. First of all it was obvious they hadn't seen the light for nearly 150 years, as the colours were bright and sharp, and secondly they were, in my opinion, visionary paintings. They were all signed EO but the name on the portfolio read 'Elizabeth Oakley'.

I was very keen to buy them, but I too, like Simon, had no money. Simon said he had tried to sell them to dealers but had got nowhere. Simon mentioned a price which was very reasonable but quite beyond me. 'I have a friend,' I said. 'I'll be back. If he likes them perhaps we can strike a deal.' I went straight to the only person I knew who had any money; my dearest friend David Hemmings. He saw the paintings, trusted my judgement that they were very special and put up the money. Well, in the first flush of excitement we tried to get galleries to promote them, sell them. David was eager to make a turn on his money. No one was interested. David moved on with Hemdale, and more movies, the portfolio was shoved under my bed.

Years passed, then David, who had left Gayle, thrown out in fact, moved in with Sue and me and suddenly said, 'Have you still got those paintings we bought?' (I had paid him half by now.)

'Yes, I think so.'

'Well,' said David, 'I've got three weeks before I start rehearsing *Jeeves*.' (He was to play Bertie Wooster in the musical, lyrics by Alan Ayckbourn, music by Andrew Lloyd Webber.) David, rather like the character he played in *Blow-Up* hated to be bored. 'I've got a friend whose wife had a dress shop in Beauchamp Place. He says we can have it for a week. Why don't we mount an exhibition of the paintings ourselves?'

'Brilliant idea, David. I think they're under my bed,' I replied.

I knew David really well by this time. I recognized the light in his eyes and even if he couldn't remember the name of the artist he could see fun ahead. I went and got the dusty portfolio, and spread out the paintings.

'What's the plan, David?' I asked.

'Well,' said David, 'two weeks to get the paintings all framed, convert the shop into an art gallery for one week and send out the invitations.'

'I'll write a catalogue, David, if you can get it printed in time, and I know the man who owns Bourlet, the frame makers. I'll get a quick and cheap deal from him, if I can,' I said. 'Also, I think we should really go for this, because I believe Elizabeth Oakley is a unique undiscovered artist, and we should contact all the major art critics and say we have a sensational new discovery.'

'You're learning a bit,' said my tutor in enthusiasm. 'Let's do it.'

I decided the catalogue would also be the printed invitation with a reproduction of one of the extraordinary paintings on the front – and a 'write up' on the other side by me. The first painting was dated 1827 and the last 1848, so only just early Victorian. In fact in one of them the young Queen is painted in a scene. The thing that struck me so forcibly was how the characters or the figures were sometimes dressed. Some were strangely 1940s, and there were also elongated figures floating or flying in the sky above the scene on the ground. I had never seen this before except, of course, famously in Chagall, and the figures were very Chagall-like in their colour and romantic dreamlike quality. I wrote in the catalogue that this artist had somehow pre-empted Picasso and Chagall. What a storm that innocent remark was to cause!

The pictures were framed. David found a printer, got out his address book and sent off the catalogues. Students from the Royal College of Art came into the dress shop on the Saturday evening and worked all night and all Sunday in shifts, battening up the walls (which were mercifully white) and putting up lights. David and I hung and priced the paintings on Sunday evening and we opened at ten o'clock on Monday morning, 3 February 1975, at a dress shop that had been fortunately called Fauve.

We had bought crates of champagne and people began to arrive. It was a sensation. Red dots began to go up like measles. I rang the newspapers. 'Get your art critics over here as soon as possible. Art history is being made. A new Victorian artist discovered,' I enthused. Would anyone come? I didn't know, but two did, from opposite ends of the spectrum. The exhibition was a complete sell-out, and I remember the famous art dealer Andras Kalman coming and buying, also the director of the V & A, Roy Strong, and the art lover and financier Sir Mark Weinberg. Although exhausted, we were very happy, especially when we opened the Sunday *Observer* to discover a glowing review of the paintings by their distinguished art critic, Nigel Gosling.

David and his new partner, Prue, who had been his secretary and who he was later to marry, found a flat the following week and moved out of our house. Sue and I were invited to dinner at his flat in Chelsea with Andrew Lloyd Webber and his first wife. I'm afraid I proceeded to have a passionate row with Lloyd Webber about art – shades of my time with Rudolph Nureyev, who had ironically been befriended and housed by Nigel Gosling when Nureyev first came to London, but more of Nureyev later. The following Sunday, 23 February, the 'shit hit the fan'.

I was lying in bed listening to the Sunday morning eight o'clock news when it said the *People* newspaper claimed there had been a huge art hoax by the actors David Hemmings and Peter Bowles. I immediately rang David, who was already up trying to learn his lines for *Jeeves*. He had heard nothing. 'I'll buy a paper, David, and come over and see you,' I said.

It was worse, much worse, than I could have imagined. The front page, huge headline: 'The Great Art Hoax'. There was a picture of the famous film actor David Hemmings and a heavy article over several pages. It said that their reporter had bought a painting (it was shown) and taken it to Christie's, the V & A

Museum, the British Museum department of watercolours and, most damning of all, to Reeves, the watercolour paint manufacturers, and they had all testified they were fake. The very respected world expert on Victorian watercolours, Sir John Pope-Hennessy, was quoted as saying they were fakes, and he was the head of the British Museum.

David and I were in trouble; that is to say, we were being libelled. We knew they weren't fake paintings, what were we to do? Many well-known people had bought them, and although I felt certain they didn't read the *People*, this story was bound to feature in other papers and they may have heard it on the radio. I rushed round to see David and whilst I was discussing with him what to do, David's phone rang. It was my wife.

'Darling,' she said, 'I have just had two of the most frightening men I have ever talked to come round to our house looking for David. I didn't tell them where he was, of course, but they knew he'd been living with us.'

'What happened? Who are they? Were they violent? What frightened you?' I anxiously asked.

'No they weren't violent, but they had an aura about them that scared me to death.' I told David. He went pale.

'I don't know who that could be,' he said.

We decided to have an early drink. It wasn't long before the doorbell rang and a nervous Prue came into the room to say that— (she mentioned a name) had come to see David. David's face, at first just pale, turned a whiter shade of ghostly.

'Okay,' said David. 'Show him in.'

In came two men, obviously the ones who had called on my wife. I immediately saw why she'd been frightened. One man was about sixty, the other in his late thirties, both immaculately dressed and both had cockney accents.

The older man embraced and kissed David, the other one, without glancing in my direction, said, 'Who's the geezer, David?'

'Oh, that's a very good friend of mine,' said David.

'Is he a shstummer?' asked the older man, meaning, I suppose, can he keep his mouth shut.

'Yes,' said David, who was very nervous, 'definitely. Would you like a drink?'

'We'd like a cup of tea, if that's all right, David?' said the older man. 'We've had a hell of a job finding you, and I'd like to tell Mum I've found you, so could I please use your phone?' David indicated the phone and politely called out to Prue in the kitchen to make a pot of tea. The man dialled a number: 'Yeah, we found him – don't know yet – call you back.'

'Now who's done this, David?' the older man said, indicating the newspaper which I only just noticed he had in his hand.

'Well,' said David, 'it's all bollocks. It's not true and Peter and I –' he indicated me – 'can sort it out. Don't worry. And it's lovely to see you and I appreciate it enormously that you were concerned for me.'

The older man, who by this time had had a sip of tea, embraced David again. 'You sure you're all right, David? You've only to drop the word and we'll be here.'

'Yes,' said David, 'I'm sure, but thank you. Thank you for coming to see me.'

'Can I use the phone again please, David?' said the older man.

The younger man had stood the whole time and not drunk any tea, but had smiled at me a couple of times. 'Yeah, he says he's okay. He can handle it. Yeah, he looks great. See you later,' and the older man put down the phone.

After a final embrace, this time from both the men, they left. David was very relieved and shaking. He explained to me that when he was in his teens he had been involved with John Daly (the other half of Hemdale) looking after and later managing boxers at Toby's Gym in Bermondsey, and had got to know and had been greatly liked by various characters of the gangster fraternity. They were men who looked after their own.

'Make no mistake, Peter,' said David, 'if we knew what this was all about – that is, if there was someone behind it, and I gave them a name, that person would have had their legs broken at the very least.' I believed him. 'They are a lovely group of people and they have always been very protective of me, but I haven't seen the Colonel for years and thank God I have never needed their deluxe services.'

'We've been libelled, David, and at the very least we owe it to our purchasers to show Elizabeth Oakley is genuine,' I suggested.

'Peter,' said David, 'I am with you a hundred per cent but I've got to learn to sing, dance and deliver this massive starring role in *Jeeves* in a couple of weeks. Could you please handle it for me?'

'Okay,' I said. 'I will.'

I decided on a triple-pronged attack. One, to see one of the great solicitors in London, Oscar Beuselinck, who I'd met when he was a director of Woodfall Films. Two, to contact the *Observer*, who had given the exhibition such a good review. Three, to take a picture to the world's greatest art institute and laboratory, the Courtauld Institute, for investigation of the paint and paper used in the painting.

Oscar Beuselinck was marvellous. Before I went to see him I had discovered that the *People*'s picture had only been shown at the front desk of Christie's to a lowish 'expert', accompanied by my Picasso/Chagall catalogue. It had not been seen by anyone at the top. They were disturbed by the newspaper articles and were very willing to retract should I get scientific proof from the Courtauld Institute.

Roy Strong said he'd loved the paintings and had found out that the *People*'s painting again had only been shown to someone with no deep knowledge. He was sure they were genuine and in fact gave me a very interesting discourse on why they were painted and of the subject matter. The Reeves organization were also disturbed, and said they had not tested anything and would be very happy to withdraw if the Courtauld's testing proved the dates, 1827–1848. That left only Sir John Pope-Hennessy from the British Museum. He refused to talk to me on the phone. I took a picture in a taxi to the British Museum. He refused to see me. I wrote to him and received a reply, which rather than retract positively said that he laid his reputation on the fact that the paintings were bogus – fakes. Sir John Pope-Hennessy was a very important man and a very dangerous enemy.

'All right, cock,' said Oscar. 'I'll write out something and send it by bike to the *People* offices, saying we're going to sue for libel. You sit there and I'll guarantee I know what the answer will be.' While we waited Oscar made a phone call. Within the hour another bike, this time from the *People* newspaper arrived. 'See you in Court,' or words to that effect, were expressed. 'Told you,' said Oscar. 'Come on, old cock, we'll go and take counsel's advice.'

And off we went to the Inns of Court. We were ushered into a very large room lined with books. At one end was a desk from which rose a very distinguished QC. He had several young people with him. After introductions he asked if I minded if his pupils listened in to what was to occur. 'Of course not,' I said. Oscar had briefed the QC quite thoroughly on the phone and now we were able to give him an actual copy of the newspaper. He read it slowly and carefully. 'Sit down,' he said. 'I'm going to ask you some questions.' He was extremely gracious but had a very strong personality.

He began to ask me detailed and penetrating questions. When he had finished he said, 'Well, I think you have a very good case for libel. You've convinced me but whether you'll be able to convince a jury on a matter of art, not something they will know anything about, with Sir John Pope-Hennessy appearing for the *People* newspaper, is another matter. You will definitely need the Courtauld's proof at the very least.'

We went back to Oscar's office. 'Well, cock,' said Oscar, 'the thing is, do you want to lose your house? Because that's the money you'll need if you lose. The *People* won't lose even if you win because it will sell a lot of newspapers on the Film Star Scandal angle. It's up to you, old cock, but my advice is to go home, buy some fish and chips, and eat them out of this newspaper —' he brandished it — 'and then throw it in the nearest dustbin.'

It was, as it turned out, very wise advice indeed.

Anthony Blunt was, I think, in charge of the Courtauld at this time. I didn't meet him but I did meet Michael Kitson, and our case was taken up by this very respected figure in the art world. He took away a painting (we kept one) and said extensive chemical and conclusive tests would be made on the paper and paint, and indeed on the brush marks to indicate the type of bristle. Very thorough indeed. It would take about one month.

David and *Jeeves* opened in Bristol. I went to see it, ominous signs. David was beginning to take over directing.

Finally Mr Kitson telephoned me. The results were absolutely conclusive on all tests. The paintings were genuine.

Mr Kitson and I had got on very well at our first meeting. He knew and liked my work as an actor and had said so. I invited him to lunch and asked him if he could bring the various results of the tests and the Courtauld's conclusions with him. He said he would. We sat down to lunch and talked of this and that. After ordering, I asked him if he had brought the papers with him. 'Yes,' he said, 'they are in an envelope in my inside pocket,' and tapped his pocket.

'Could I have them, please?' I said, 'as I would love to read them.'

'Before I give them to you,' he said, 'what use do you intend to make of them? Do you intend to sue the paper? I mean, will you present them in court?'

'You bet your life I'll use them. Sir John Pope-Hennessy I am sure will appear for the newspaper, and he absolutely refuses to retract.'

Mr Kitson became very shifty. 'Then I'm afraid I can't give the papers over to you. My name is on them. I have recently applied for Sir John's job, which is to become vacant, and if my name is used against him in court I won't get the job. He's very powerful.'

I was flabbergasted. Mr Kitson was making it quite clear that personal ambition was more important than the reputation of an artist, let alone the reputation of a couple of actors. Yes, Oscar Beuselinck was right: I metaphorically bought the fish and chips and threw the newspaper into the dustbin. *Jeeves* was a disaster. Poor David.

The *Observer* newspaper, who possibly felt angered that their art critic had been made a fool of, came to our rescue. They decided to send over their top investigative reporter, John Clare who is now a very distinguished educational journalist, to get to the bottom of this whole matter. Who was Elizabeth Oakley? How had the paintings emerged? Was there someone behind the smear? Before John Clare came over to see me I had discovered from Simon Gough that he had bought them in Bermondsey market from someone known as Silk Shawl. Sue and I, and our three quite young children, all crushed into my old 356C convertible Porsche and drove at six o'clock in the morning to Bermondsey to see if we could locate Silk Shawl.

We were apprehended on the way, which made an exciting start. I don't know what the police thought we were up to but I managed to prove I wasn't abducting anyone. Yes, everyone at the market knew Silk Shawl but not his real name. It was still dark at that early hour and prospective buyers and dealers were going around with torches examining objects. A very mysterious atmosphere pertained in the gloomy dust, and no one liked my enquiries. I'm not sure but I think there is a legend (which might be true) that under some ancient Act of Parliament even stolen goods can be sold at this market before 8 a.m., without prosecution. We didn't find Silk Shawl but discovered he often had a stall there, and we all enjoyed a terrific fry-up breakfast at a local café.

John Clare was as formidable as the QC had been. Many, many questions. 'I'll come back to you when I've made some enquiries,' he said before he left. He rang a few days later. 'I've discovered quite a lot,' he said. 'We've got to go to a small town in Sussex. Bring your painting.'

We arrived at a small antique shop and spoke to the owner. Yes, he'd seen paintings like that before. He'd bought and sold some and he knew where they came from, and he gave us an address.

The tiny cottage was in a small Sussex village and it was very empty. There had been a very old lady living there and she had died, then someone came and cleared the house out, neighbours told me. Well, I won't go into details about this except to say that it transpired a fifteenth-century carved coffer had been taken from the house and it had ended up in Bermondsey market. It was sold immediately but was first emptied of its contents; a portfolio of paintings all signed EO. The portfolio had the full name of Elizabeth Oakley on it and an address in Wales. The address in Wales turned out to be rather a grand house.

David was interviewed on Michael Parkinson's show about the scandal and we were approached by descendants of Elizabeth Oakley. They lent us Elizabeth's journals. She had not only written down when she had bought paint and brushes, but had given the days and the number of days she deliberately fasted. What a revelation. Elizabeth fasted. There is no doubt in my mind that some of the 'visionary' paintings were indeed visions, brought on by her fasts.

The *Observer* gave us the front-page headline: 'Oakley is a great artist – official' There was a whole-page account by John

Clare, and to top it all off they gave Elizabeth and many of her paintings the main coverage in the *Observer* colour magazine.

John Clare was to come into my life again a few years later, in the strange case of the Controller of the Supreme Council of Great Britain – but that's another (and weird) story.

CHAPTER 13

LIFE'S NOT ALL ACTING

I shall be seventy-three next week and have been married to Sue for forty-eight years. I have three children. One, Guy, I have mentioned. My second son is Adam, who was born fourteen months later in a hospital that refused fathers to be present at the birth. The consequence of this was that for about two years Sue felt I didn't love Adam as much as Guy. She knew it was wrong and didn't make sense, but psychologically that's how it felt. My daughter, Sasha, was born two years later at home in our marital bed – wonderful. I am very lucky and don't I know it. I could write chapters on the happiness that my wife and three children give me. But I'm not going to. What follows are various tales and incidents from my unprofessional life.

*

Sue and I were in a restaurant in Chiswick many years ago, and sitting at a table near ours was Tommy Cooper with a group of friends. I had had drinks occasionally with Tommy, as he lived not far from me in Hammersmith, so we spoke briefly. Then into the restaurant came Bruce Forsyth with a small entourage. The two great showmen spotted each other immediately but made no contact. Not many minutes passed before Tommy Cooper began to tell jokes to his friends in a voice loud enough to be heard by other diners, producing roars of laughter. Bruce Forsyth then began to tell jokes in a raised voice too, again roars of laughter from adjoining tables. These two great comics still gave no acknowledgement to each other but were professional enough (and also so they could be heard, I suppose) to always wait until the other had finished his little routine and the laughter had begun to subside.

The restaurant began to be filled with electric anticipation as the competition mounted, and mount it did, because it wasn't too long before Bruce Forsyth and Tommy Cooper were standing on their chairs and addressing all the assembled diners like an audience. I remember Tommy took off his jacket, and although he didn't have his fez he did have a lovely pair of braces. It was an extraordinary experience and both comics hugged each other after what must have been at least an hour of gladiatorial battle.

*

I was in a Royal line-up once with my wife standing beside me. Princess Margaret was coming down the line and was being introduced, in between chatting to her hosts, who walked with her. I was at the height of my fame at this time and I saw her spot me several paces away. As she drew opposite me, she had a cigarette holder primed with a cigarette in her hand.

'Would you give me a light?' she said to me and then turned away to say something to her companions. I searched in my dinner jacket pockets and found an old book of matches. Princess Margaret turned back to me, the cigarette holder now firmly in her mouth and her head cocked forward in anticipation of a light. I struck the match, her head jerked back. 'Oh no. Sulphur, I can't stand sulphur. Haven't you got a lighter?' This was said in a quite loud and very imperious voice.

Before I had time to make my reply a figure stepped into the small space between Princess Margaret and myself. It was my wife. 'How dare you speak to my husband like that? I think you are very rude.'

Princess Margaret was shocked. I was shocked. Princess Margaret handled it pretty well, her demeanour changed completely to that of one woman speaking to another. 'I didn't mean to be rude,' she said quietly to my wife. 'I'm sorry to have upset you but I really do have a problem with sulphur.' And on she swept.

Two years later I was at a large private party at which Princess Margaret was also a guest. My wife was not with me. Princess Margaret again spotted me and immediately came over. 'Good evening, Mr Bowles,' she said. 'You will be my bag man for the evening.' Her eyes were twinkling as she handed me a bejewelled lady's clutch bag. 'In there,' she said, 'are my cigarettes and a lighter. When I require a cigarette I shall ask you to give me one and then light it for me with my lighter.'

Upon that she spun on her heel and walked away. I, of course, felt more than obliged, commanded in fact, to follow her, clutching the clutch bag.

She didn't humiliate me for too long, however. After a few minutes she turned to me and asked for a cigarette, and I lit it with her lighter. 'Thank you,' she said and then held out her hands indicating she would like the return of the bag and its contents. I placed it in her free open hand. 'Quits now, I think, Mr Bowles,' she said with a charming smile and disappeared into the crowd.

*

I sometimes worry that the dramas people view, especially in America, can sometimes affect their natural instinctive behaviour. People copy the often not very well acted, overblown, sentimental or hysterical reactions made by actors in substandard soaps or films. They overreact or dramatize ordinary things in real life. I had an example of this on a Pan-Am plane flying to New York one winter.

My wife and I had booked business class and had heavy coats with us and wanted to put them in the wardrobe for the long journey. There was a little queue of people with the same idea. When we reached the stewardess who was hanging the coats, she said, on viewing our large heavy coats, 'You're giving me problems. I've got problems and you're giving me two more. I can't take any more problems.' This was said in a slightly hysterical tone with both arms raised in the air. If Mr Winner had been doing his adverts then I might have said, 'Calm down, dear.' As it was, I said for her not to be upset, as we would sit in the front row of the ordinary class, where we could see there was stacks of room and we could lay our coats across seats. 'You'll have to be refunded, fill in forms, that's more problems for me,' said the stewardess. I assured her that we would be perfectly happy without a refund and went and sat down.

Our seats were near the galley where the stewardesses made coffee, etc. Some time into the night, with the light glowing in the galley and our reading lights on, I caught 'our' stewardess's eyes as she was making some coffee. She smiled at me. I smiled back and then said, 'Oh good, you must be relaxing now. That's the first time I've seen you smile.' A bit personal, I suppose, but I stupidly meant well.

The reaction was enormous, I was dragged immediately into a soap opera. The stewardess strode over, her teeth clenched, and stood before me. I had no seats in front of me, so she was able to hitch up her already shortish skirt and bestraddle me. One of her legs on either side of mine. She put a finger into my face and said, 'What did you say to me back there?' pointing to the galley. 'What did you say to me just now?' She was serious. She was deadly.

'I'm sorry,' I said. 'I've obviously offended you. I didn't mean to, and I'm sorry.'

'What did you say to me?' she enquired, her voice was becoming threatening.

I replied that I had meant it in the nicest way, that I was just pleased that I had seen her smile for the first time. Her finger jabbed again, I could almost feel her hot breath.

'Listen,' she said. I was listening. 'I'll tell you what happened back there.' She again indicated the softly lit galley. 'I looked at you, you looked at me and there was a warm moment between us. You just killed it, okay?'

With that she pulled down her skirt and strode off.

I hoped the pilot was happier in his job than the stewardess, who I learnt later was the chief stewardess.

Too many bad TV programmes watched in empty hotel rooms between flights. My wife, by the way, said nothing on this occasion; perhaps she thought this woman might be armed!

*

In the early years of our marriage, when we could afford to have a live-in au pair but certainly couldn't afford to dine out, we used to go to the Connaught Hotel. I've always liked to give my wife the very best and we have always liked to 'strut our stuff' even when we had little to strut. Every other week or so Sue and I would get bathed and changed, and go by tube to the Connaught, walk into the bar and have one drink, which we would nurse with olives and nuts, and then come home by tube. When the children were teenagers and I was better off and we wanted some time to ourselves we would go to different London hotels for the weekend. On this occasion we went to an hotel we had never been to before, the Berkley, and we didn't go by tube but in that new Rolls-Royce I had just bought. We drew up at the entrance and a spectacularly dressed and top-hatted doorman opened the car doors.

As he took the keys from me to park the car, and I started to take out our weekend bags, the doorman said, 'Oi, Pete, you're not kipping here, are you?' I indicated I was. 'I am surprised Pete.' I had, of course, never met him in my life before but was used to this friendly approach. 'All the big stars stay at the Intercontinental. I used to work there so I know. Oh, by the way, is this the missus?' I assured him she was, and not an extremely glamorous mistress. He looked slightly disappointed. 'Pleased to meet you,' he said to Sue, doffing his hat. I was by now standing with my two small bags waiting to go in. The doorman was reluctant to let me. 'Have you stayed here before, Pete?' he enquired. I said no, I was a 'first-time caller'. 'Well, Pete, I'll tell you something,' he said. 'This place is really a very expensive block of council flats.' (It had recently re-opened after refurbishment.) 'And I'll tell you something else, Pete. You see that place over there?' He pointed to a large house nearby. 'That's the vicarage. We have lots of Bar Mitzvahs here, and the old vicar knows when one is on, because come midnight, he'll come over to me and say, "Oi, pack it in, it's gone midnight and you're making too much noise." Anyway, have a nice weekend, Pete. I'll put the Roller away but next time try the Intercontinental.'

We went in at last. It was like walking into a very grand jeweller's. There were separate leather-covered tables in the foyer. The sort of table on which they lay out an expensive piece of jewellery or watch. The staff around these several tables wore striped trousers and dark tail coats. This was where you signed in. Very grand. We signed in, and the bags were whisked away. One of the tail-coated men took us up to our deluxe room. There were two single beds in it.

'I'm sorry,' I said, 'but we must have a large double bed. That's what I expected.'

'That's no problem at all, Mr Bowles. I'll send the maid in immediately to make it into a double.'

The bags had not yet arrived, but the maid did. She was middle-aged, probably middle European, and not at all happy. 'Why you want beds made up now? Can't you wait till tomorrow? I go off duty soon and I have only just made up these single beds, now you want me to do it again.'

I didn't answer, but indicated to Sue we should leave the room immediately. As we walked down the corridor looking for the lift, the porter with our bags strode towards us. I shook my head, and before I could speak, he leant against the wallpapered wall of the corridor and disappeared through a concealed door. It was becoming truly surreal. When we arrived in the foyer our faces must have indicated displeasure as we were immediately surrounded by a group of stripe-trousered, tail-coated men. I explained the problem with the maid. Their reaction was unsurprised and not very concerned.

'I'm sorry, Mr Bowles, but you can't get the staff these days. We'll move you to another floor, as presumably you won't want to see that maid first thing tomorrow morning.'

Some of the staff then asked me for my autograph – saying they weren't supposed to but in my case couldn't resist. I was flattered but couldn't help thinking the doorman was right and real stars stayed at the Intercontinental. This was years ago, of course, and I'm sure the Berkley Hotel, which is one of London's great hotels, is quite different now.

*

Sue and I were about to enter a very small lift in a house in Carlton House Terrace. We had been invited to a party and had been told by one of the uniformed policemen nearby that the lift would take us straight to the party. As we were about to work out the mechanics of the tiny lift, which held a maximum of four, two more people got in, a man and a woman.

'Oh I'm so sorry,' said the woman and she stepped out again. The man backed out too. 'Oh no, this is silly,' said the woman, 'we are obviously going to the same party. Let's go together.'

Her companion shut the gate. We stood almost nose to nose.

'Perhaps we should introduce ourselves,' said the woman. 'My name is Margaret Thatcher.'

Mrs Thatcher at this time was very much the Prime Minister in her second term of office.

'And this is—' She introduced the man, who was obviously a bodyguard.

I introduced Sue and myself.

'Oh I know who you are,' she said.

Mrs Thatcher and my wife then had quite a long conversation about coats as my wife was wearing one and Mrs Thatcher wasn't. 'I only ever travel in cars, my dear,' she said, before saying, as we had been standing there some time, 'Well, I suppose someone had better press the button.'

Coming from the lips of the Prime Minister it had a peculiar nuclear ring to it in my mind. We shuffled around, pressed a button and ascended, then Sue and I shuffled around again in order to let Mrs Thatcher and companion alight first.

The party was very jolly and in full swing when our hostess started to introduce her most distinguished guest to her other guests. 'Oh Prime Minister, can I introduce you to the actor Peter Bowles and his wife, Sue.'

A couple of drinks in, the witty, quick as a flash, Peter Bowles said, 'Oh we've met before. We were rather intimate in a lift.'

'I beg your pardon?' said Mrs Thatcher in a very loud voice indeed.

The world reeled, the party ceased, you could hear ice tinkling as it melted in glasses. I have never felt so stupid in my life. I didn't know what to say. It was a true 'I wish the floor would open up and swallow me' situation. The party waited; the hostess had aged considerably.

Mrs Thatcher suddenly smiled a warm, truly amused smile, touched me gently and said, 'I think you meant to say we were rather close in a lift, don't you?'

I gulped, 'Yes, Prime Minister,' and Mrs Thatcher swept on.

I decided to leave before more drink and trouble, when a voice bellowed from across the room, 'What's it like working for a bunch of Reds?'

It was Denis Thatcher, who must have come later. I was unable to reply to his odd demanding question. Seeing the puzzlement on my face he continued to bellow, 'You work for the BBC, don't you? What's it like working for a bunch of Reds?' The party was really enjoying this. I again was unable to reply. 'Oh don't worry about me,' he yelled, 'everyone here knows I am right of Genghis Khan.'

I hope I was able to thank our hostess for a lovely party, but I do remember leaving very quickly after these exchanges.

*

A brush with history came my way about thirty years ago when I was on holiday at a wonderful resort in the British Virgin Islands. There were lush and beautifully tended grounds surrounding a beautiful half-moon bay. A sort of paradise. One day as I strolled through paradise I noticed a late-middle-aged man sitting on a rock on his own. He had a short grey crew cut so was obviously American, but what drew my attention to him was that he was weeping. It was a soft weeping, which was so distressing I felt compelled to enquire what was troubling him, perhaps I could help or comfort him. I couldn't help or comfort him, or perhaps I did in a small way by listening to what he had to say to me.

He apologized most politely for disturbing me, and then through his drying tears told me his story. It was short and to the point. He had bouts of depression, he told me, and had been haunted and troubled for many years. The reason being that he had been a member of the aircrew on the bomber that had dropped the atomic bomb on Hiroshima.

There was nothing I could say to this, but I did hold his very masculine hand for a good few minutes. I thanked him for sharing his most intimate story with a stranger and walked away.

Of course this chance encounter had quite an effect on me.

*

I was sitting on a bench on the promenade at Eastbourne eating some fish and chips, when I saw coming along from my right what appeared to be an elderly married couple. The wife was holding the arm of her husband who was obviously blind as he was tapping a white stick ahead of him and wore very dark glasses. They passed in front of me in silence but two or three paces past me I heard the woman say to her husband, 'You'll never believe this but we've just passed Peter Bowles sitting on a bench.'

'You don't need to tell me,' replied her husband in a slightly peeved tone. 'I would recognize Peter Bowles anywhere.'

*

I was desperately out of work, very overdrawn, depressed and on Social Security – not unusual for an actor – but dispiriting all the same. The phone rang. It was David, my dear friend David, who at the time was riding very high both in film fame and his company Hemdale.

'Would you and Sue like to come with Gayle and me to see a gala performance of *Swan Lake* at Covent Garden tonight? Oh, the dancers are Margot Fonteyn and Rudolph Nureyev.'

'I don't know, David,' I said, and indicated I didn't think I could afford it.

'Don't be silly,' said David. 'I've got four tickets in the stalls and you'll be my guests. Oh and it's a black-tie job.'

'Thank you, David, we'd love to come.' Anything for a diversion, I thought, and Fonteyn and Nureyev were such massive world stars, especially Nureyev, at that time. 'But I have to warn you, David, that although Sue, I'm sure, loves ballet, I've never seen one.'

'That's okay,' said David, 'neither have I. See you outside at seven-thirty.'

Well it was amazing, of course, but I was terribly intimidated by the atmosphere. I'd never been to Covent Garden before, never experienced the audience of a ballet, especially a gala ballet, and I was in the stalls and everyone seemed so very rich and I felt so very poor and desolate. In the bar at the interval, I suddenly found myself saying, and it was a shock to me, but not to David, 'David, I'm so sorry to ask this, but could you possibly lend me two hundred and fifty pounds?'

I had never before or, thank God, since, asked anyone except a bank manager for a loan.

'Of course, Peter,' said David. 'Better still, I need help on a film script I'm writing called *The Last National Servicemen*. If you could give me a hand tomorrow night I'll pay you two hundred and fifty pounds and I'll be bloody grateful as I've got to deliver the script the day after tomorrow.'

Dear generous David. He'd let me off the hook of feeling embarrassed asking for a handout, and I did help him on his script.

The curtain fell and the audience went mad. I too thought it was wonderful. The delicate moving pathos of Fonteyn, the electrifying vigour, the astonishing leaps of the creature called Nureyev. But the audience clapped for almost half an hour. I'd never witnessed anything like it before. I felt strangely disturbed and I suppose jealous that this profession of ballet could command for its great stars a mountain of flowers, and I mean hundreds of bouquets, and dozens of curtain calls, whilst the stars of my profession, Olivier, Gielgud, Richardson, would

receive nothing remotely like that even after a truly great performance. Yes, I felt poor and desperate and I was a little
sickened. It didn't bode well for what was about to unexpectedly happen.

'Come on,' said David.

'Yes, come on, Sue,' said Gayle, 'we're going round to see Rudi.'

And we were ushered through the seething crowds, past the
stage door to Nureyev's dressing room.

There was possibly the greatest, most famous male star in the
world, in one of the grottiest dressing rooms I'd ever been in. It
was quite a large room but there was only a smallish oblong of
carpet over the linoleum. Serried rows of water pipes lined the
walls and were be-strung with well-used jock straps, dating
back to when the theatre was built it seemed. Perhaps it was a
tradition for any incumbent star to leave his marker, by way of
his jock strap on the pipes! There seemed to be only one chair
(this surely can't have been so!) and Nureyev leapt from it as
soon as we entered. He had been putting heavy grease on his
face to remove the make-up and immediately wiped his hands
and embraced David and Gayle. Grinning broadly, he then
shook hands with Sue and me. He easily and politely tossed
aside our congratulations and said, 'You will now come to my
house for supper.' And with that he pulled leg warmers over his
tights, then corduroy trousers and a jumper over his bare chest,
and headed for the door. 'Have you got your car, David?' he
asked. David did have his car, which was at that time his own
chauffeur-driven Rolls-Royce Phantom. 'Sue,' he said to my
wife as we clattered down the stairs, 'you will come with me.'

There must have been two hundred people at the stage door.
Nureyev was polite but firm. 'No, no, I never, never ever sign
autographs,' he said and took Sue's arm. I later discovered that
he had a convertible Triumph Vitesse round the corner. Sue
had a lovely, jolly exciting drive.

Nureyev's house was abutting Richmond Park. It had the

most enormous furniture in it. It was, it seemed to me, like a set from *Ivan the Terrible*, but there was a warm welcome from his housekeeper and lots of lovely food on a table in the drawing room, in front of a roasting fire. Everything went well during the meal. Much much laughter. Wonderful, crazy stories from Nureyev and impossible fantasies from David, plus splendid conjuring tricks, for David was a member of the Magic Circle and a very accomplished magician.

We were sitting cross-legged in front of the fire when trouble began. I had been rather quiet during the dinner. Outclassed, out-starred, although obviously very welcome. I decided to amuse Nureyev with my story of Mark Burns and the frog, and attempted to get on to the bit about his arrest and the Turkish cavalry. I only got as far as the frog.

'You English are so sentimental about animals,' said Nureyev. 'What is the point of this story, if it's about someone throwing stones at a frog? Who cares? Only an Englishman.'

It was said in a light-hearted, bantering way, but I didn't respond well. As an actor, I had lost my audience. He wouldn't let me finish my story, and if he didn't care about the frog the story had lost its point.

I exploded in defence of the English and cruelty to animals, especially frogs. It was awful. Very boorish of me, very rude; a disaster. I'm still ashamed of it because this great man, this gracious host who was simply bursting with physical energy, could obviously see something was wrong with me, he knew something was bothering me other than frogs, and he showed concern. He got up and asked Sue if she'd like to see more of the house. I learnt later that Sue had told him of my asking for money during the interval and my long period out of work. He had said he completely understood my outburst now.

When they arrived back in the room, Nureyev suddenly said, as if to change the subject and certainly to change the atmosphere, 'I hear Sean Connery is in London.' He called to his housekeeper. 'Darling,' he said, 'I would like to meet Sean Connery. Find out where he is staying, and tell him that Rudolph Nureyev would like him to come over now, tonight, for a drink.' Sean Connery at this time had done two or three *Bond* films and was the only other Massive World Star. It was 1.30 in the morning and about thirty minutes later, as Sue and I were about to be driven home by David's chauffeur, the doorbell rang and there was Sean, and I don't think he and Nureyev had ever met before.

It was my first glimpse into the stratospheric and heady world of 'the beautiful people'.

*

I'll end this chapter with an insight on how English and possibly stupid I am.

I was sitting in a pub having just ordered a pint of beer and a ham sandwich. The beer had arrived but the sandwich was still being made. Suddenly in front of me stood a familiar figure in T-shirt and jeans.

'I'm so sorry to disturb you, Mr Bowles,' said the familiar figure, 'but I am a huge fan of yours. Oh my name is Quentin Tarantino, by the way. I was sitting in the restaurant across the road with my girl when I saw you come in here, and I wondered if you would care to join us for a spot of lunch.'

The possibly stupid Englishman thanked him most kindly for his obvious compliment, and then found himself saying, 'Thank you so much for your invitation but I'm afraid I've just ordered a sandwich.'

With an 'Okay fine. Rain check. Love your work,' he was gone.

I could have been a killer in movies but somehow I didn't want to disappoint the waiter.

CHAPTER 14

THE FIRST CHANGE OF LIFE

It was 1975, and for most of the 1960s and part of the 1970s I had been doing television. In fact I had not done any theatre since a Sean O'Casey play at the Mermaid Theatre in 1964. (Incidentally the dressing rooms often flooded and we had to put our socks and footwear on at the side of the stage!) I was quite desperate to get back onto the stage.

As I have mentioned before, my attempts to get into the National had failed. I had even written a personal, heartfelt letter to Laurence Olivier personally, begging him to take me on in any capacity whatsoever. I received a printed card saying, 'We thank you for your letter. If you are in a play within travelling distance from London let us know.'

I decided for the first time in my life I would ask God for help. I am not religious or a church-goer, but I got married in church and believe there is something controlling us. When I am in a church, usually for architectural reasons, I always say a 'thank you' prayer for the many, many good things in my life. However, this is 1975. I have done TV for eleven years and feel I must get back into the theatre somehow. There was and still is a snobbery in the acting world – if you are successful on TV, especially pulp TV or sitcom TV or soap TV, you almost certainly can't act on stage, so 'they' don't employ you. Let alone Lindsay Anderson's 'he can't act, I've seen him wear a suit' political prejudice. I went into a modernist church of no architectural merit whatever with the express purpose for once in my life of asking God's assistance. 'Please help me. I am going mad.' I was becoming severely depressed at this time due, I know, to frustration. I wanted to act on stage.

The very next morning I was contacted by my agent, who told me I had been offered not one but two new plays and a new TV sitcom series. One play was by a good writer called Don Taylor – a rather strange thriller. The other play was by Alan Ayckbourn, then (and now) at the very zenith of his fame. It was called *Absent Friends* and was the beginning of Mr Ayckbourn's darker plays. The television series was called *The Good Life*.

Well, God had certainly answered my prayer. The scripts of the plays arrived along with two scripts of *The Good Life*. I read everything closely. The Don Taylor play was good, and my part, which was eventually played by Brian Blessed, was tempting. The Ayckbourn play was terrific. A small cast, and my part was very good indeed. That was the play I wanted to do. Hurrah. The TV series was also good. Ordinarily I would have done it like a shot, although in my heart of hearts I felt the part of Jerry, slightly wimpish and very put-upon, was something I had done too often before. I turned down the TV and decided to do *Absent Friends*.

I quickly discovered, which was another bonus, that in *Absent Friends* I would be starring alongside my old RADA friend Richard Briers, and I had been recommended by the great impresario Michael Codron on the strength of a TV I had just done on the philosopher Wittgenstein. TV at last had paid stage dividends, as it was to again many, many years later, in another life-changing way, with Sir Peter Hall.

When I arrived for the first rehearsal and read-through, after the usual hugs and kisses Richard Briers said to me, 'Why aren't you doing *The Good Life?*'

'How do you know about that?' I asked.

'Well, I'm doing it,' said Richard.

'How can you be?' I asked, genuinely puzzled. 'This play and the series clashes.'

The very experienced actor of sitcoms looked back at me equally puzzled. 'They don't clash, Peter. They record sitcoms on Sundays. I've often done a play and a sitcom at the same time.'

No one had told me. Stupid!

'Would you like to do it?' said Richard.

'Yes,' I said, knowing I could really do with the money.

Richard very sweetly excused himself and went straight to a phone. 'Sorry,' he said when he came back, 'it has just been cast with my other old friend, Paul Eddington.'

Never mind, I thought. On with the play.

Eric Thompson, father of Emma (whom I met then, aged about twelve), was director, and the wonderful Ray Brooks was in it also. He amazed me by going off in the lunch break to do several voice-overs. He was the king of voice-overs at this time. I'd only done one VO in my life before and I knew they paid good money. The one I had done, a few years earlier, was for the Milk Marketing Board. I had to say, 'Milk. ARE YOU GETTING ENOUGH?' Slightly suggestive, but very popular and I received £3000 in repeats, which at that time was equivalent to a year's salary. The Milk Board asked me to do it again the following year.

'Be at the recording studio tomorrow at four o'clock,' said my agent.

'But I'm doing a TV,' I said.

'Ask the director to let you off. You're getting one hundred and seventy-five pounds for the TV' (an *Armchair Theatre* directed by Philip Saville) 'and this VO pays three thousand, and I may be able to get you more.'

I had received my agent's call in the TV rehearsal lunch break, I went straight to the director. Perhaps I didn't put my position strongly enough. I certainly didn't mention money – that would have been pathetic. After all, the class of work is the thing and the *Armchair Theatre* was classy TV.

'Four o'clock tomorrow, Peter? No, I am very sorry, but I'm sure I will have got to your scenes by then.'

He didn't. Sad, isn't it? I know this all sounds very mercenary but the reason I've gone on about it is that *Absent Friends* ran for twelve months. I don't know how many VOs Ray did in that time (he told me he averaged about five a day!) but Richard did two series of *The Good Life* plus one repeat. There was hardly a night went by, it seemed, when there wasn't a knock on my dressing-room door and Richard would shout, 'I've had another cheque for *The Good Life*.' I'm only joking, Richard, honest.

It was towards the end of *Absent Friends* that my front-door letter box rattled. A script had been hand delivered, I'm almost certain by the playwright himself, Tom Stoppard. It was called *Dirty Linen*, one of the funniest plays I had ever read, about the sexual shenanigans of politicians. A theme, of course, that will never ever date. There was a handwritten note from Mr Stoppard (now Sir Tom Stoppard) asking if I would play the part of Withenshaw, the north country Labour MP and chairman of the cross-party committee that was the action of the play. North country? I almost always played posh parts or foreigners, could Mr Stoppard have made a mistake? Tom Stoppard had left his phone number for me to call and give my answer.

'Are you sure you want me to play this bluff brash north country MP?' I asked Mr Stoppard.

'Peter, you can play any part you like but I think you would be wonderful as Withenshaw,' said Tom.

That was enough for me, he had faith.

It was to be produced at a lunchtime theatre called the Almost Free and was to be directed by the polymath American Ed Berman. I could play it at lunchtime and be on in *Absent Friends* in the evening. It was a socking hit. After *Absent Friends* closed *Dirty Linen* transferred to the Arts Theatre where the play ran for seven years. I played the first six months and I don't think I have ever had a happier time in the theatre. I got to know Stoppard well because he often attended rehearsals. The cast were so good, so friendly and we were all thrilled to be in such a big hit. Everybody came. Dame Margot Fonteyn came twice to the matinees with friends and each time took the cast out to tea. I remember seeing Robert Wagner and Natalie Wood queuing for tickets, and also seeing John Cleese, who had been sitting in an end of row seat, actually – yes, really truly – rolling in the aisle. He fell out of his seat onto the floor utterly helpless with laughter. The women's rights movement threw flour bombs at us on the first night as they thought it sexist. The delightful, sexy, Luan Peters, who played the secretary that everyone had slept with, spent most of the play in her underwear, and I remember she got cold as winter drew on and made her entrance one night incongruously carrying a paraffin heater, which she placed by her near-naked body. I think the management turned the heating up after that.

I shared a dressing room with Richard Goolden of 'Mole' fame. He was in his late eighties and brought in a programme of a play called *The Whip* that had been produced at the Coliseum before the 1914–18 war. The play was about the Derby and he had seen it with six horses at full gallop on moveable rollers on the stage. The huge crowd watching the Derby were Covent Garden porters brought in for this one scene – about a hundred he said – and paid two shillings to cheer and shout. The audience would cheer and shout too, as the rollers were manipulated so one horse would lead, and then another. The whole thing was stopped, never to be done again, when one of the 'rollers' jammed and the jockey was thrown off into the orchestra pit, and died impaled on the neck of the double bass.

Richard Goolden also told me of seeing a play, again at the Coliseum, where naked women stood around a huge pool in a harem and two elephants made their entrance down chutes into the water. The front two rows of the stalls were issued with sou'westers! He brought in an illustrated programme, and indeed the ladies around the pool were naked. So nothing is new.

Another member of the cast was Frederick Treves, whose grandfather (or great-grandfather) had been Sir Frederick Treves, who had treated and looked after the Elephant Man. I had never heard about the Elephant Man before (nor had anyone else, it seemed, in 1976 London). I thought the story would make a marvellous film. Freddie brought in Sir Frederick's papers and various newspaper articles and posters of the time. I wrote an outline and tried to interest film producers. No luck, absolutely not a chance. 'What a gruesome goulish tale – box office death' was the response I got. Well, we all know the great success of *The Elephant Man* film with John Hurt many years later. That's show business.

Which reminds me, when I was at the height of my popularity I was asked by Equity to address the Royal Television Society on the subject of cable television. Equity was against it or apprehensive about it for a number of reasons. I have never made a public speech before and I would be addressing my powerful peers. I was up all night writing my speech. It was printed in the *Guardian* and quoted in parliament – yes, I'm in Hansard – and, as we now know, it had no effect whatsoever. But the real point of this story is that after the speeches there was a dinner and I sat next to Michael Peacock, the man who had launched BBC2 and was now in a powerful producer partnership with John Cleese.

He said to me, 'I'd give my right arm for a TV series that I could sell to the networks in America. That's where the real money is.'

'I've got one,' I said. I hadn't, but I'd learnt by now from David Hemmings not to miss an opportunity.

'Have you?' he replied in an excited tone. 'Please come and see me at my offices tomorrow morning at eleven o'clock, I long to hear about it.'

I spent another sleepless night trying to think of an idea, no luck. Tired and with feelings of embarrassment beginning to flood over me, I caught a cab for the appointment with Mr Michael Peacock. During the cab ride the idea came to me – it was, I thought, terrific. *To The Manor Born* had been a huge hit in America, so had *The Irish RM*. My idea was to have me playing the British Ambassador in Washington appointed by a Labour Government, and Penelope Keith playing my rather forceful wife with extreme Conservative views. Comedy, drama, conflict, witty, intelligent, modern, contemporary, new, well acted by favourite stars – success! Michael Peacock thought so too.

'I know the very man to write this: Michael O'Shea,' said Mr Peacock. 'I know he's the Queen's Press Secretary but he's also a marvellous writer, and this ambassador in Washington idea will be right up his street.'

It was a very exciting meeting, I can tell you. After a week or so I received a sheaf of notepaper all headed 'Buckingham Palace'. They were Michael O'Shea's first stab at writing an episode. I didn't like it very much. It needed a lot of work. I went in to see Mr Peacock.

'Okay,' said Mr Peacock, 'I see what you mean, but I know O'Shea is the man to write it, let's give him another chance. I'll have a chat with him, and give him your notes.'

A week or so went by and another sheaf of papers from Buckingham Palace arrived. I read them. I was not happy. I didn't think Mr O'Shea was the man to write up my idea. Mr Peacock rang.

'Have you got the new script sheets? Aren't they marvellous?' he exclaimed.

'No,' I said. 'I'm not happy with them. I think we should try another writer.'

'Well I don't,' said Mr Peacock 'I'm very happy with this script and I'm going ahead with Michael O'Shea.'

'Just a minute,' I said, 'you can't do that. I came to you. It's my idea. I think we should look elsewhere.'

Michael Peacock's tone suddenly changed. 'Grow up,' he said. 'You brought me an idea, only an idea, nothing on paper. I'm going ahead.' And he put the phone down.

The moral, apart from 'growing up', is that if you have an idea in the back of a cab, have a piece of paper and pencil as well.

What happened to that idea is very interesting – but I'm not going to tell you because it doesn't concern me. Although it might still concern Rupert Everett.

*

As I say, *Absent Friends* ran for twelve months and after the first few months I noticed that many of the audience had arrived by coach. It was my first experience of coach parties – when you left the theatre they were lined up and down the road with lots and lots of (usually) ladies, waving and smiling. Now this was before the time of the boffo musicals and as usual the West End theatre in general was in a terrible state. Dwindling audiences, theatres and plays closing even after goodish notices. Theatre was dying. I had an idea! Little did I know it was the beginning of a whole lot of ideas for the rest of my career – which I always wrote down on paper as it happens, except in cabs of course.

Anyway, this idea was as follows. Why not put the West End ttheatre coaches into reverse? That is, why not have a traveling coach or coaches of actors who would enact or sing scenes from West End shows, they woud also bring autographed programmes, posters and reviews, they would come and perform at your local Women's Institutes, clubs, village halls or local hotels. Just for one evening. But they would only come if you could guarantee at least one coach load of people who would come to London's West End theatres. Great! You would have a wonderfully entertaining free evening plus a ticket to a show in London.

There were lots of hugely talented out-of-work actors who would jump at this chance of showing off their talent to the London producers, as they checked out that the clips from their shows were being done properly. Then there was the fun of doing the shows and also the camaraderie. Oh, and if you booked a full bus you could expect at least one member of the London cast to come and say hello after the West End show. I thought this idea would help solve the problem of dwindling audiences. After all, the impresarios were tearing their hair out. Backers were losing money. 'Well done, Peter,' they would say. 'We'll give it a try.' They didn't.

I went first to Michael Codron.

'I have an idea, Michael.'

'Does it begin with an R,' said Michael, 'because I only do new plays not revivals.'

Michael, of course, was famous at this time for encouraging and discovering great new playwrights. I explained my idea and he was most polite but unenthusiastic in his response.

'Peter,' he said, 'I don't really believe in publicity. I believe in the word of mouth. It's word of mouth that makes a hit, so I wouldn't want any of my shows to be involved in your scheme. But take it to the chairman of the West End theatre managers, David Conville.'

I did. I was invited to his gracious home in Putney, given a glass of champagne, listened to politely and given the brush-off. It would never work, seemed to be his considered opinion. He didn't seem to know quite why, but he was sure it wouldn't. So my plannings, costings and already tentative business contacts had been a waste of time. I would have to think of something else. I did.

The Theatre of Comedy.

*

There are two masks, Comedy and Tragedy. They are always depicted side by side, equal billing in the representation of DRAMA. I had felt for some time that the comedy mask had slipped. Tragedy had top billing and looked down on comedy. I began to notice, that with the advent of the National Theatre under Sir Laurence Olivier and the gushing forth of the *Carry On* films, that really 'serious' actors rarely did comedy unless it was a Restoration comedy by people like Farquhar, Sheridan, Goldsmith or Molière, in other words 'classical' comedy. An actor who specialized in modern comedy was slightly looked down on – not comedians playing in comedy, that's a different thing. Sitcoms were looked down on by the 'serious' side. This was made graphically clear to me after the first series of *To The Manor Born* when a most senior drama producer at the BBC called me aside in the canteen and said, 'You do realize you'll never work in drama again.'

'What do you mean?' I replied, my stomach churning.

'You have joined the other side,' he said and walked away.

I will talk more about this incident and its consequences later on.

In contrast to producers, directors and even critics, the snobbery existing between 'serious' acting and 'comedy' acting doesn't always exist between actors. A very good illustration of this was when I was at a party at which most of the guests were politicians. There was one other actor. It was Ian McKellen, and we fell on each other for comfort in this alien atmosphere. Suddenly a handsome, middle-aged woman came up to us and poured compliments over me, saying what a huge fan she was of *To The Manor Born*. I thanked her and introduced her to Ian.

'Are you an actor too?' she enquired, not recognizing him as a politician, I suppose.

'Yes,' said Ian, his face darkening a little.

Ian McKellen had opened at the National Theatre in *Coriolanus* only the week before, to outstanding reviews. I had seen his performance; it was thrilling.

'Are you in anything at the moment?' asked our handsome fellow guest.

Ian explained politely that he was playing *Coriolanus* at the National Theatre.

'Forgive me,' said our lady, 'but my husband is so busy we never find time to go to the theatre.'

She then poured more gushing praise on me and departed.

'Christ,' said Ian McKellen. 'I've got no money, I drive a scooter, I've given up smoking to play fucking Coriolanus, I'm a star at the National Theatre and no one knows who I am. Quite honestly, Peter, I would give my right arm to be in a sitcom like you.'

He meant it, and I thought I'd give my right arm to be playing almost anything at the National.

I think Sir Ian McKellen is all right now, though, don't you? But he had to do it through his own guts and initiative with his film of *Richard III*.

*

I decided what was needed was a Theatre of Comedy. In fact, a National Theatre of Comedy, which could put on Chekhov, Joe Orton, Shakespeare, Ayckbourn, Frayn, Stoppard, Nichols, Restoration plays and modern farce. I hoped the idea would attract the foremost actors, directors and playwrights of the day. I approached many of them; I had a very positive response.

'At last,' said Leonard Rossiter, 'a chance to show those toffee-nosed bastards that comedy is not to be laughed at.'

I thought he summed it up well and totally. I got a little group together, which included at that time John Mortimer, Michael Frayn, Leonard Rossiter, Richard Beckinsale, Ronnie Barker, Eric Thompson and Richard Briers. Everyone was enthusiastic about the policy and the name, Theatre of Comedy, because it could embrace so much writing; but obviously what we needed was a theatre. The old Lyric Theatre in Hammersmith had been pulled down, but they had almost finished building a new Lyric, and as I lived in Hammersmith I approached the council. They liked the sound of the idea. They were looking for a policy for the new theatre, could I come and outline my policy?

Richard Briers and Leonard Rossiter (who were much more famous than me at this time) and I addressed the council. It went down well; we even came up with the idea of a Festival of Comedy to which companies from around the world could be invited. All very ambitious and very exciting. But of course I didn't have any idea where the money would come from at this stage. I suppose in my innocence I just presumed the Hammersmith and Fulham Council would fund it. Time passed. Then I suddenly had a phone call late in the day from someone on the council who informed me that they were going ahead and were about to issue a statement to the press the next day. They had approached an administrator and artistic director (David Giles) and they would be announcing a Policy of Theatre that had a strong comedy bias, including a Festival of Comedy. The official told me my name would not be associated with the statement, and he was merely ringing out of courtesy. I think he wanted me to congratulate him. When I pointed out forcibly that whilst I thought his team and policy were to be applauded, if comedy at the Lyric was the thrust of the press statement, mine and my colleagues' names must be mentioned and given credit. He refused and said that the Comedy Theatre idea wasn't a patent. Suffice it to say I went round to his house that evening and made him an offer he couldn't refuse.

So everything was on. I was possibly to be the artistic director and the National Theatre of Comedy would launch at the Lyric. But first it would be nice they suggested if I invited the councillors to my home to meet all of my supporters from the theatre world. Perhaps a lunch on Saturday, it was suggested. It was all arranged. My wife organized the food and I organized red and white wine. There would be about twenty people altogether. On Friday afternoon the council rang me. They wanted to know what 'beverage', as they put it, I would be serving with the lunch, which was to be a buffet. Slightly baffled I told them red or white wine, or tea or water. Whatever was preferred. 'Oh no,' they told me, 'there cannot be any alcohol present or on view as this could be construed as bribery.'

I was not used to the way of councils. I was a fool where angels fear to tread and I had gone one step too far. I was so angry and non-plussed, I cut off my nose and cancelled the whole damn thing.

Then through the good offices of Sir John Mortimer, I was approached by the governors of the Old Vic. The Old Vic was in serious trouble at this time, and at a secret meeting (it was held at the Garrick where no business is supposed to be discussed), I explained my policy to the trustees of the Old Vic. They loved the idea – where was I going to get the money from? Yes, ideas are cheap if you can't follow through. I realized I was really an actor not a businessman.

About five years later, on 1 February 1983, I received a letter from a very good businessman and a very good writer of farce. It was headed on printed notepaper: the Theatre of Laughter.

The letter was from Ray Cooney. He had had the idea of setting up a National Theatre of Comedy, it said, and he went on to mention the people he'd approached with this idea, many

of whom were members of my old team, and that he already
had the chance to acquire a Theatre, the Shaftesbury. There was
no hint or mention that he knew that I had been promoting the
same idea a few years before, but would I be interested in being
involved and perhaps interested in becoming a shareholder in
the venture. I rang Ray and invited him to my home for a chat.
I did, of course, mention the coincidence of us having exactly
the same idea and indicated I'd like to be involved.

The one cavil I had was with his company name, 'The
Theatre of Laughter', which I felt would limit the idea. I felt it
would suggest broader comedy, whilst not necessarily a broader
policy that would include Chekhov, Anouilh, Beckett or
Shakespeare. I suggested the company name should be the
Theatre of Comedy. Ray thought this a good idea.

I joined his executive team. The first production was to be a
pantomime. I excitedly expected us to commission a brand-
new pantomime, but Ray felt a star-filled traditional Paul Elliott
pantomime would be just the thing. I had an enormous feeling of
disappointment and wasted opportunity. I realized I shouldn't
have interfered with Ray's original title, the Theatre of Laughter.
I made my excuses and left.

CHAPTER 15

THE COMEDY YEARS

Maybe I had tickled it with Guthrie Featherstone QC MP in *Rumpole of the Bailey*. It was certainly an eccentric role with lots of accidental and unconscious comedy in the playing of it, and of course beautifully written. As I mentioned in a previous chapter, the door was really opened when I was offered the part of Hilary in an episode of *Rising Damp* called 'Stage Struck', in 1977. I have been very pleased to discover that this is a favourite episode of many fans of the series.

As I have explained, I have something of a reputation for being 'difficult', but I had been warned that Leonard Rossiter could be especially difficult and that I must handle him with kid gloves. I was mystified as I had spent a very happy year with Leonard at the Bristol Old Vic. We all know what a wonderful cast it was in *Rising Damp* and I was greeted warmly by everyone, especially by Leonard, as we considered ourselves friends. Not a hint of difficulty, I thought. What were they talking about? Then we came to our first big scene together and I made a suggestion to Leonard regarding something in the scene. I immediately felt a frisson from everyone else in the room, and an intake of breath. I felt that perhaps they were all going to take cover.

Before Leonard could reply to my suggestion, the director, imagining he was going to quickly defuse the situation, said, 'No, no, the scene is perfect as it is.'

Leonard wheeled on him. 'Just one moment.' 'Peter has made a very interesting suggestion. We are going to work on it and when we are ready you can work out your shots and write your camera script. Until then, please keep quiet.'

Yes, Leonard was a man who was 100 per cent interested in getting the scene as right as possible. We two 'difficult' actors had a great time together, but everyone in the cast was a joy to work with and a master of comedy.

Comedy is a funny thing. My first line on entrance was 'Hello ducky.' I'd done it in rehearsals, done it on camera rehearsals, everything seemed normal, nothing unusual, but when we came to the recording in front of a live audience and I said, 'Hello ducky,' the whole audience and studio collapsed with laughter. The cameramen were laughing, the audience was hysterical. The recording had to be stopped. We couldn't continue. We did it again, the audience loved it again (thank goodness) but at least we were able to continue. The show was written by that genius of comedy writing Eric Chappell, and my performance must have stuck in his mind because his next series was *Only When I Laugh* and I was offered my first comedy starring role. This was after the success of *Absent Friends* and *Dirty Linen*. I'm sure this had no influence, however, as on the whole TV and theatre don't mix, as I was to learn – later.

The series was also to star James Bolam, an old friend from the Royal Court days, and featured another actor who I grew to like enormously, as a friend and as a huge comedy talent, Richard Wilson.

Now fortunately this didn't clash with *Rumpole of the Bailey*, but as I was beginning to rehearse and record this series, out of the blue I was offered another comedy series called *To The Manor Born*.

I hope the Channel 4
Chairman drove past
this every day.
My mum loved it.

Archie Rice. I thought
Hewison's cartoon for *Punch*
summed it all up.

THE ENTERTAINER —
PETER BOWLES as Archie Rice
Shaftesbury Theatre 5 June 1986
Punch issue: 18 June

*I have a go, lady,
don't I — I have a go.*

HEWISON
'86

My Old Vic 'corrupters' and dearest friends, Bryan Pringle and James Villiers in later life.

John Osborne a great friend and host (whose is that car?).

The Irish Resident Magistrate.

There were even more laughs off stage. Sir Michael Gambon and me as Vic Parks in *The Man of the Moment*.

Bryan Murray and me looking dodgy. *Perfect Scoundrels*.

George Grant from *Running Late*. We won the Golden Gate Award at the San Francisco Film Festival.

Look into my eyes. *Gangster No. 1* with Richard Johnston.

It was Bliss. With Dame Judi Dench in *Hay Fever*.

Mad and bad – Byron in the film *Shelley*.

Psychopath and killer – Root in the play *Wait Until Dark*.

It's not *Macbeth* but it is Don Armardo playing Hector in *Loves Labour's Lost*.

Sir Peter Hall and me about to launch into *Loves Labour's Lost*.

We filled the 1,300 seat Piccadilly Theatre – Tumbrels welcomed, with Eric Sykes and Carmen Silvera.

Our silver wedding with Guy on the right and Adam and Sasha on the left. Bob in front.

A family celebration. The gang's all here. (2009)

My agent rang me and said, 'I thought you'd like to know that the BBC wanted you to be Penelope Keith's leading man in a new starring vehicle for her. I have of course said you can't do it as it clashes with *Rumpole of the Bailey*.'

Bells rang, fire engines wailed, police cars turned on their sirens. Situation comedies record on Sundays, *Rumpole of the Bailey* recorded on a Thursday – maybe something could be worked out. It was. Verity Lambert at Thames TV was understanding, John Howard Davies from the BBC was understanding, rehearsal rooms were in the same area of London. I rehearsed one show in the morning (*To The Manor Born*) and another in the afternoon (*Rumpole*). I was given the Rumpole Thursday recording off, but by then we had already done three episodes of *To The Manor Born* because each episode of *Rumpole* took three weeks to rehearse and in sitcom you only rehearse for a short week and only mornings at that. Yes, it is very hard work, I can tell you; but the rewards can be great.

The amazing thing was that I was going to be starring in two situation comedies for two rival channels, sometimes in the same week!

Now of course you have no idea if the work you are doing is going to be a success. You can only judge the quality of the writing and hope for the best. As we know now, both series were huge successes. In fact one can definitely say that *To The Manor Born* was a phenomenal success.

Only When I Laugh which was rehearsed in London but recorded in Leeds, was huge fun. James Bolam was another 100 per cent man, tremendously exciting to work with. We were a very happy team with brilliant scripts by Eric Chappell. It was during this series that James Bolam tipped me off that Peter Nichols had written *Born in The Gardens* and that there was a good part for me, but more of that later.

As I have mentioned, my part in *Rumpole* as Guthrie Featherstone QC MP was a character role. This was also the case with Archie Glover, the part I played in *Only When I Laugh*, or H A PPY. as all the children called it. The part of Richard de Vere in *To The Manor Born* offered a different possibility. First of all it was a romantic part, the first I had been offered since Byron years before. But how to play it? It was a sitcom not a play or film, and there is of course a strong tendency in actors (or at least there was) to be funny, not quite real, comic, get laughs, be amusing – after all, that's the function of an actor in a situation comedy, isn't it? To complicate matters I heard that an episode had been recorded for radio sometime before with Bernard Braden playing my role as a brash American; there were hints that perhaps I could play him as a rich Arab. The implications were that he should be a foreigner, and therefore that carried with it the sitcom cliché of Funny Foreigner; Manuel in *Fawlty Towers* being the classic example. It was decided by the 'powers that be' that I would be Czechoslovakian and I would have my Czechoslovakian mother living with me. I decided that whatever happened I wasn't going to be a Funny Foreigner. It seemed clear to me that Penelope Keith's character wouldn't fall for a Funny Foreigner.

Oddly enough there was no discussion about all this, I had to make my decision myself. I thought of Robert Maxwell. He was a Czech who had come to Britain and was now presenting himself as the quintessential Englishman, beautiful Savile Row clothes, and no accent. I decided I must have come to England very young, and in my formative years worked in East End markets, developing my skills and intelligence into creating Cavendish Foods, and of course learning how to speak perfect English. Then I decided to play him absolutely real, a real man, and the only real man that I knew was myself. I would play Richard de Vere from inside myself, as real as myself, and let the situations I found myself in – devised by Peter Spence (the writer) – provide the comedy. We did the first 'stagger through' of the first episode in front of the head of BBC Comedy, the brilliant, charming John Howard Davies (the original Oliver in 'David Lean's *Oliver Twist*). I was very, very apprehensive. Penny was very funny – real, of course, but she had created a strong character and persona. The same with the beautiful Angela Thorne, who transformed herself into the kind, mousey, nervous friend, she was very funny too. The 'stagger through' finished.

'Well done, everybody,' said Mr Howard Davies. He had a few words with Penny and the director, Gareth Gwenlan, and began to walk out of the rehearsal room. I caught up with him.

'Was I okay?' I asked fearfully. 'I mean, is it all right for me to play him real and straight like that?'

John Howard Davies gave me a big reassuring smile. 'Peter,' he said, 'that is exactly how it should be played, and I cast you in the part because I knew that's how you probably would play him. Keep it up, don't worry, have confidence.' And off he went.

What John Howard Davies said to me changed my whole approach to acting, changed my theatrical life. At the age of forty-three I had learnt that 'acting' wasn't the true way for an actor. 'Being', doing as little as possible to express your character's emotions clearly, and letting the audience's imagination do the rest. That was true acting.

The shows went out on Sundays. After Episode One I got up as usual to get the morning papers. To get to the paper shop I had to walk a little way down the traffic-jammed Great West Road. Horns began to sound, hoots, honks, deep-throated blasts. What was going on, were they frustrated at the jam? As I turned to see what the commotion was really about, windows came down, saloon drivers waved, cab drivers waved, lorry drivers gave the thumbs-up. Something extraordinary had happened, something that cut across all classes in Britain's class-ridden society. The noise I was hearing was the vocal expression of the pleasure given to over twenty million people

with the first episode of *To The Manor Born*. Well done, Peter
Spence, well done, Penelope Keith, well done, Angela Thorne;
well done, Gareth Gwenlan and Mr John Howard Davies. And
I was part of it too.

One of the big plusses in the developing relationship of
Audrey fforbes-Hamilton and Richard de Vere was that I found
Penny so attractive and exciting to work with. I have a very
strong wife so I had plenty of experience in getting along with
strong women and, believe me, Penelope Keith is a very strong
woman indeed. I loved it.

As the series continued the viewing figures broke all records,
causing pubs and churches to complain of falling customers
and congregations on Sunday evenings (this was before recording machines, remember). The press began to analyse the
reasons for the phenomenal success. They got it wrong; they
have always got it wrong. They all said the public was drawn to
it because it was about that British thing called class. It wasn't;
it was about that universal thing called romance, escapist
romance with delightful unforced humour and charm. If it had
just been about class, then all the classes of our society would-
n't have liked it. From 'the man and woman on the Clapham
omnibus', the builder, baker and candlestick maker, as well as
the upper-class landed gentry – they all switched on.

It didn't pay much. At first I was offered £250 a week for my
part but I eventually doubled it to £500 an episode; and for the
first two series Daphne Heard, who played my Czech-speaking
mum (she made up the much-praised authentic accent) had to
pay for her own digs in London as she lived in Bristol, so all her
fee went in rent! Penny and I put a stop to that for the third
series; we had been ignorant of the situation before that. Oh,
and I wasn't invited to the BBC press launch of the series or to
the BAFTA award gala. In the BBC's eyes it was Penelope
Keith's show, I suppose. It's a funny thing, comedy.

Only When I Laugh was continuing, of course, and topping

even *Coronation Street* on the ITV ratings. It was enough to turn a young man's head. Except at forty-three I wasn't young, and I had three teenage children who kept my feet very firmly on the ground, not to mention Sue, who wouldn't have put up with a big head for one single solitary moment.

Before the first episode of either *To The Manor Born* or *Only When I Laugh* had been transmitted I had followed up James Bolam's advice about Peter Nichols's *Born in The Gardens*. Having been in his film of *A Day in the Death of Joe Egg* I was able to phone him at home, and he expressed delight in offering me the part. The play was a four-hander: two women, two men. The leading woman was to be Beryl Reid and the other man was Barry Foster (of *Van der Valk* fame and a distinguished stage actor).

The play was to be tried out at the Bristol Old Vic. I found myself on the train from London with Beryl Reid, who I had done two televisions with at sometime or other. The read-through of the play was to be in the circle bar. I knew the theatre well, and the straightforward way to the bar was through the foyer and up the main staircase. As we ascended together the theatre manager appeared at the top of the stairs, and then gushed down towards us.

'Welcome to the Bristol Old Vic, Miss Reid,' said the manager. He ignored me. 'We feel very honoured to have you here. There's just one thing: in future could you use the stage door, as actors aren't allowed up these stairs.'

The answer from Beryl was immediate. 'You mean the servants' entrance? Fuck off. I'm going back to London.'

And she turned on her heels. It took a lot of persuading by that stupid man to get Beryl back up those stairs.

We opened and had been playing to packed houses for two weeks. I was staying as a guest in the flat of the Bristol theatre's resident stage manager. It was Sunday morning and my 'landlord' said sweetly, 'I've been invited to a sherry party across the road at eleven-thirty, would you like to come?' I said I'd love to. After all, I'd never been to a sherry party before.

It was pretty packed when we got there, all Bristolians of the middle-class type. The opening remark to me from another guest was, 'Where are you living?' I pointed through the window to the house opposite. 'Oh dear, the unfashionable side,' said this woman, who really wasn't Lady Bracknell – or perhaps she really was – in any case, I broke away to look for mine host.

The Kafka nightmare was only just beginning. Mine host turned out to be a local solicitor. I thanked him for his hospitality.

'I understand you're an actor,' he said.

'Yes,' I replied truthfully.

'Working at the BBC Bristol radio, I suppose.'

'No,' I said, 'I'm working at the Bristol Old Vic, in *Born in The Gardens*, which opened last week.'

It seemed a reasonable enough statement to me. But not to him, oh no.

'Excuse me,' his face was beginning to change shape. 'You are not in *Born in The Gardens*. My wife and I saw the play last night and you certainly weren't in it.'

This was spoken in such a way as to suggest he felt he might have a dangerous lying psychopath in his house. I have to emphasize here that there were only two men in this play, both with large parts. Barry Foster was about five foot seven, with very bubbly white/blond hair, and I am six foot two, with dark hair and a moustache. I also had a solo speech to the audience during the play.

I affected polite puzzlement, 'Yes, I was in it,' I said. 'Perhaps you didn't like the play.' I was offering him some excuse, I suppose.

'We loved the play, but you were not in it.'

This man was a lawyer, remember, a seeker of the truth. A

moment of awkward impasse, then he said, as he quickly turned away, 'You must have been playing a very small part. I'm afraid I never remember very small parts.'

I decided to get out of this alien mad house as soon as possible, but as I reached the door my sleeve was plucked. It was the hostess.

'Excuse me,' she said, 'my husband says you told him you were in the play we saw last night.'

'Yes,' I said, 'I did, because I am in the play you saw last night.'

I tried to be polite but I was desperate now for a proper drink. Obviously sherry was driving these people insane. The proof of this was about to be delivered.

'Well what part did you play?' she asked with a deeply confused frowning face.

'I played the part of Hedley, the MP,' I replied.

She took two steps back, several emotions passed over her face, she looked me up and down and then she said, 'Well that can't have been difficult for you, can it? You look just like him.'

I tried to get my wife a sherry in a pub recently. They told me they didn't stock it anymore as there was no call for it. I'm not surprised.

*

As I'm writing about my so-called Comedy Years I'm reminded of the very first comedy role I played professionally. It was Algernon in *The Importance of Being Earnest*. It was part of a season of plays that included *The Diary of Anne Frank* – so not all comedy – and it was in Cardiff. I was, I think, twenty-one at the time. Earnest was being played by a much older actor called Alan Foss. He was bald and wore a wig for Earnest. We shared a dressing room, and had got on very well during rehearsals. I only refer to Mr Foss's age and lack of hair because it must have been part of the fuel for what was about to happen.

The show went very well. On the first night and after the final curtain call, Alan Foss immediately tore off his jacket and, in front of the still assembled cast, punched me as hard as he could in the face. I staggered, and he was restrained, which gave me the chance to ask him through the blood pouring from my nose why he had hit me. 'That was for getting so many laughs,' he screamed from his now purple face, his wig dangling over one ear. We didn't share a dressing room after that, and I don't think he understood that the laughs were Oscar Wilde's. I continued to get the laughs.

*

Born in The Gardens ran at the Globe Theatre in London for ten months and during that time I did another series of *To The Manor Born* and I think two of *Only When I Laugh*. The filming for *To The Manor Born*, that is the exterior scenes which are inserted into episodes later, was done in Somerset before the M3 was built. After the first night of *Born in The Gardens*, and for about two more weeks, I had to walk straight out of the stage door into a large hired car driven by my wife to get to Cricket St Thomas in Somerset and be in make-up at 7 a.m. The BBC wouldn't pay for a car, so I had to hire one (for about half my fee) big enough for me to sleep in (sort of) on the back seat during the three-and-a-half-hour journey, often in fog. They would film with me until about 2.30 p.m., then while Penny and the others broke for lunch Sue would drive me back to London, arriving just in time for a quick lie-down in the dressing room before going on stage and the whole cycle starting again.

Yes, hard work, yes, very tiring, but I had waited so long for some sort of recognition it was more than worth it.

Born in The Gardens had opened and we had started the second series of *To The Manor Born* as I have said, but what I perhaps have not made clear is that the first series had still to be shown. It was transmitted a week or two after we had opened, so on the Monday of the honking horns and thumbs-up, I made my entrance that evening to a surprising and rather shocking huge round of applause. This did not go down too well with the rest of the small cast, however, especially Miss Reid. There was nothing I could do about it, though, and it continued for the ten-month run of the show. Another sign that something extraordinary had happened as far as I was concerned was that there was always a crowd of fans at the stage door. I was forty-three, I had been on the television and stage many, many times but had never had stage-door fans. Something was definitely happening to me through my playing of the multimillionaire Richard De Vere.

There was, I'm afraid, to be a severe reaction for my 'serious' acting ambitions as I discovered later.

Only When I Laugh, although recorded on Fridays in Leeds was a little easier than *To The Manor Born* which was recorded on Sundays in London, because the management kindly let me have Thursday and Friday evenings off, whilst a specially engaged actor took my part for two nights.

I did four series of *Only When I Laugh*. When they asked me to do the fourth series (I was by now also doing *The Irish RM* and *Lytton's Diary*) I said to my agent that he should suggest I would do the fourth series if they gave me a series of my own. He thought this was extremely outrageous of me and didn't want to do it – but he did. From that came *The Bounder*, again written by that master of comedy Eric Chappell. I also had the joy of working with someone I had admired for years: George Cole. I remember being astonished at the press launch of the show when George was asked by a journalist if he had ever played comedy before. I tell you, it's a funny old game.

As I am writing this the papers are full of the money the BBC spends on executives' salaries, expenses, junkets, etc. When *To The Manor Born* finished, after having played for, I think, twenty episodes over three series, and having been watched by the largest audiences ever recorded for a show requiring actors, the BBC management said they would like to have a party to celebrate the ending of this wonderfully successful series. That's nice we all thought, thank you. The BBC spokesman then continued, 'So if Penny and Peter could possibly supply the drinks, we the BBC will supply the sandwiches.' Penny and I bought wine, I seem to remember, and trays of sandwiches were provided by the BBC, the cast clubbed together and bought our wonderful producer/director Gareth Gwenlan a present, and I was never offered another job by the BBC for twenty-six years. Thank God for the competition of ITV.

It was during the recording of the second series of *To The Manor Born* that I was approached in a friendly manner by a senior drama producer in the BBC canteen, who congratulated me on my success but said to me, 'You do realize don't you, that you will never work in drama again.'

I felt my blood run cold. 'Why do you say that?' I asked.

'Because,' he replied, 'you have joined the other side.'

I mentioned this earlier and make no excuse for mentioning it again, as it changed my life dramatically once more. I discovered I was completely innocent in the way theatre and TV worked, that there was a sharp division at this time, 1979, between sitcom actors, TV actors in general, soap actors in particular, and serious theatre actors. Not, of course, among the actors themselves – the Ian McKellen story is a perfect example of that – but among the producers and directors. It was all changed for ever when Dame Judi Dench and her husband, Michael Williams, decided to a sitcom. They got the head of BBC Drama, James Cellan Jones to direct their series. The first time, I think, that a drama director had joined 'the other side' – and as far as I know there has been no journey the other way with sitcom directors.

Anyway the chilling statement, which felt like a threat, but was just a practical statement made me start to write the outline and format for a drama series. The series was to become *Lytton's Diary*. It was to be about a 'star' gossip columnist. There was a true star gossip columnist on the *Mail* at this time called Nigel Dempster, and even the broadsheets were beginning to have gossip columns. There wasn't the absolute hysterics about gossip there is today, which mostly concerns celebs and soap stars. Then it was more about the so-called privileged people.

My interest and awareness of gossip columns had always been there because my parents read the William Hickey page in the *Daily Express* every day. They did this because they could follow the lives, or at least the gossip of the lives, of the people they had either worked for or met through their time in service. Also, I think my mum liked the *Express* because it was a Beaverbrook paper.

*

Just to keep some sort of track on the timing of events, I began the fight back into drama while still recording *To The Manor Born* but before *The Irish RM*. That is, if you're still with me.

CHAPTER 16

LYTTON'S DIARY

I had two experiences that opened up the gossip column idea.
One was that I had been in an office when I saw and heard
an aide ring the *Daily Mail* Dempster office with some gossip
about the state of his boss's marriage. His boss being a well-
known film star who was standing beside him. I was amazed at
this, and was told by the star that it was good publicity, one, and
two, if they went too far he/she would sue the paper for libel.
A win–win situation. The other revelation to me was when I
was having lunch with a famous and highly respected film
writer. We were in Julie's Bar in Notting Hill, I remember.
After a drink or two he told me that often, just for his own
amusement, he would pick up tittle-tattle or intimate details of
his friends at dinner parties and then pass this on to Nigel
Dempster's office at the *Daily Mail*. I hadn't mentioned any
interest whatsoever in gossip columns and this was told to me
out of the blue. I was astonished. Here was a wealthy, highly
successful man who had this secret 'vice', if I might call it that,
of being indiscreet about his friends just to see the story in the
newspaper and to know he was the source. I passed no adverse
comment on this, but thought it was seriously weird. When
Nigel Dempster became a friend a year or two later I was to

discover this happened all the time, it was often how he got his stories.

Once again I was untutored in the ways of setting up or pitching a big TV series to the ITV networks. I say ITV because the BBC was an absolute non-starter. I was seriously damaged goods in their drama department.

I decided first of all to write storylines for the series, stories that would be strong enough to make the front page of the newspaper. I wrote about fifty of them, just a few lines or half a page. I was amazed at how rich the seam was. It was just at this time I was sent a musical play by Tina Brown, who was regarded as 'up and coming' (they got that right). She was wondering if I would like the part in it of a gossip writer (shades of Osborne's Paul Slickey). I didn't, but wondered if she would like to write a TV pilot/series about a gossip writer. We had two very fruitful lunches at the newly opened Langan's. I have in front of me a note from her saying thank you, after the second of these meetings, 'for what was perhaps the most exciting and creative lunch I have ever had'. But she had just been appointed editor of *Tatler* so wouldn't have time to join me on the project. I think she has had a few more exciting lunches since then, don't you?

I then contacted an old friend, Philip Broadley, who had a fine reputation in writing TV plays and episodes for very successful television series. I wondered if he would be excited by the idea, and if so we could collaborate on developing a script. He was excited and he set to work.

My creative mania was running high, and although I had not approached any TV company with the idea yet, I knew who I wanted to do the graphics or titles for the series: Mark Boxer. Now Mark Boxer was the top serious lampooning cartoonist of his day. As famous as Matt of the *Telegraph* is now. Mark Boxer featured on the front page of *The Times*. I had never met Mr Boxer so I just rang *The Times*. They had never heard of him.

'They' not being someone on the switchboard. 'They' being the editorial staff. 'Mark Boxer? No, whoever he is he doesn't work for *The Times*, sorry.' I persuaded them to look at the front page of that day's *Times*. 'They' were mildly surprised and unembarrassed to see a Mark Boxer cartoon prominently positioned. 'Oh yes, never seen him, know who you mean now. He just sends the cartoons in and we print them.' Very hard bitten and unsentimental these newsmen (a good tip I was to discover). Anyway, they were able to furnish me with a means of contacting Mr Boxer. This famous, highly regarded, sophisticated and extremely handsome man was interested enough and gracious enough to come to my home. I liked him enormously. He loved the idea for the series and expressed great interest in doing the titles but as it turned out the eventual producers decided to open the series in a different way and Mark Boxer followed Tina Brown by becoming the next editor of *Tatler*.

I did learn two interesting things from the charming Mark Boxer, though. One was that he felt that actors never ever got the upper classes 'right'. In his experience no TV play or series had managed to really 'crack the code'. 'You all tend to think if you wear a Turnbull and Asser shirt and cufflinks, plus a "posh" accent, highly polished shoes and a Savile Row suit, you are "upper class". Upper middle class, yes; upper class, no; aristocratic class, absolutely miles off.' He told me all the secrets. I didn't ring the gossip columns but I had valuable knowledge as an actor.

Mr Boxer looked through some of my storylines. 'My God,' he said, 'who told you this?' He suddenly seemed very serious and not a little disturbed.

The storyline that had caused this reaction was something I had completely made up with no knowledge whatsoever. But knowing through my interest in art that our 'great' auction houses were (and may be still) staffed at all levels by members of the true aristocracy or upper classes I invented this.

Over the years, centuries, sometimes great English titled families, when short of funds, have had to sell their family portraits by Gainsborough, Lawrence, Reynolds and so on. In the world of the 'upper-class club' when these family portraits reappeared, many years later, for assessment and sale at one of the great auction houses, the living descendants of the family would be discreetly contacted and, all things being equal, if the family were keen to buy back these heirlooms but didn't have the big money for a big-name painter, the auction house would assess the portrait as being 'in the style of' or 'from the studio of' or 'in the manner of' Gainsborough, Reynolds and so on. This way the painting could be returned cheaply to its proper place.

Mark Boxer was aghast. 'You should never have been told this,' he said, as though someone had broken the code of a secret society.

'Mark, I promise you I made it up, for no reason. I just thought it was a good idea.'

'Well,' said Mark, 'it is such a good idea that the people in the right place have already had the idea, and under certain circumstances this does happen.'

I don't know how Mark Boxer knew these things. I didn't ask him, but I didn't use the story.

After many meetings, script conferences, drinks and suchlike, Philip Broadley came up with a marvellous 'pilot' script on the solving of the Lord Lucan mystery. He also came up with the name of the hero and the series became *Lytton's Diary*. It had the right ring to it for those upper-class roguish days – it was years later I discovered he'd got the name from the street next to his. A true writer indeed.

So here I now was. I had an idea, I had storylines and I had a fully written exciting pilot script. What I didn't know, but learnt later to good effect, was that you only need one of these things: a good idea, written down on half a sheet of paper.

John Frankau had now taken over from Verity Lambert as the

head of Thames Television drama. Thames Television was the London division of the big ITV four – Granada, ATV, Yorkshire and Thames. I had done a small part in a television that Mr Frankau had directed many years before. Somewhere I had his telephone number and one evening I rang him at his home. I opened with 'I have the best idea for a TV series you have ever heard.' I didn't get any further.

'If it's that good,' said the very practical John Frankau, 'you had better come over to my home tomorrow morning at seven-thirty and pitch it to me while I have my breakfast and before I go into the office.'

Yes that was it. That was the first absolutely positive indication that I had smashed the glass ceiling. I had had ideas before but could never get put through to anyone, or no one rang back. The reality of having 24 million viewers per episode of the sitcom was hopefully about to pay off, and in drama too.

Mr Frankau had his boiled egg and I did my first sales pitch for a TV series. Mr Frankau liked it a lot.

'Leave the script,' he said, 'and if I like it as much as your pitch I would like to commission thirteen, one-hour episodes.'

I left, never even touching the ground, let alone the toast and coffee I'd been offered, and rushed home.

While I was excitedly telling my wife what had happened, the phone rang.

'I've read the script – you're on. Please get your agents to contact us so we can start drawing up a contract.'

My agents, who I saw that morning, didn't believe me, or didn't believe Mr Frankau. It seemed incomprehensible to them that this had happened and from an actor too, and my agents were well-known people. No, they wouldn't contact Thames TV. I rang the most powerful literary agent in London, Anthony Jones, and the 24 million viewers paid off once again. Come over tomorrow and tell me about it. I did.

'I love it,' he said. 'You've cracked it. Many writers have

tried to set up a series in a newspaper office but haven't got off the ground. You, an actor, have cracked it. I would like to handle this for you.'

Then silence. I waited and waited. My agents were not too pleased I had gone to Anthony Jones. They believed me now. Thames TV contacted me. 'We've heard nothing. What's going on?' was the question. I rang the most powerful literary agent in London once again.

'What's happening? Why haven't you rung Thames?'

I had gone one step too far. I was not a star writer, after all – I was an actor, no matter how 'popular'. The general gist of his remarks as I remember them was: 'I can't have you ringing me up like this, suggesting what I should or should not do. Find someone else.' And he put the phone down. I returned, tail between my legs, to my actors' agency and they did the deal.

Then, as these things happen, John Frankau left and Verity Lambert came back, and I had to pitch the whole idea again. She liked it. I suggested Ray Connolly to write it. Verity liked him too. I had always admired Ray Connolly as a writer and as an interviewer (the 'Ray Connolly Interview' in the *Standard*) and also for his many extremely informed articles on the Beatles, which incidentally he is still writing as John Lennon had been a personal friend.

It was decided that six pilots for different possible series would be made but only two series actually commissioned. Then Verity Lambert left Thames for independent pastures and Lloyd Shirley took over. He loved the recorded pilot written by Ray (poor Philip's script having come and gone) and commissioned a full series of six one-hours. The other pilot commissioned was called *Wooden Tops*, which when made into a series was called *The Bill* and is still running twenty-nine years later.

Lytton's Diary was cancelled after two highly successful (around 14 million viewers) series, even though a third had been commissioned by Lloyd Shirley, because a new head of

Thames Television Ltd had been appointed. The rumour was that he'd cancelled it over the head of Lloyd Shirley because he thought the subject meretricious. He himself had come from the world of serious documentaries. He was also my next-door neighbour with whom I got on very well. It's a funny old game, drama.

Incidentally, and just to bore you a little more with my sitcom versus drama theme, I was offered a job from the BBC at this time. It was to be a *Play of the Month* starring Paul Scofield, very prestigious. I read the script hungrily. My part turned out to be about one and a half pages long. I wrote a very polite note of decline to the director. He sent me an equally polite note back saying how sorry he was, but that he thought I was making a mistake as he felt he was offering me an oppor-tunity to 'break back into drama'. The director, I seem to remember, was Stephen Frears. In the light of his distinguished career perhaps I *was* mistaken!

A very important bonus of making *Lytton's Diary* were the friendships I made: Ray Connolly, of course, Chris Burt the producer (who later did *Sharpe*, *Morse*, etc., etc.), and espe-cially Nigel Dempster and his wife, Camilla. Nigel was the most delightful companion, with old-fashioned good manners and a very quick wit and devilish sense of humour. I rather foolishly thought it wise to be a little careful in what I said to him about myself and my friends. Quietly insulting, I realized after a while, as Nigel was completely and utterly discreet as far as his friends were concerned. Although I remember him saying once to me, 'If you ever do get into trouble, Peter, please tell me first, as I'll be able to break it gently in my columns and thus spike the guns of the other papers.'

Talking of other papers reminds me that when the first pro-gramme of *Lytton* finished at 9 p.m. there was an immediate phone call. It was the *Daily Express* saying they had written a knocking piece about the programme for the morning paper, but now having actually watched it they were going to sing its praises – a great compliment to the professionalism of Ray Connolly of course. The other interesting 'other papers' thing was that the next morning my phone rang at 7.30. 'Robert Maxwell here,' said a strong deep voice. 'Saw your programme last night, loved it. Keep up the good work.' I thanked him and he rang off. Maxwell, of course, at that time was the owner of the powerful *Daily Mirror*.

Nigel Dempster even invited me to edit his column one week, and took me all over London to various houses and events. I saw quickly how people revered him and indeed were not a little scared of him. I invited him to have lunch at the Garrick Club. He was very reluctant. 'Are you sure you know what you're doing, Peter?' he said. 'They won't like to see me there.' They did. In fact members kept coming over to my table in order to be introduced.

I also had the fun and interest of spending days in Nigel's office at the *Mail*, listening to the banter, and hearing the tips and information that flooded in, and the dogged follow-ups by Nigel's staff, to check if the story 'stood up'. Sometimes Nigel knew things about someone, but would offer not to print them provided that person gave him something a little less embarrassing that he could publish. It was quite tragic that he died so young and so cruelly. I am pleased to say that Camilla became, and remains a very close friend of Sue and I, and is very much part of our lives.

In 1986, while I was doing *The Entertainer* at the Shaftesbury Theatre, I was visited in my dressing room by a very powerful and well-known American television producer Don Taffner. He felt certain that *Lytton's Diary* could be developed internationally with stories being shot all over the world: the Oscars, Cannes Film Festival, Prix de l'Arc de Triomphe, St Moritz and so on. He would like permission to approach various countries for the finances. I gave it willingly. The TV companies abroad were very interested in the idea. I was about to be launched as an international TV star – well, nearly. There was a problem. They would need a network showing in Britain, which meant contacting Thames TV, the original producers. They refused. I presume they still felt the subject was meretricious. I never discussed it with my neighbour. I suppose I was too busy playing Archie Rice. Anyway big boys don't cry. They just move house.

CHAPTER 17

FAME AND FANS

'Oi, Pete!' is a very familiar and welcome call I still get from men across the street or working on building sites. 'Look, there's your man,' used to be the cry in Ireland from men, women and children.

The 'Oi, Pete!' is because my popular fame came through television. I was and, through repeats, still am someone who visits people in their home, and usually in programmes that have, thank goodness, given them pleasure.

If you are a film star it is different. There is a gentle nudge between friends and a hushed awed whisper of 'Oh look, isn't that so and so?' should the film star dare show himself on the high street or public transport. For the stage star it is quite different: no one recognizes him at all – unless, of course, he has already been successful in film or television. But I am very lucky; I feel free to walk the streets, happy to take the tube and find that people near me, as opposed to on rooftops, greet me with a warm smile and a gratefully received compliment.

Fame, or indeed any remembrance at all, is a very transitory thing. Especially for stage actors. The distinguished producer Thelma Holt was shocked to discover some members of the Royal Shakespeare Company standing in front of the bust of Sir

John Gielgud in the foyer of the newly named Gielgud Theatre discussing who this John Gielgud might be. I was shocked too, Gielgud had died only a few years before and was probably the greatest classical actor of the twentieth century. Unlike Sir Alec Guinness, he hadn't been in *Star Wars*, so was unknown to these actors. Actors of my age knew all about Macready, Kean, Kemble, Irving, Ellen Terry and Sarah Siddons before we even went to drama school. However, being a film star is no guarantee of enduring fame either, as I have spoken to many young actors who have never heard of Burt Lancaster, Cary Grant, Gary Cooper or even Spencer Tracy. Bubble reputation indeed.

The first time I experienced the need for people to have 'a little contact with fame' was many years ago, and long before I was in any way famous. I had appeared in one or two television plays, though, and as the people who wanted my autograph were members of my own family they would have probably have watched them.

Nothing too odd about what I have written so far but what I am about to write, I think, shows the extraordinary pull and effect that being seen on television can have on people.

As I have mentioned, I am half Scottish from my mother's side of the family. My Scottish Uncle George had died. He was only in his early fifties but had had a rotten war, which contributed to his early death. It was and no doubt still is, both here – certainly in working-class Nottingham – and in working-class Scotland, the custom to lay out the body of the deceased in an open coffin in the front or 'best' room. That was where I said my goodbyes to my much liked Uncle George. There were many relatives filing round the coffin, most of whom I'd never met before. I had sat down in the tiny room on one of the borrowed simple chairs hard up against the walls. Tea had been served and I became aware to my considerable embarrassment and consternation that a queue was forming at my chair. It was all my Scottish relations who wanted me to sign their funeral programmes.

So while the body of my dead Uncle George lay very cold in his coffin just two feet away from me, a little juggling act with cups of tea and signed funeral programmes took place. Joe Orton would have loved it.

Because I have done so little new television over the past eighteen years people in general think I've retired. Even the young people who are now enjoying my old programmes for the first time on repeat channels think this old geezer has retired. He hasn't. Actors don't retire as a rule because all humans get older so there are always older parts to play. Certainly for men, and certainly in stage plays.

There are people, of course, who like your work or persona so much that they want a little piece of you. This is usually a simple autograph, which is always a pleasure to give. Then there's the signed photograph sent through the post, which is a little difficult as the photo they want signed can't be fitted into your local post box in that large and politely stamped envelope. Then there are the batches of photos and playbills that they would like you to sign. I am sometimes circumspect about these, as there is quite a market for signed photos on the internet, which is often where these articles will end up.

I, and no doubt many stage actors, have notes sent round in the interval either asking if they can meet you after the show, or asking you to please phone this number tonight. These missives in my experience are almost always from American ladies who are staying in very expensive London hotels. The note is often a card showing their high-powered executive position in life. I never respond. I bet I've missed some interesting experiences.

Actors are famously shy. People who approach you are usually nervous so the main duty is to try to put them at their ease. All the people I have mentioned so far, on the whole, are true fans, a little forward sometimes, but not too unsettling.

However, I had a real fan who began to unsettle me, in that she lived in Europe and yet came to every first night of every play I appeared in, anywhere. It could be a provincial city or it could be the West End. She was a handsome young woman who always sat in the front row, centre, and always watched only me. No matter who was speaking her eyes were glued to me. It was unnerving. She climbed onto the stage the very first time she came to see me. It was *Pygmalion* at Chichester, where the stage was easily accessible. She did, however, come on stage to give me a large bouquet of flowers. She was married with a husband and two small children. She always found out through the internet where I was appearing and always came. This went on for several years and I became very concerned at the money it must be costing her family in tickets, hotels and flights. As she often wrote to me via my agent with pictures of herself and her family, I could see they were not exactly rich. I eventually wrote what I thought a reasonable letter to her, mentioning the cost of her coming to see me, and suggesting that when she came, perhaps she could sit somewhere other than the front row. I received a very angry letter back and have not seen her since.

The next two fans I tell you about were really disturbed and strange.

As I have mentioned, I played Balor, the most evil man in the universe, in the first episode of *Space 1999* to be shown in America. I didn't know it had been shown when I got a phone call from the film studios where the series had been made. They said a very large parcel had arrived from America addressed to me. Would I like to come and collect it? I did. It was a parcel the size of a door (I had a lot of trouble getting it into the car) and inside the parcel was a full-length oil painting of me as Balor. There was also a charming, almost poetically written letter from a young girl studying at a well-known American university. She said she hoped I liked the painting. I had inspired her. She was studying art. She also enclosed her photograph, and she was beautiful and looked about nineteen.

At this time in the early seventies I had never had a fan letter before, let alone a painting in a parcel and I made the grave, grave error of replying to the artist at the university, giving my home address. An exchange of letters followed. Hers were always very poetical and reminded me of Sylvia Plath. Then one day I received a disturbing letter about how the other students were jealous of her talent (which judging from the painting was pretty feeble) and she had been tied up and severely beaten by them. I replied the best I could. Then came a very deranged letter, explaining that she had decided she only wanted one thing in life, which was to be my sex slave. I don't think I'd ever really heard that expression before. Anyway this time I wrote a very sensible, grown-up, married man with three children reply, saying calmly that I wouldn't be writing any more and I didn't think that she should either.

Some months later I returned home from rehearsal, and as I put the key in the door, my wife rushed to see me and explained quickly what to expect in the kitchen. There sat a middle-aged woman in some sort of tracksuit. She had blagged her way into my house by saying I had arranged to see her. She was American, she was the 'beautiful young girl' who had been writing to me, and she was obviously of disturbed mind.

I had three young children in the house. I had to get her out as quickly as possible. She might have a gun or knife. I calmly suggested we should walk down to my local pub. She agreed. I showed no surprise in her appearance or deception, only in her arrival. In the inevitable explanatory conversation at the pub it transpired she was indeed at this university, that's why my letters reached her, but she worked as a waitress in the university refectory. She had a husband who was a long-distance lorry driver. He was away at the moment so she had drawn out all their money, flown over to England, booked, liked a good American, into the Hilton Hotel, and come straight to see me. She was quite adamant that the only thing she wanted in the world was to be my sex slave. The sex slave of the most evil man in the universe.

When I said, as gently as I could, that this wasn't possible, she began screaming at the top of her voice. It disturbed the pub, I can tell you. I did what I had only ever seen done in films – I gave her a quick but not hard slap in the face, and she immediately stopped screaming and let me lead her into the street. She said she was sorry for the deception and everything. She would go back to her hotel, and straight back to America. Bye, bye. Phew.

In the middle of the night there was a banging on the front door. She was back. I put on a dressing gown, grabbed keys and spoke to her on the doorstep. She had returned to her hotel, she told me, to discover an urgent message from the American embassy. Her husband had been killed in a car (or lorry) crash – but that was not all, oh no. The FBI wanted to talk to her as she had travelled here on a false passport. She couldn't go back to America. She was now all alone in the world. Could she come and live with me? I told her this time to fuck off, shut the door and went back to bed. At about 6.30 a.m. there was another banging on the door. It was short and I ignored it. When I got up I found a letter from her. It wasn't written by Sylvia Plath this time but by some cage fighter who obviously was suffering from a very serious bout of Tourette's syndrome. But anyway, the writer was on the way to the airport. I never heard from her again. I wish I'd kept her last letter, though. It was really punchy.

It was when filming for the first, and not-yet-shown series of *To The Manor Born* that I made another innocent mistake. We were on location somewhere in the countryside and several local people had come to watch. Among them was a particularly striking blonde girl of about eighteen or nineteen, and this old fool of forty-three was rather flattered by her attention, and chatted with her between takes. We were only at that location for one morning and I never saw her again. About three years later, after the complete series of *To The Manor Born* had been shown and I was still engaged on *The Bounder*, I received via my agent a letter from my long-ago 'flirt'. I knew it was her because besides reminding me of our meeting she enclosed a photograph and I recognized her. She told me a little bit about herself, such as that she was twenty-one, an only child, and she lived with her mother at home. No mention of a father. Okay so far. However, she went on to say that I was appearing – that is to say she could see me materializing – in her bedroom and her bathroom. This was, she said, very exciting and gave her great pleasure. She thought I would like to know. I ignored the letter and threw it away.

More letters began to arrive via my agent. They became more explicit and more sexual in nature and things were developing, in that she could now see me sometimes in my home as well. After receiving this last letter and chatting with Sue, we decided to show the letter to my doctor, as the poor girl obviously needed help of some kind. My doctor agreed and suggested that Sue should write to the girl's mother enclosing her daughter's letter, and he also made a few suggestions as to what Sue should say. Gentle, sensitive, concerned, understanding things, because after all the letter spoke for itself.

A reply was received from the girl's mother, again via my agent. The mother had been pleased to receive our letter. She wrote that she knew her daughter had been writing to me, and what she was writing was true. She knew it was true because she saw me as well. Blimey.

I persuaded someone at my agency to write and request no more letters were sent to me, and my agent agreed not to forward them on to me if there were any. A letter was sent, however, and my agent didn't send it on, but read the contents. It was so disturbing he rang me. At this time I was recording *The Bounder* in Leeds in front of a live audience. In this letter the girl said she was coming to one of my shows; she had to speak to me, etc., etc. She would, however, come in disguise. Perhaps, she said, even dressed as a nun. I still had her photograph and copies were distributed to the staff at Yorkshire Television. I was nervous but I don't think any nuns came and I never heard from her or her mother again. I hope twenty-five years later that they are both okay. Oh dear.

I often think in these days of massive paparazzi attention and the proliferation of gossip magazines at the newsagents how lucky I was to have had my public exposure and fame before this explosion occurred. The only 'gossip' thing that happened to me was that when Stringfellow's opened, Mr Stringfellow invited me for supper with his wife and mum and dad. While I was there an extremely glamorous young woman came to our table and asked me for a dance. As Sue wasn't with me I was happy to dance with her. What I wasn't conscious of was that photos were being taken. What I was conscious of was that the girl was dancing really close. Very nice, I thought. Two days later it was all over the popular press that I was cheating on my wife with a mystery girl at the new Stringfellow's club. Incidentally, when I left that night, still innocent of the set-up, for that's what it was, Mr Stringfellow offered me his chauffeur-driven Rolls-Royce. I accepted. I have never been to Stringfellow's again, I'm afraid. However, some years later three young women who worked at Stringfellow's rented the basement flat next door, and used to sunbathe naked in the garden. I tried not to look. Not too often, that is.

The televisions I have made have been sold all over the world, and it is so very nice when going abroad to have people who enjoyed the shows smile, and want to shake my hand.

A very particular and most charming and, of course, flattering example of this was when I took Sue to New York for the first time. After checking in at our hotel we went for a walk on a sunny evening to Greenwich Village. There was a lovely open-air restaurant there and fortunately they had a table. I had noticed when we arrived that there were two large black limos outside overseen by obvious security men with walkie-talkies (before mobile phones). A table near us had a group of about six dark-suited men. They stood out because (a) it was a hot evening and they were very formally attired, and (b) five of the men were obviously with an Alpha male, their leader. They showed him deference and often laughed loudly at things he said. I, coming from the culture of American films shown in England, had a strong suspicion they were Mafia, and they were with a big gang boss.

I leant over to another table away from the suited men and whispered sotto voce, 'Excuse me, but would you know who that man at the other table is?'

Before I was able to receive a reply a big voice said, 'You may not know who I am, Mr Bowles, but I know who you are.' The man who had spoken got up and held out his hand. 'My name is Koch,' he said. 'I'm mayor of this city.' As I took his hand he pumped it warmly and said, 'I love your TV shows, Mr Bowles, I'm a fan. Welcome to New York.'

I'd like to think Boris Johnson might do that. Mark you, I think any American actor would know exactly who Boris Johnson was.

CHAPTER 18

AT LAST AN ENGLISHMAN

I can't remember the name of the film, I can't remember the name of the restaurant, but I can remember the name of the TV series. It was *The Irish RM*. My wife and I had often been to our local cinema but had always gone home straight afterwards for our supper. This evening, for no particular reason, we decided to eat in a little Italian restaurant that we had never been in before, and in fact have never been into again.

While we were eating, a young woman stopped by our table to say hi. It was someone who I had met as a friend of David Hemmings (yes, David again). I introduced her to Sue and she introduced us to her fiancé. In the quick conversation that followed it transpired that her fiancé, James Mitchell, who had been a lawyer, was about to go into television production and his first venture was to be Somerville and Ross's *The Irish RM*.

The bell of Big Ben rang because some six years earlier I had been sent the novel (there were several of them) *The Irish RM* and a draft script for a TV series to be made by a man called Ronald Inkpen. Mr Inkpen was the producer and he wanted me to play the RM of the title, the resident magistrate, Major Yeates. I couldn't believe it, this was a wonderful, wonderful part, a huge starring role. I was still doing *Dirty Linen* at the Arts

Theatre and was not a star. Honestly, my first thought was why isn't it being offered to someone like Michael Caine or some other big star. Mr Inkpen wanted me. He gave me proposed shooting dates but said he couldn't quite make a formal offer until he had tied up his American co-producers. As I understand it, Mr Inkpen, poor man, had a fatal stroke as he was boarding the plane at Heathrow to raise the money in Los Angeles. I heard no more, but I was hooked.

I began in an amateur and totally inexperienced way to look into the 'rights' position. They were held by now with Ulster TV. I looked into purchasing an option. I spoke to many people for advice, not the first or last time. This was fatal. One of the people I had asked for advice went ahead and purchased the option himself. (I don't know where I thought I was going to get my money from – dreaming again.) Then, oh the cheek of it, he offered the part of Major Yeates to me. Anyway it all fell through, the IRA began to explode bombs in London – no one was interested in putting on national TV a big series called the Irish anything, it seemed. Then suddenly, years later, Mr James Mitchell is about to make *The Irish RM*. It was being financed by Channel 4, which had just started, and Ulster TV. The other thing that had happened in the years since my first encounter with *The Irish RM* was that I had become a star, a TV star. I had just finished *To The Manor Born* which on its last episode had 25 million viewers. Channel 4 was at this time getting about 1.5 million for its top show.

'Have you cast the major?' I asked.

Mr Mitchell was very surprised I knew the books at all, it seemed no other English actor had heard of them. 'Actually not quite, nearly, but not quite,' replied Mr Mitchell. 'Why, would you be interested in playing him?'

'Yes,' I said as calmly as a man with 25 million viewers could. I'm joking – I wanted that part, I felt just like any other desperate actor about to see his chance walk out of the restaurant.

'I'll call your agent tomorrow,' said Mr Mitchell, and he did.

The deal was quickly done and at last I was to play the part. I had of course seen the scripts by this time and thought they were terrific.

The first and only read-through was in a large church hall in London. Apart from the actress playing my wife all the other actors were from Ireland. They had been flown over for the read-through and I was soon to learn, for the rehearsals also. The director had recently won awards for his direction of *Private Shultz* on TV, starring Ian Richardson and Michael Elphick. His opening remark to the forty or so actors gathered round a large table was that he was going to have all six scripts read that day – six hours of reading. I got off to my 'being difficult' start by saying that I couldn't possibly do that, (after all I was in almost every scene) but I would happily read three scripts. He was not pleased but accepted the fact. The director then made the extraordinary statement, extraordinary not only to my ears but to every Irish man and woman there, that he intended to direct the whole series as a documentary of Irish life and it was not, in his opinion, comedy. When he said comedy he looked at me with quite an aggressive look in his eyes. Of course as we began to read these wonderful scripts, the great Irish actors began to release their talent and the predicament of the English magistrate was revealed as the Irish people ran rings around him. There were gales of laughter. Documentary laughter, one could only presume.

The next surprise was that it was proposed that we would rehearse the various episodes for two weeks in a rehearsal room. Not just the simple interior dialogue. Oh no. The director had us miming walking over muddy fields, clambering over imagined fences, driving a pony and trap and of course riding horses. The director was working out his camera shots, I suppose. I didn't mind doing any of this, it gave me a chance to get to know my fellow actors, but it did seem odd and it never happened again in the second or third series with different directors. Then we were off to Ireland for the big adventure.

I had only been to Ireland once before, rather briefly. There used to be an Irish Film Festival (perhaps there still is) and after *The Charge of the Light Brigade* had been released, my dear friend from the film T. P. McKenna asked me if I would like to be officially invited. I hesitated. 'Oh don't worry,' he said, 'I know everyone involved, everything will be paid for and you'll be treated just as if you were a film star. Please come.' The festival was held in Cork. I was booked into a nice hotel and that same evening was to be the opening of the festival. This opening was of course televised across Ireland and was composed of all the stars being brought, one by one, onto the stage of the main cinema for a short interview, and then the first film of the festival being shown. After this, there was to be a grand ball and reception at the Cork town hall. No one had told me to bring a dinner jacket. I stood in the wings as each dinner-jacketed, evening-dressed actor/actress was called onto the stage. They were all starring in various films to be shown. Some I knew of, others I didn't. Then the big finale. 'Ladies and gentlemen,' said the beautiful lady compere, 'now I would like to introduce you to one of Ireland's greatest actors, a man who is loved by us all and who has recently starred in that great film *The Charge of the Light Brigade*. Ladies and gentlemen, would you please give a huge welcome to Ireland's own star of stage and film, Mr T. P. McKenna – and his friend.' Yes, and his friend! I was not on the official list. As T. P. strode on smiling I grabbed his hand, so we walked on as a strange pair. T. P. McKenna and his friend. His friend never spoke during this televised interview except to interrupt T. P. An interruption he has never forgiven me for. He mentioned his age in his interview. He said he was thirty-two. 'No he's not,' suddenly piped up his friend. 'He is thirty-seven.' Huge, huge laughter from the packed cinema.

After the film we went onto the reception come ball. Drinks

were flowing, everyone was excited. I was at the bar with T. P. when I was approached by a member of the Cork committee of the festival. He ticked me off roundly for not wearing a dinner jacket, but before he had finished my 37-year-old-going-on-32 friend turned on him. 'How dare you talk to my friend like that? He is not only a friend, he is a guest of this country and more particularly a guest of Cork. You are behaving like a provincial,' said the Dublin man, T. P. McKenna, and with that he tore off his bow tie, and threw it into the air. Then he took off his dinner jacket, threw it on the floor and stamped on it. Then he asked me what I would like to drink. What a dear, dear friend, then and now. As for myself, I left the festival by first plane the following morning.

T. P. had given me the most marvellous tip on where to stay for my sixteen weeks in Dublin, while filming *The Irish RM*. The once very famous Gresham Hotel in O'Connell Street had the most luxurious, large hotel suites in Dublin. There were three of them and they occupied the whole top floor of the hotel and they had a 'secret' lift, which was only supposedly known by the residents of the suites. The most important part of T. P.'s tip was that one of the suites had been completely refurbished for Richard Burton and Elizabeth Taylor when they had made a film in Ireland a couple of years before. I asked Channel 4 to book this suite for me unseen.

When I arrived I was quite unprepared for the grandeur: huge drawing room with a large open fire, the most sumptuous chairs and sofas, oil paintings, swagged curtains, a large modern kitchen, and the most over-the-top glamorous bathroom I had ever seen. Everything was gold plated, even the taps were gold dolphins. The shower head was a gold 'putti' and of course the toilet-roll holder was gold plated too. There was a 'servant's' entrance into the suite, via the kitchen, while the main entrance was through double doors into a large furnished hall with rooms leading off. I'm not going to describe the bedroom, as you must be sick of this by now. The reason I have described it so much is that it was the first (and last) time I had full 'film star' accommodation, and the apartment was to feature quite heavily in unexpected ways during my stays in Ireland.

I did three series of *The Irish RM* so had three years of staying at this hotel. The filming took place about thirty miles outside Dublin in County Kildare, which stood in for County Cork.

A very strange, and for me disturbing, thing happened as we were just about to start filming the third episode. The director, who had always been polite but rather taciturn with me, called me aside.

'Peter, I have just watched a rough cut of the first episode. You're very good.' I recognised the tone of surprise in his voice behind the compliment.

'Thank you,' I said. 'That's a relief because all these Irish actors I'm playing with are marvellous.'

'No,' said my director, 'you are really very good. I have to tell you I didn't want you for this part, I thought you were just a sitcom actor. You were cast over my head. I wanted Ian Richardson.'

His fierce look in my direction before the read-through was now making complete sense. It wasn't his fault, just another continuing example of how the so-called 'serious' theatre looked down on comedy.

My wife had never been to Ireland and after we had shot a couple of episodes she came over for the weekend. She was to do this every weekend from then on during the course of the series. Sue arrived on Friday evenings, and although I would be shooting the next day, she would come on the set and we would relax on Sundays together. So here we were in our palatial apartment on Sue's first trip to Ireland. It was, of course, at a time when things were still really bad with the IRA, with kidnappings as well as murders. All the apartments had really spacious terraces, big enough to eat or dance on. At about 1 a.m. we became aware of very loud party noises coming from the next suite. I went onto our terrace and saw many men and women in evening dress dancing and drinking on the next-door terrace. They were very loud and seemingly rather drunk. I had as usual, to be up at 6 a.m. and it was obvious I wasn't going to get any sleep. I gave it another half-hour and then phoned the night manager. He said he would have a word with them. I don't know what he said but not long after my phone call there were heavy bangings on my hotel doors and loud cries of 'Fuck off back to England, Englishman.' Soon there were also Irish rebel songs being sung very loudly. The abuse and threatening behaviour was coming from both men and women. We were very disturbed indeed and my wife was extremely frightened. I rang down again. The manager this time was unhelpful.

'I can't help you, Mr Bowles. Sorry.'

'There is riotous and threatening behaviour outside my door, and I am going to call the police,' I said.

'They won't come,' said the manager. 'First of all this is an hotel, I am in charge. And secondly the people who are outside your door are some of the most important people in Ireland, even the police won't want to deal with them.'

I rang the police and explained the situation. They were quite marvellous. They seemed to know who I was. They explained with some force that no one was too important if they were breaking the law, and they would be right over. They came. I saw them after they had dealt with the situation. There was silence now and the next-door terrace was empty. There was a gentle knock on my door. Outside stood six of the biggest policemen, or Gardai, I had ever seen. 'You'll have no more trouble tonight, Mr Bowles.' Of course I invited them in for a drink as a way of saying thank you. They were delighted. A bottle of Bushmills was opened, and although I didn't get any sleep that night I had a very jolly time with the Dublin police.

The directors of the Gresham were on the film set at lunchtime next day, begging me not to say a word to the press, as there would be enormous trouble. I agreed.

This, I'm afraid, was not the only time my wife and I had trouble at the hotel. Again it was a Friday, although a different year. Again terrible raucous sounds of people enjoying themselves, just enjoying themselves with blisteringly loud music. I had another early call, I phoned the manager.

'I don't know what I can do, Mr Bowles,' he said. 'It's the Queen pop group. They have had a concert tonight with another two to come and they have booked two floors of the hotel plus that suite next door.'

'Okay, I understand your position but please ask them to quieten down.'

Well, once again, I don't know what was said, or if he mentioned what I had done before, but the noise did subside, there seemed to be much flushing of toilets, and then a loud hammering on my door.

'Peter Bowles, Peter Bowles,' the voices said, 'we used to think you were a great actor, now we think you're just a c★★t.'

They were quite right. I've always been a big rock 'n' roll fan, and especially of Queen. Perhaps I'm just a spoilsport. The directors of the hotel were on set again the next day. They offered to book me into another hotel for the next couple of nights, as they couldn't possibly ask Queen to leave. And would I please not mention any of this to the press. Of course, I understood and agreed.

The amazing thing is that the press never seemed to get a sniff of either incident. This is even odder, because I discovered that a press photographer was present, incognito, in the hotel foyer every night in order to catch me should I come back to the hotel with presumably someone they felt I shouldn't be with.

The filming of *The Irish RM* was tremendous fun and it was a rewarding experience for me to work with such terrific actors. Also I became a lifelong friend with Bryan Murray, who played Flurry Knox. Niall Toibin, who played Slipper, also became a true friend. One day he invited me to the national hurling final at Croke Park, Dublin.

A very fierce and somewhat dangerous game I had never watched before. Suddenly the puck, if that's what you call the hard 'ball', was lofted into the air towards the watching crowd. I don't know what the capacity of Croke Park was then but many tens of thousands of eyes watched the ball fall from the skies and into the hands of a spectator. It was a man, and every eye in the stadium watched him put the ball in his right-hand pocket and open what appeared to be his programme. All the players stood stock-still and a hush fell over the ground. Time passed, a few seconds, I suppose, but it seemed much longer, then we all saw a man next to the ball pocketer say something to him. There was no reaction. Time stood still again. The players and the crowd watched, then the man spoke to the ball holder once more, again no response. Still complete silence over the whole ground, no one called out, there was no jeering, just silent watching. Then the man who had spoken twice and been twice ignored drew back his right arm and hit the ball man hard on the side of his face. There was a great 'whaaaing' moan from the crowd then again silence. Then we all watched the man who had received the blow, but who seemingly had 'ridden' it, calmly and without taking his eyes from his programme put his hand in his pocket and throw the ball back onto the pitch. A huge roar from the crowd and the fierce battle was resumed as if nothing had occurred. It was one of the strangest events I have ever witnessed.

Another great Irish occasion I witnessed while making *The Irish RM* was the Goffs horse sale. This was held in a huge horseshoe-shaped building, with the bidders sitting in ranked steep-sided sections looking down on a parade ring surrounding the auctioneer.

What was exciting, apart from the atmosphere of beautiful horses and staggering sums of money, was the arrangement and behaviour of the 'tellers' who encouraged potential, or already bidding clients, to bid even higher. The tellers were all very attractive girls in very fetching short skirts. They quickly positioned themselves by a bidder and when the bidder faltered they would turn and face them in ways that seemed to call into question the very testosterone and masculine pride of the often Arabian-clothed bidder, encouraging them to make another bid. The girl herself would then turn back around from her client and shout 'Here!' with raised arm to the auctioneer. Very stirring stuff indeed. Horses, big money, Alpha male pride and sex – and this was before I went to the Irish races. But that's another story.

The great joy for an actor working in Ireland is how the Irish people accept and welcome anyone who is interested in the arts. It's because, on the whole, so are they. Unlike England, where people who attend ballet or opera are one group; theatre lovers and art lovers another, film and books people possibly another. The Irish people I met in pubs and private houses, no matter what their jobs (class as such doesn't seem to exist), had something to say about the arts, no matter what branch. You are a slight oddity in England being an actor, in Ireland it is just your job, like any other. It was a joy for me and very relaxing.

The series was shown on Channel 4, which had only been broadcasting for about a year, and, as I said, it had not been getting good viewing figures. Their top programmes were usually imported from America and getting about 1.5 to 2 million viewers. People still hadn't found the Channel 4 button.

The first episode of *The Irish RM* received extremely good reviews and suddenly Channel 4 had a big hit on its hands. The ratings suddenly went up to over 5 million for *The Irish RM*. A headline in the *Evening Standard*, which I cherish, said: 'BOWLES SAVES CHANNEL 4'. Not bad for a programme whose title confused most English people, who kept calling it *The Irish PM*. Terry Wogan, who was an enormous star on radio at this time, never stopped talking about the programme, starting a national debate as to whether Anna Manahan as the housekeeper, Mrs Cadogan, was wearing her cap back to front. (I think she was!)

Another series was commissioned, this time with two different directors.

I remember getting a phone call in my grand suite from the so-called Witch of Fleet Street, Jean Rook. She explained she was going to print a story in, I think, the *Express*, on how I had personally ruined an English family's holiday by refusing to give their ten-year-old son my autograph. Would I like to comment before she printed the knocking story? The incident had happened earlier that week and I remembered it. We were actually shooting, the camera some way from my position was turning and was about to pan onto me, at which point, on a signal from the first assistant, I would start walking towards the camera. Just before this happened a young boy came up and asked for my autograph, without taking my eyes off the first assistant's upraised arm I politely said I couldn't now but would later, and he ran off.

Ms Rook said my refusal had caused the boy such distress that the parents decided to cancel their holiday four days early and return to England, where they had rung and told her all about this cruel act from a self-important star inflicted on their young lad. Fortunately Ms Rook believed my side of the story and cancelled the article. But it makes you think, doesn't it!

We worked very long hours, of course, I never got back to the hotel before 9.30 or 10.00 p.m., just time to grab a hamburger and retire. I never went out for a drink in the evenings. I learnt early on this was very dangerous: people would line up drinks for you and you had to return the compliment, and so on ad infinitum. I discovered that most of the Irish actors I worked with who were over the age of about forty had given up drink all together. They had learnt that a successful acting career and Irish drinking habits didn't mix too well.

Talking of drink, I was having a drink on this occasion in a famous actors' pub in Dublin. I had been talking at the bar with a leading Irish actor and friend. After he had left the bar I was approached by a youngish American woman. 'Excuse me, could you tell me where I might meet men who have syphilis?' she enquired.

I indicated my surprise and shock at her politely spoken but bald enquiry. 'No, I couldn't. Why on earth do you ask?'

'Oh,' she said, 'I am a doctor specializing in venereal diseases. The annual world conference of venereal specialists is being held in Dublin this year, and I hoped you could help my research.' All this was said in that maddening American manner that some Americans have.

'Why on earth did you think I could help you in your search for syphilis?' It suddenly sounded like the name of a lost cat.

'Well,' she said, 'the man you were talking to was gay – I could tell from the way he walked out of the pub. You were obviously friendly with him, so I presume you are gay too.'

She didn't care, did she? My anger at her cool rudeness was overruled by my intrigue at this sudden diversion from the humdrum life I lead.

'I'm not gay,' I replied, 'and I have no idea if my friend is. Actually I think you are being rather rude.'

'Oh I'm sorry,' she said, 'but there are gay men in Dublin who have syphilis and I'm determined to find them.'

I didn't wish her luck, and the lady doctor left the pub, seemingly sober, to continue her quest. I didn't think that her questions would go down quite so incident free with any Dublin man she might approach. Silly woman.

Many of the scenes in the series were shot in magnificent Irish stately homes, of which there were many, and all, it seemed, slightly crumbling. The families who lived in them were always tremendous hosts and very kind to me. So kind, in fact, that on two occasions when we had shot on a Saturday and I had been invited to spend the night and the following Sunday as a guest, I had woken in the night to find a naked young woman climbing into my bed. Not an easy situation this. I always imagined there was the odd shotgun kept in these houses, and I felt a riled boyfriend or husband wouldn't hesitate to use it. Also, conversation over the grilled kidneys and bacon at breakfast might be a little tricky. I made my excuses, and the ladies on both occasions sighed, kissed my forehead, and left in a glimmer of ivory skin.

The whole of the third series was to be directed by the great Roy Ward Baker. Roy Ward Baker, I knew, had directed many good British films, including *A Night to Remember*, still the best film of the sinking of the *Titanic* ever made. Mr Baker, whom I had never met before, called my home in London a couple of weeks before shooting and asked me over to his house for a chat.

He was in his sixties then, I imagine, and is still with us in great age now. As he offered me a sherry (of course) he said, to my amazement, that as I would expect to be shot on my 'best side' he needed to know in advance what side that was. This was real old-time big-star treatment that I had never encountered before, only heard of in hushed tones, and certainly not for a man. I decided to take the offer in my stride without surprise and after listening to Mr Baker's tales of how whole sets had to be turned around to accommodate Dirk Bogarde's 'best side', I told him what I thought mine was. Oh yes, I knew all right, but had never dared mention it for fear of ridicule, especially from my wife.

After six weeks of shooting I could bear it no longer. I took Roy aside.

'Why are you deliberately shooting me in every single scene

on my bad side Roy? I don't really mind' (I did) 'but I am confused.'

'Oh God!' said Roy. 'I'm so sorry. I must have made a mistake. I thought you said this side. I'm so terribly sorry, Peter.'

We had a good laugh and decided not under any circumstances to worry about good or bad sides any more.

These years were an extraordinary time for me because in
between the breaks of the series *The Irish RM* I was filming
Lytton's Diary, and in the breaks between the series of *Lytton's
Diary* I was recording the final episodes of *Only When I Laugh*
and then the brand-new series of *The Bounder*. A very heady,
wonderful, magical time for me, especially as everything was
well received by the public and critics alike. Little did I know
that as an actor who wished to be regarded as an all-round,
complete actor, I was digging a very large hole for myself.

CHAPTER 19

A FEW ODD THINGS
BEFORE MOVING ON

It was about 12.15 a.m., I was standing on a street in one of our larger provincial cities looking for a taxi. I had just been to a theatrical first-night party, but had never visited the city before. The streets were almost deserted, hardly any cars, no taxis, no passers-by, when suddenly I saw approaching from my right-hand side, and approaching at some speed, a very large group of naked young women. As I stood slightly open-mouthed and quite sober I observed that the girls were well built, that is to say they were full bosomed and well hipped with strong legs. The very epitome of healthy, sexually alluring, naked-fleshed femininity, and they were coming towards me at speed. I was recognized; they stopped in a concertinaed colli-sion of breasts and buttocks, with much laughter and delight. I saw they were wearing some sort of footwear and carrying some sort of clothing under their arms.

'What is it? Am I dreaming?' I asked. 'Why are you naked? What are you doing, what's going on?' They were really pleased to see me; that is to say they were really pleased to see me seeing them, naked, appreciating them naked, reacting so strongly, and with such male pleasure. 'We are the local

University Women's Rugby Team,' they chorused amidst great
laughter, and whilst jumping up and down with excitement
went on to tell me they were running naked to some destina-
tion I'd never heard of. 'We're doing it for a bet,' they squealed,
'and you're coming with us.' Then in a collective and well-
trained scrumming maul they began to pull my trousers down.
I'll stop there.

*

I have been fortunate to have many of my suits made by a
Savile Row tailor. These have all been for TV shows I have
done. On going in for a fitting one day I noticed a long cloak
in deep purple and covered in frogging and gold braid, hanging
up in a plastic bag. I asked the tailor if he specialized in military
or ceremonial wear. He told me he didn't, this was a special
order, and was in his view a little strange.

Apparently a man had come in and given very precise draw-
ings of a cloak he would like made, stating that if he liked it he
would order thirteen uniforms. All these orders would be paid
for in cash.

I enquired who this man was. 'He calls himself the
Commander of the Supreme Council of Great Britain and has of
course left a deposit and also his card.' The card did not have the
'Commander' title but did show the man was a titled nobleman.
At another fitting I enquired further. 'Oh he loved the cloak and
we are now making the uniforms,' said my tailor. As I was writing storylines for *Lytton's Diary* at this time I thought I would
like to know more about this. There had been, in the not too
distant past, the three-day week and rumours of a revolution. A
friend of a friend of mine was reported to have bought arms,
which included a tank, to defend his estates in Devon. I decided
to contact the wonderful investigative journalist John Clare, who
had helped me so much over Elizabeth Oakley.

After a few days he rang me. He was serious, terse and to the point. 'Walk away from this, Peter,' he said. 'Just leave it, walk away.' His tone was so positive I felt too chilled to ask anything further. I just thanked him and he rang off.

A few days later I got a phone call from a man who said, 'I believe you are interested in my organization and have been making enquiries about me. Would you like to meet?' Worried how he had got my phone number I politely said it was only casual intrigue, and I had no further interest, certainly not in meeting. I didn't hear from him again. But I did hear lots more about him – not about the Supreme Council of Great Britain, but about him personally, but then that's his life not mine.

*

I did a guest star spot on one of the *Morecambe and Wise* shows. I played a psychiatrist and Ernie had brought Eric to me to be psychoanalysed. I'm sure you can already imagine how funny it was.

The rehearsals got off to a very jolly start. They were very friendly and full of fun. The only thing was they never said any of the extremely funny lines that were scripted. They ad-libbed at every rehearsal so I was never quite sure when my cue was coming. After a day or two of this I started to ad-lib myself. The atmosphere changed immediately. 'No, no, Peter, we do the jokes,' said Eric. 'You do the script.' I understood completely. On the studio day we had one rehearsal before the studio audience arrived. Eric and Ernie still ad-libbed all their lines and I spoke my lines when I could. Good fun, I enjoyed it. I sat at a desk. They sat side by side, facing me. I mention this because when the audience were in and the show was actually recorded Eric and Ernie were dead line perfect. I heard their written script for the first time. A huge surge of adrenaline went through my body and I upped several gears. It was, of course, hilarious. What I didn't know, and they teased and congratulated me afterwards, was that all their lines were being shown behind my head

on a rolling teleprompter. They had enjoyed the rehearsals without getting bored, if you see what I mean.

A few years later I bumped into Ernie in Westminster Abbey.
I told him I was going to be Archie Rice in *The Entertainer* and
was starting tap dancing lessons. 'Oh, I can help you with that,'
said Ernie, and he proceeded to show me how to do the 'time
step'. As I started to copy him I looked down at my drumming
feet and saw we were both dancing on the grave of Byron. After
all my research on Byron I felt he wouldn't have minded.

*

I used to be a friend and admirer of Mike Pratt. Remember
him? He was Randall in the original *Randall and Hopkirk
(deceased)*. Mike died, poor man, whilst still in his forties. I had
gone to see him at the newly opened Bush Theatre in London.
It was and still is a highly regarded fringe theatre held above a
pub in Shepherd's Bush.

'Don't wait for me downstairs in the bar,' said Mike on the
phone. 'I'll meet you after the show in a pub further up the
Uxbridge Road.'

'Why, Mike?' I asked.

'Because,' said Mike, 'the income tax people are trying to
serve some sort of papers on me and that's where they will be
waiting. After the show I always climb out of the lavatory
window at the top of the pub and then cross the rooftops to a
pub up the road,' he said naming it.

I arrived early for the show, into a crowded downstairs bar. I
had just ordered myself a drink when the whole pub went pin-
dropping quiet. It was as if someone had turned a switch. Very
eerie. I had only experienced this once before when four 'uniformed' members of the IRA came into a pub in Cork for a
drink. No one spoke until they had drunk and left. Although
this was Shepherd's Bush I couldn't imagine it was the IRA this
time. I turned and there coming towards me was the biggest

man I had ever seen. He was, I soon discovered, Britain's tallest man and stood 7 ft 6½ ins.

'Hello,' he said to me. I had been standing, but I immediately sat down on a stool, it felt more comfortable. 'I wonder if you could help me?' he went on.

'I'll do my best,' I said.

There was no other sound except the sound of our voices. Everyone else was listening and looking open mouthed.

'I'm supposed to meet a man in here, do you know him?' and he mentioned a name.

'No, I'm afraid not,' I said. 'Would you like a drink?'

My new friend accepted a pint of bitter and held it in his hand like a thimble. He was very nice, and although this was thirty years ago I suppose I could find his name, but I'm not going to. 'Does this man know you?' I asked.

'No,' he said, and then he told me his story.

He had been listening to a commercial radio station the night before, when on came an advert for security men for a Rolling Stones' concert. He had rung a number and a man had agreed to interview him in this pub. I asked him how he'd got here. 'Oh my friends take me around on the back of their open lorry. They're driving around Shepherd's Bush Green now, waiting for me.' He then pointed to his boots. 'I have to have these specially made,' he said. 'They are size twenty-five and cost me two hundred and fifty pounds a pair. I get through a few pairs too, as I work on a building site.'

I felt sorry for this nice gentle man. 'Did you tell the man you were to meet how tall you were?' I asked.

'Oh yes,' he said.

'Well,' I went on lamely, 'if he was here I expect he would have recognized you.'

'Yes, I suppose you're right,' sighed this giant. 'He's not turned up, I suppose. Thanks for the drink,' and he stooped his way out of the pub.

Oh I've just looked him up, it must have been a young Chris Greener.

Just an odd story that's all.

*

I was and always have been a fan of Eddie Cochran. When I was at the Bristol Old Vic, during a week I wasn't performing at night, Eddie and Gene Vincent came to the Bristol Hippodrome. I saw what tragically turned out to be Eddie Cochran's last performance, as on that Saturday night – 16 April 1960 – he was killed in a car crash on his way back to London.

It was the first and last time I had ever seen rock 'n' roll on stage. It was a revelation. I knew within a few moments that if I had been born in England a few years later I would have been a rock 'n' roll singer. No actor could ever command the emotional response, the naked no-holds-barred, total excitement that these two artists, Eddie Cochran and Gene Vincent, got from the British audience that night.

First, Gene Vincent: black leather, a mop of black hair and a gammy leg. He looked dangerous, like a street fighter. He swung his stiff, injured leg like a weapon. There was something oddly homo-erotic too about his behaviour. At one point he beckoned a yellow-headed guitarist from his backing group, got him to kneel in front of him, and while he sang some rock 'n' roll ballad, played with the young man's hair. I have read somewhere that Joe Brown was in Vincent's backing group. Could that tousled boy have been Joe?

Then there was Eddie: the curtain rose, the stage was pitch black. Then the loud 'de de de de de de – de de', 'de de de de de de – de de'. Suddenly a sharply focussed spotlight lit a tightly-clad, red leather bum, and the bum was twitching and swinging in time to the music. The expectation was electric, sexual excitement was crackling through the auditorium. Then just as suddenly, all the stage lights came up and Eddie Cochran turned, guitar in hand, singing 'C'mon everybody'. There was an explosion of noise, of sheer erotic pleasure from the crowd. Eddie's voice was so masculine, so raw, so experienced. It was unbelievable that he was only twenty-one. It made me feel very immature and I was twenty-three. Eddie was wearing dark glasses, some sort of pale shirt and red leather trousers. When he'd finished his first number he held up a hand, the audience went quiet as they knew he was going to speak to them. Then Eddie announced, 'I'm a gonna do something I've never done before. I'm a gonna . . .' (pause) 'Smile.' And he did. The audience's response was roof-raising. He did a similar trick with his sun glasses after another number. He got the audience quiet and then said, 'Now, I'm a gonna take off my . . .' (pause) 'Glasses.' And he did. Pandemonium.

Yes, I love Eddie Cochran. Gene Vincent was good, but not like Eddie. He was 'Somethin' Else'.

*

Peter Langan, the revolutionary restaurateur, was a great friend of Sue and myself. Peter had adored Sue ever since we first met him, when he had immediately enquired of Sue if she was wearing stockings and suspenders. 'Of course,' said my wife. Oh yes, Sue could handle boys/men like Peter Langan with total ease and amusement.

We found out later that he often asked beautiful women this question on first introduction – and some became mightily offended.

It was our silver wedding anniversary and we threw a big party in our house and garden. Peter arrived with two paintings from his collection as a present for Sue and a really huge tin of Beluga Caviar for Sue's mother, who was a Moscow-born Russian and was also celebrating her eightieth birthday with us. I got nothing, but then I don't wear stockings and suspenders. Sue has just reminded me I got a painting too.

The party started at about 12.30 p.m. and by about 10.30 p.m. everyone had gone except Peter. He wasn't drunk. Although he had, of course, been quaffing champagne all day but he wasn't drunk, but we wanted to begin tidying up and start getting ready for bed. I gently suggested I could easily call Peter a cab. 'Oh great,' said Peter, and then he gave me his address in Essex to give to the cab firm. The cab arrived and after quite a bit of banter and cajoling Peter finally left, happy and jolly. We were happy and jolly, but completely exhausted. About an hour later, when Sue was already in bed, the front door bell rang. It was Peter, looking very hangdog and worried.

'I am so sorry, Peter,' he said to me, 'but on the way home I remembered something. I'm so embarrassed and ashamed and you please, please mustn't mention this to Sue, but the fact is I had a bit of an accident in my underpants during the party and I hid them somewhere in the house. Please, please don't tell Sue.'

'Where did you hide them, Peter?' I asked.

'I can't remember,' said Peter, and tottered back to the waiting cab.

I told Sue immediately of course and she felt sorry for Peter. We both looked everywhere in what was rather a large house. They were nowhere to be found. Short of employing sniffer dogs there was nothing more to be done. We eventually decided that Peter was playing a wicked trick on us, and was feeling he had been ushered out of the house before he was ready.

That house is now owned by a member of a very famous family, and I still wonder if they found a very dirty and full pair of 'Peter Bowles's' underpants.

I miss Peter, as do all his many friends.

*

I was a member of a panel of six people, all so-called celebrities. We had been asked to judge a beauty competition, to be broadcast live on television later that night. I had never done anything like this before, which is why I had agreed to do it. Also I'm a man, I'm afraid.

I soon discovered, and was pleased to discover, that all the judging took place during the day. That is, each girl comes to meet the panel and is spoken and chatted to for some time. She then appears in her costume and ball gown, again in a private room with only the panel in attendance. We were three men and three women. The whole process took several hours, starting early in the morning. After we had seen all the girls, rather like a jury – I have served on one, so I know – the merits of all the girls were discussed in detail and we decided on the final line-up of eight contestants, and then the first three: third, second, first, in that order. We wrote down the names of the finalists and of course the name of the absolute winner and handed them to a member of the studio staff.

When the show was to go out live, in front of an invited audience, with the girls parading around and then being interviewed by a 'name' host, we would be sitting watching and pretending to be judging – and then at the end hand in our scores to be counted. All fake but all quite usual.

We were just having some welcome refreshments some little time after we had handed in our real adjudications, when the red-faced producer came into the room.

'I'm sorry,' he said in flustered tones. 'Could you choose someone else as the winner?'

'Why?' we asked.

'Erm,' he said, 'I don't quite know what to say. I'll be back in a minute.'

He wasn't, but another man was. Before the other man arrived we all came to the same conclusion, and we were disturbed and mystified. The other man who arrived was obviously, from his dress and manner, a chief executive of some sort. He got straight to the point.

'The girl you have chosen is black. I'm afraid this is giving us a terrible problem. You will have to choose someone else.' (All the rest of the girls were white.)

We were now truly shocked. We were, it seemed, actually being told to change our choice purely because of colour. We made it clear that we were most upset with what we were being asked to do, and what's more we certainly were not going to do it.

'Oh look it's absolutely not a racist matter,' said the executive sounding extremely shocked that we might think it was. 'It's a practical matter. The winner of this competition always get lots of modelling work from our sponsors to promote their clothes and it's been made quite clear to me that it would be awkward and not useful to them if the winner was black.'

'Then it is a racist matter,' we said, 'and although it may not be your fault we are absolutely not going to change our choice. Whether the girl gets work or not is one thing. She will be thrilled to win and so will her mum and dad and sisters. That's that, and we think the less said about this again the better.'

The executive left, crestfallen. The beautiful, charming, intelligent, graceful young black woman who won this competition was overjoyed.

Times, and televised beauty competitions, if there are still such things, have, thank God, long moved on.

*

It was my sixtieth birthday and I had arranged to meet some friends for lunch at the Garrick Club. Whilst in the gentlemen's loo there, relieving myself before lunch, a gentleman standing in the next stall to me, suddenly said, 'Good Lord, it's Peter Bowles, isn't it? I've just a few minutes ago finished writing your obituary for *The Times*.' It seems they start on your obituary at sixty and then just top it up. It made me even more determined to keep going.

*

When I was playing a matinee of *Born in The Gardens* the cast heard squeals and little shrieks coming from the wings and from the auditorium. There was also the glimpse of running policemen. The audience was disturbed and so were we. As I have mentioned elsewhere, we were playing at the Globe Theatre, now named the Gielgud. (Who is this Gielgud?) When the curtain came down we discovered that police and immigration officials had raided the theatre and 'arrested' the whole of the front of house staff. It was pouring with rain that afternoon and many of the packed audience had to wait some time to get their macs and brollies from the cloakroom as the key was held by one of the suspected illegal immigrants now held at Savile Row police station.

*

I always used to park my car in a little cul-de-sac off Savile Row when working in the West End. On climbing into it after a show on this particular occasion I noticed one other car, lights out, but four men sitting in it, parked just across from mine. Before I had a chance to start my engine another car drove into the short snub-nosed mews. As this car parked beside the other, all the men from the first car got out. I became interested and watched. Two men got out of the newly arrived car and one of them opened the boot. There were now six men altogether and they were all of Asian appearance. The man who had opened the boot began to hand out blouson windcheater-type jackets on the back of which was a particular emblem. He then began to give each man a handgun or revolver. I decided to get the hell out of it. As soon as I started my engine one of the men ran over and banged on my windows. I knew at once that he had recognized me and he gestured to me to get out of my car. No fear – I quickly put my car in gear and shot off. As I drove away

I almost immediately passed Savile Row police station. I felt I should report what I had seen. I didn't. I was too frightened. I had been recognized. They would know it was me who had informed on them. I studied the papers closely for days. No news of any Asian gang attacks. I was a coward all the same and have always felt a little guilty at my lack of civil morals.

I've depressed myself now. I'll try to cheer myself up.

*

I was invited to America to promote *The Irish RM*, which was to be shown on PBS Masterpiece Theatre, introduced by Alistair Cooke. Our first stop was Los Angeles, which neither Sue nor I had ever been to before. To our surprise, when we arrived at Heathrow we were met by Special Customer Services who escorted us to the VVIP's room. The VVIP's room in those days, early 1980s, consisted of a sort of storeroom full of old boxes, various bits of equipment, a few tatty 'sit up and beg' chairs, and the whole of ABBA pop group. ABBA were at the very zenith of their fame but they too were in the makeshift VVIP's lounge. We all got on famously. They were most friendly and charming. There was quite a long wait and they avoided boredom by going out individually, one at a time, to shop. This way, they said, they were never recognized.

On arriving in Los Angeles and making our way to the airport exit, I was amazed to see Charlton Heston leaning against a huge black limo and waving and smiling at me. I sort of waved back in a daze and then realized he was not waving and smiling at me but at his daughter, who was directly behind Sue and me. She was returning from a term at RADA. What is more, Charlton Heston drove off in his VW and I was surprised to discover from a liveried chauffeur that the limo was ours. I cannot tell you how exciting all this was to this English actor and his wife. The limo had ice buckets full of champagne and racks of bottles of every spirit imaginable.

The first person we saw on arriving at the hotel was the then very famous John Carson (Heeere's Johnny) sitting in tennis clothes with racket in the reception hall. We checked in, and as I was bursting to go to the loo, I enquired where the downstairs gents was. I walked across the large lobby to the appropriately marked door. Whilst performing my task, another man joined me in the next stall. (I seem to have a lot of urinal stories.)

'Mr Bowles,' he said, as he performed his task. 'I watched you cross the lobby. You walk real tall and you hold yourself real well.'

I couldn't believe what I was hearing. As I broke away to wash my hands he joined me at the next basin.

He continued, 'I'm doing a movie starting in a few months. There's a great part you would be perfect for. Would you mind giving me your agent's card?'

He then gave me his card. I still have it. He was quite well known.

'I'm so sorry,' I said, 'I don't carry an agent's card or any sort of card. I'm afraid I'm working at the time you mention but thank you for asking.'

I had been in the Beverly Hills hotel five minutes and I'd already been offered a film. Amazing place, Hollywood. All sorts of extraordinary things happened in our two weeks there, but the most extraordinary, flattering and unforgettable thing happened to me on our return to Heathrow. On entering the arrivals hall, where hundreds of people were waiting for their loved ones, I was aware that they had all begun clapping and to my absolute astonishment I realized they were clapping me. No greater return to one's own country could be imagined. Not by me anyway. It's not happened again – but I am very, very lucky and grateful that it did happen once.

I feel better now.

CHAPTER 20

A THEATRE ACTOR AGAIN

I had just finished these many years of television series when I got a call from David Aukin. When David Aukin had been the director of the Hampstead Theatre he had several times asked for me, so I knew he liked my work. He was now the head of the Leicester Haymarket Theatre, which at this time was the most powerful producing regional theatre in the country. He wanted me to play the lead in a Feydeau farce translated and adapted by the great Irish writer Hugh (Jack) Leonard. It was called *Some of My Best Friends are Husbands* and was to be directed by Robin Lefevre, a front-rank director whose work I admired.

I liked the play but I felt very strongly that I didn't under any circumstances want to come into London in a comedy or farce. When I took my first leading role in the West End I wanted it to be in a serious drama. It was agreed that we would do the play for one month in Leicester and then go on a sixteen-week tour. I arrived in Leicester a very nervous man. As I have indicated, I had never led a company before, never ever been the absolute star of a stage play before. I was very nervous and apprehensive. This was compounded into almost terror when on arriving at the theatre I discovered it was completely sold out for the month – and I hadn't started rehearsals yet.

Anyway it was a joy to do and we broke box-office records wherever we went, an important factor for my next offer.

The cast were a delight and I worked with my old friend Richard Wilson and met a young man who I thought was very talented, and who became part of my life in later years: Richard (Bill) McCabe. I broke my ankle during one performance and had to play this fast-moving romantic farce in plaster and crutches. I think I beat Anthony Sher and his Richard III to it. It was, as I say, a very successful tour and doubtless because of this I was made an extraordinary offer by David Aukin with the London producer Richard Armitage. They said, 'Peter, we will put on in the West End any play you wish to do.' It was an electrifying moment, which took place, funnily enough, in the street. I'm sure they were hoping I would come up with a comedy. I didn't. I thought, what is the most difficult dramatic part outside of Shakespeare I can think of. In a fraction of a second I said, 'I'd like to play Archie Rice in *The Entertainer*.'

I had seen Laurence Olivier play the part at the Royal Court twenty-five years before, and knew it had never been done in the West End since Olivier had played it at the Palace Theatre. I was forty-nine, the same as Olivier had been in the role of Archie, and I had many times been to the old Collin's Music Hall in Islington while at RADA. Collin's Music Hall was where Olivier had done his research for Archie. Looking back, we could have seen the same acts. What I didn't know was, that at the very moment I was speaking, the National Theatre were about to announce to the press that they were doing it with Alan Bates and Joan Plowright. Also at the moment I was speaking, for reasons I won't go into here, John Osborne was withdrawing his consent to the National.

It was a miracle for me on that account, of course, but it was also a miracle that Mr John Osborne happened to be a great admirer of my work. After a very enjoyable meeting with him, he gave the production of *The Entertainer* with me playing Archie his enthusiastic blessing.

There is, I believe, some porn film called *Debbie Does Dallas* or *Doreen Does Doncaster* – well, the announcement that 'Peter Bowles does *The Entertainer*' was received with about the same artistic expectations, much to my innocent surprise.

The challenge of playing Archie Rice was obviously a big thing in my life. Mainly because it was a huge test of my talent and also a huge responsibility in relation to the faith put in me by Mr Aukin and Mr Armitage. The responsibility towards the playwright, John Osborne, particularly at this point in his life, was, I need hardly say, paramount.

I was also offered choice of director. I decided I had got on very well with Robin Lefevre, enjoyed his direction and admired his Scottish grit. I trusted him. Robin had given me the best advice any newly fledged leading actor could be given. 'Peter, go to bed every afternoon, rest for at least two hours, sleep if you can and on matinee days try and sleep in between the shows or lie down and completely rest. Do not go out after the show drinking. Once the show has opened your job is to go onto that stage as full of inner energy as you can muster.' I think I have done twenty-seven plays since that advice was given to me. Thank you, Robin – it was the best advice that a middle-aged actor could have received.

Robin's advice to me before we started on the journey of *The Entertainer* was: 'From the first day of rehearsals you must inspire confidence in the rest of the cast. They must be immediately convinced they have a leading man. Learn to tap dance automatically, learn to sing without strain and learn the songs. Also learn all the front-cloth speeches.' Robin knew as I did that the true heart of the play, and therefore the true heart of Archie Rice, lay in the family scenes. That's where the play would succeed or fail. I could fail during my front-cloth turns. I couldn't fail the author or the cast in the family scenes. The family scenes were what he would spend most time on.

For six weeks before we began I did everything he had suggested. I employed a tap-dancing teacher and a singing teacher.
I worked every day on both skills and learnt the big front-cloth
speeches. A wonderful cast was assembled including Sylvia Syms
and Frank Middlemass, as Archie's wife and dad. Sylvia Syms, I
soon discovered, was to be one of the finest actors I've ever
worked with.

The first day of rehearsals arrived, the first time the cast had
all met each other, and I had never worked with any of them
other than Robin Lefevre before. After the read through, we
started on the first family scene. I was, of course, carrying my
script, as I had made no attempt to learn any of these scenes. I
would learn them as I got to know the other characters. I spoke
my first line. Then an extraordinary thing happened, a truly
shocking thing happened. The director suddenly shouted,
'How dare you come to my rehearsals and insult my cast by
knowing your lines?' It didn't make sense on any level.
Certainly the volume with which it was delivered didn't. It
was out of left field, inexplicable, and I thought, very rude. I
asked as politely as I could if Robin and I could have a quiet
word in another room. I apologized to the rest of the bewildered cast and went to have a word with my trusted Robin
Lefevre. I won't go into the language used, particularly mine,
but the gist of it, if you can believe it, was that Mr Lefevre
wanted to make it quite clear to me and the rest of the cast that
he was in charge, and that this production of *The Entertainer* was
his and not a vehicle for Peter Bowles. I explained to him in
calm and 'friendly' terms that I had enough on my plate without having to deal with his insecurities, hang-ups and ego. We
kissed, made up and everything went on perfectly normally for
the next four weeks. I tell you, it's a funny old game, drama.

As I've indicted, there had been great rumblings in the press
and profession about me playing Archie Rice. This included the
staggering rudeness of the chairman of Channel 4, who told me

to my face that a sitcom actor playing Archie Rice was a direct insult to Laurence Olivier. In Brighton, when we were on tour, people shouted at me in the street, 'You'd better be good. Lord Olivier used to live in Brighton.' My first intimation that I was going to break through all this prejudice and doubt came after the first night of our four-week try-out in Leicester, and it was not the cheers of the audience but the words of Nancy Meckler, a leading director of serious drama (and also David Aukin's wife). In the bar afterwards she said honestly, 'I have to admit you really surprised me tonight. You are going to be wonderful, but until tonight I had serious doubts.' Poor David Aukin – he must have been getting this at home!

The one person however, who did have doubts was John Osborne. We had supper after this first night and he made it quite clear that I had only reached base camp on the Everest of Archie Rice. His words not mine. The thing about John was that almost everything, and especially theatre, had to be 100 per cent or not at all. No excuses, ever.

There was terrible headline gossip in the press that Mr John Osborne had been heard to say in his hotel bar that he wasn't going to let it come into London. I tackled him about this immediately. He absolutely denied it. I believed him. Then another bombshell: it was announced the play would be coming into London but to the Shaftesbury Theatre. Now the Shaftesbury worried me on two counts. One, it was far too big, with 1300 seats, not the 700 or 800 seats of many other West End theatres. Two, but this was a silly personal thing, the Shaftesbury was the home of the Theatre of Comedy and it was written up in neon lights outside the theatre. I pathetically tried to get this taken down. I failed.

I could tell – you couldn't miss it – that John Osborne was still not happy with my less than 100 per cent performance as the short tour after Leicester progressed. Yes, the audiences were cheering, but Mr Osborne wasn't. The last date before the London opening was the Theatre Royal Bath. Robin Lefevre was not available for this week and we were told John Osborne would take over the direction. Monday, cheering. Tuesday morning, notes from Mr Osborne to the cast; he clearly and understandably feels there is work to be done. His notes are politely and graciously given. He is a great man of the theatre, not just a playwright by any means. Tuesday night, cheering. Wednesday, notes in the morning, with a matinee in the afternoon. Suddenly the morning has gone and we have to perform.

'I've got some notes for you, Peter, important ones, but there's no time now. I'll give them to you tomorrow,' said John.

I found myself replying, 'John, I can't go on knowing that there is something you're not happy with, important things. You must tell me.'

'I'm afraid it would take too long,' said John. 'It can wait until tomorrow.'

My 'difficult actor' side kicked in. 'John, unless you tell me your notes now I'm not going to perform this afternoon. The understudy can go on.'

This, of course, was like a red rag to John Osborne. His voice deepened and struck a cawing penetrating timbre. 'All right,' said this formidable man, 'I want to see from you, acting that I have not seen on the English stage for twenty-five years.'

'You're going to get it this afternoon,' I replied.

This was an echo of Tony Richardson all over again. It was the most inspiring, succinct note that any actor could receive. At least the sort of actor I am.

The matinee audience didn't just cheer, they stood and cheered. John and his wife, Helen, came into my dressing room. Helen was crying. John took me in his arms.

'That's it,' he said. 'You've done it.'

I knew exactly what was new, what I had released. I knew I could repeat it.

'I wasn't going to let you get away with that challenging note, John. Thank you,' I whispered in his ear.

The first night in London came and went. The reviews for John Osborne's play and Robin Lefevre's production were stonking raves. The reviews for my performance were more than I could have hoped for, especially from John Peter in *The Sunday Times*, who wrote:

> The production is dominated by Peter Bowles's Archie, one of those dilapidated but tenacious men who can only express affection by intimate malevolence. The performance has an edgy, unpleasant brilliance. If Osborne's achievement is to have made heroes out of unpleasant people, Bowles's is of making this unpleasantness almost heroic. He asks for no sympathy. He offers no faded glitter. When he says that behind his eyes he is dead he is not quite telling the truth; there's a beast of prey lurking behind those beady eyes, poised to pounce. There's nothing ingratiating about this Archie, but a sniffy, rodent-like wariness in the way he observes the world; a creature of the moral undergrowth. Bowles has had to wait long for his first West End starring role, and has seized it with magisterial assurance.

The most important thing for me, though, as it would be for any actor, was that I had pleased the living author. Not possible, of course, in most 'classics'. If you'll forgive me, here is John Osborne's letter to me on the first night, written on his personal notepaper.

My dear Friend,

Well, you've done it. It is indeed <u>astonishing</u> – not that you could do it – but you could attempt so much more. I hope you have amazed yourself. You are indeed AN ACTOR.

You'd better keep your hat and scarf for a glass case in the Garrick.

With congratulations, affection and abiding admiration,

John

John and Helen's friendship to myself and my wife became one of the highlights of my life. I spent many all-night sessions talking and laughing with John in his eyrie in Shropshire and I miss them both terribly.

Then I was out of work for nearly a year. Not turning down work. I had no offers whatsoever.

'I can't get you a job,' said my agent. 'You are too well known as a personality.'

I changed my agent.

CHAPTER 21

FIRST COMES THE KNOCK
ON THE DOOR

They say first comes the telephone call, but I wasn't receiving any. I had done it with *Lytton's Diary* – I decided to try to do it again. That is, not wait for the phone to ring, but to try to develop ideas for a television series myself – starring me.

We had a cottage in the country at this time, 1987, which I had bought a few years earlier. It straddled the borders of Dorset and Wiltshire. The cottage was just in Dorset but the land was in Wiltshire. You could see the tarmacadam of the tiny lane change colour at the border. Strangely, after we had bought the cottage, we discovered that it had been owned by the people opposite us in London. The wide road of Castelnau, Barnes, however precluded neighbourly friendships.

Which reminds me of something that I am so very happy with in my life, but have forgotten to mention. As you know, my wife gave up what would have been a successful career. I, thank God, was succeeding and she was able to join in that success. The first thing I had done with our money from the beginnings of my TV success was to buy Sue a house. A very particular house. There is a small group of beautiful Regency houses in Castelnau, Barnes, known as the Forty Thieves. They are the finest houses in Barnes. Sue had lived in New Malden when a schoolgirl, always travelling by bus down Castelnau on the way to St Paul's Girls' School in Hammersmith, and she had told me she had always coveted one of these impossibly expensive houses because they were so beautiful and unusual. Simon Jenkins when he first saw them couldn't believe his eyes. In 1981, one came up for sale and after the usual heart-stopping dramas I bought it. A year later I bought our first cottage.

It was the cottage that gave me the idea for what was to be a half-hour sitcom. We had a chimney fire and as the cottage was thatched we quickly rang 999 and started to move furniture out. Two fire engines arrived, one, as it turned out, from Dorset, the other from Wiltshire. It was a very narrow lane and they were parked nose to nose. I had never met firemen before and I was mightily impressed. At first, however, they seemed more pleased to see me than attend to the fire and insisted on taking off their boots 'so as not to spoil your carpets'. Anyway they were wonderful, all of them, and soon put the raging fire out and doused the thatch, which was just beginning to smoulder. I asked one of them if they would care for a thank-you drink.

'You'll have to ask the boss,' said this red-helmeted man, and he pointed to a man in a white helmet. I spoke to him.

'Well,' he said, 'I'm sure we'd love one, but we're from Dorset – your cottage, I can see, is in Dorset, the fire was in Dorset – so we'd prefer it if the drink could wait until the Wiltshire men have gone. Oh, and if you don't mind, I'll have whisky,' he said, 'but the men will have beer.'

This extraordinary exchange and rivalry, which I won't go into further, was the germ of the idea for my comedy of living in the country.

I worked out storylines of episodes, and on learning that Channel 4 were looking for a situation comedy I took the idea to them. They loved it. So much so they said they would like it to be six one-hour episodes. Exciting stuff. I also began to develop an idea for *First Loves Found* that I mentioned was inspired by my curiosity as to what had become of my first love, Rachel. I developed this as a drama series and took it to the BBC. To my amazement they loved that too, and wanted to commission a series.

All this takes time, of course, and time was passing. Still no actual acting work being offered.

I decided I couldn't handle these large, possible commissions on my own, and approached Verity Lambert, who by this time had her own company, Cinema Verity, and was respected and admired as one of the greatest independent producers in the country. We formed a partnership together to get things moving. Channel 4, of course, wanted a writer. I had heard a play on the radio, that had the right blend of truth and humour. It was by Stephen Fagan. He wrote a pilot, and from this six more scripts were commissioned. Channel 4 loved them. Then there was a change in the commissioning editor. The new man decided it was in his words, 'Brilliant, but I'm afraid it's too funny for Channel 4 – our remit, you know.'

First Loves Found was commissioned. Ten one-hour scripts were written – then rewritten with foreign locations – as they thought it could be a world-wide hit. Budgets were made up, casting was discussed. Then a new head of BBC1 was appointed. He didn't like the idea so the whole thing was shelved.

I'm telling you all this to give you a glimpse into the difficulty of getting anything actually 'on screen' in television. It all took a year or two, and during this time I got a knock on the door. It was Bryan Murray, my old friend and acting companion from *The Irish RM*. He had been having a rough time too in the acting stakes. When I had poured a drink he explained why he had come to see me. One rainy day, during the long hours of waiting in a field in Ireland, I had come up with an idea for Bryan and me to do a series about a couple of con men called *The Lizard and the Leprechaun*. We worked on the idea and took it to James Mitchell, the producer of *The Irish RM*. He turned it down. I immediately forgot about the idea and got on with my acting life. Bryan Murray had not forgotten, and here he was telling me eight years later that he'd heard TVS were looking for a comedy drama series. What about *The Lizard and the Leprechaun*? I could have kissed him, in fact I think I did. I've certainly kissed him many times since.

I'd learnt a lot since my Michael Peacock 'grow up' days, so I sat down and with Bryan's assistance wrote a letter outlining the idea to the managing director of TVS, Greg Dyke. No messing about, straight to the top. I got a reply by return of post – he liked it – and within a week Bryan and I were in a meeting to discuss writers. Greg Dyke was a man of positive action. TVS didn't like the first script by Keith Waterhouse, who was their suggestion, so we suggested ours, Ray Connolly, who had written such brilliant scripts for *Lytton's Diary*. They loved his pilot script and we were off, and with a new title, *Perfect Scoundrels*. We did three series over the next three years and would have done a fourth if TVS hadn't lost their licence. Of course there were many dramatic and unusual stories concerning *Perfect Scoundrels*, including the firing of two producers, two directors (but no actors), also the scientology religion, the script and the locations.

This is one location story. I had arrived early with all the electricians. The house for the scene was in deepest Surrey, and had just been opened up. It was a very grand house in large grounds, uninhabited but fully furnished. The first thing that struck us was that it had the atmosphere of the *Marie Celeste*. Someone who lived there had abandoned ship quite suddenly, and they had abandoned ship on their fortieth birthday. There were birthday cards displayed all over the drawing room. There was also a grand piano with sheets of composed music lying on it and on the floor around. The walls were adorned with framed gold and platinum records. Oh, and on the birthday cards was written 'Happy Birthday, Rod'. Yes, the house obviously belonged or had belonged to Rod Stewart. All his clothes, I was told by nosy crew members, were still in the cupboards. It seemed, according to the gardener, that Mr Stewart in true rock 'n' roll fashion had left suddenly for America with instructions to sell the house as it stood, lock, stock and barrel. The house, as we now found it, belonged to some obscure bank. Funny old game, rock 'n' roll.

I was at last, during this time, also offered a theatre job. It was a wonderful one. To star opposite my old friend Michael Gambon in Alan Ayckbourn's new play *Man of the Moment*. Mr Ayckbourn was to direct the play himself and it was to be produced by Michael Codron. Of great interest to me was that I was to play an East End bank robber, Vic Parkes by name. Another break from 'posh' parts – and there would be no mistaking he was English.

The play was a smash, I almost wrote 'splash' as three-quarters of the stage was taken up by an eight-foot-deep swimming pool. The play ran for a year, but Michael and I left after six months, after the most hilarious and interesting time that I had had for years. Oh the things I could tell you about Michael and me in that play.

For many years I had had in my head the idea for a film based on some real-life experiences of mine in Nottingham and elsewhere. A very strange, haunting, disturbing drama of lies, ambitions, deceit, friendships and child murder.

I took my film idea to Verity. It was called *The Backward Glance*. I had written a good detailed outline and she thought it was thrilling. 'The BBC are doing a new series called *Screen on One*,' she said. 'They are looking for six new films. I think this could be one of them.' We went together to see the head of this new BBC film project. I pitched the idea and read him the outline. Before we had left the room he had promised us £1 million to make the film, given provisos of writer, script and so

on. My emotions on that walk back to Verity's offices in
Shepherd's Bush were only comparable to my feelings of happiness on the trolley bus in Nottingham on knowing I was to be
playing Mark Antony in the school play that evening.

That most distinguished playwright Simon Gray was
approached. He wanted to write it. The BBC were thrilled we
had got such a wonderful writer, and the meetings, lunches and
drinks began.

During all this time of Simon's writing I was doing *Man of the
Moment* and *Perfect Scoundrels* so I was very busy acting again.

The final lunch with Simon Gray was on the script-deliver-
ing day. We had a nice relaxed lunch with a large brown
envelope on the side of the table. No mention was made of it
until the bill was being paid.

'Oh, here's the script,' said Simon picking up the envelope,
'but before I hand it over you must know I have completely
changed the story line' (the main character remained the same)
'so I don't want Peter's name attached to it. Also I never do
rewrites so this is it.'

I was speechless. I staggered home with the script and, without opening it, wrote a frank letter to Simon. I rang Verity and
read her the letter. That is, a copy of the letter – the original I
had already sealed, addressed and stamped for delivery.

Verity said, I think you have every right to say what you say,
but if you send that letter Simon will withdraw his script and
there will be no film. By the way, have you read his script?' I
hadn't and said so. 'Well, don't send the letter yet. Read the
script,' said Verity wisely.

I read the script. It was the best script I had ever read. The
words and scenes were delivered and written like bullets or
shells from a powerful gun. Such passion, such bitter humour,
such energy. It was quite, quite brilliant. I rang Verity again –
and I have still got the stamped, sealed, addressed and unopened
letter to Simon Gray in my files.

Running Late, for that is what it was called, went out on a Sunday evening and rather like after *To The Manor Born* I was walking down a street on the Monday morning. The street was Piccadilly. No honking horns or thumbs-up from taxi drivers this morning, though – however, a large and extremely charismatic man hove into view. I recognized him immediately.

'Good morning,' he said, 'my name is Peter Hall. I saw *Running Late* last night.' He paid me wonderful compliments on my performance and then said, 'I would very much like to work with you. Would you like to work with me?'

I, who had been longing to work for this legendary man, who had been the creator and artistic director of the Royal Shakespeare Company and for fifteen years the artistic director of the Royal National Theatre, said, 'Yes, Sir Peter, I would.'

'Oh good, I'm pleased,' said Sir Peter Hall, and he moved on.

A few days later the script of Terence Rattigan's *Separate Tables* arrived at my home. Sir Peter wanted me to play the male lead in the two plays. The play was to be produced by Bill Kenwright.

I have now, in 2009, done ten plays directed by Sir Peter Hall. The influence he has had on my development is incalculable. From the very beginning he raised the bar and extended the horizons of what I thought my talent was capable. He gave me complete confidence to try anything and always made me feel as though it had sprung entirely from myself and he was simply nudging. I was being directed by the man who had directed every truly great British actor of the last half of the twentieth century. I was a very, very lucky man.

The backing, enthusiasm and confidence I had from Bill Kenwright has also been very important to me. I have done eight plays for Bill Kenwright, probably the greatest impresario since Binkie Beaumont.

Just to end and bring a conclusion to my frustrated 'classical' aspiration that has often reared its head in this book, I was at last, in 1997, offered a major classical role. The offer, of course, came from Sir Peter Hall. It was to play Arnolphe in Molière's *The School for Wives*, and it would be produced by Bill Kenwright. I panicked. I wasn't sure I knew how to deliver the verse, translated by the brilliant Ranjit Bolt. Peter Hall invited me to lunch and after he spoke two lines of the script to me, it clicked. So that was all right. It wasn't. The panic was still there. I couldn't learn the lines. My agent also represented the hypnotist Paul McKenna, and suggested I rang him. Mr McKenna was miraculous. I spent twenty minutes with him, I thought, but it was actually one and a half hours. I had been hypnotized without my knowledge. Mr McKenna refused payment and wished me luck. I went home and immediately and easily began to memorize the huge and complicated role.

The first night came at the Piccadilly Theatre. Bill Kenwright – who on his first-night present had written, "'I want to be a classical actor" . . . you are, you are!! This one *proves* it,' (he had signed it Binkie) – rang me at about 3.30 a.m. that same night.

'Bowlsie,' he said, 'I thought you would like to hear what Benedict Nightingale of *The Times* has said about you.' He then read the following over the phone:

> I cannot believe anyone now thinks of Bowles as a television actor of limited range. But if such an invincible idiot still exists, he should at once be taken by cart or preferably tumbrel to Peter Hall's revival of *The School for Wives*. There Bowles is giving a performance that should establish him once and for all on the top table, alongside the deftest, wittiest and most complete actors we possess.

I felt great peace from this.

Between 1992 and 2009 I have starred in twenty-five plays, many in the West End. Seventeen years of the most glorious theatre work with a tremendous diversity of parts: comedies, dramas, thrillers, by Shaw, Coward, Rattigan, Shaffer, Ibsen, Ayckbourn, Anouilh, Gray, Chekhov, Molière and Shakespeare. *The Browning Version* turned out to be a socking success, and as I write this Danny Moar, another producer who has shown great faith in me, has just offered me Sir Anthony Absolute in Sheridan's *The Rivals*, to be directed by Sir Peter Hall.

So as the man said, 'Ask me if I'm happy.'

PICTURE CREDITS

Courtesy of Peter Bowles: 1, 2, 3, 4, 5, 6, 7, 8, 9, 10, 11, 15, 20, 49, 50
Arnold Allen: 12, 13
Desmond Trip: 14
Ian Jeayes: 16
ABC Weekend TV: 17
United Artists Film Co: 19
Anglia TV: 22
Yorkshire TV: 23
Courtesy of Sir Mark Weinberg: 24
Mirropix: 25
Zoe Dominic: 27
BBC: 29
Press Association: 30, 31, 44
Thames TV: 33
Hugo Dixon: 34
Bill Hewison: 35
Little Bird Film Co: 38
TVS TV Co: 40
Alistair Muir: 42
Catherine Ashmore: 43
Nobby Clark: 46, 47
Bill Kenwright: 48

ACKNOWLEDGEMENTS

With loving thanks to my sister, Patricia Ashdown, who did all the typing, and Malcolm Mackenzie for his expert help with the photographs. Also to Jane Pizzey, Managing Editor at Simon & Schuster, UK, for her charm and patience over the final draft and Tim Binding at my agents PFD for suggesting the title.

INDEX

(key to initials: PB = Peter Bowles; SB = Sue Bowles)